Fifty Years in the F[illegible]

The Working Life of Herbert Allingham

dear Emma,

I think you may have this on your kindle – I wanted you to have it "for real"

Herbert and Margery Allingham

In memory of JOYCE ALLINGHAM
(1913–2003)
and
my father
GEORGE AUBREY JONES
(1918–1983)

Fifty Years in the Fiction Factory

The Working Life of Herbert Allingham

JULIA JONES

Foreword by Jenny Hartley

'This is who I am,' she said slowly. 'Not a lady with servants to wait upon her, but a work-girl with only her own hands to keep her from starvation'

GOLDEN DUCK

First published in 2012 by
Golden Duck (UK) Ltd.,
Sokens,
Green Street,
Pleshey, near Chelmsford,
Essex.
CM3 1HT
www.golden-duck.co.uk

ISBN 978-1-899262-07-6

Design by Megan Trudell
www.emdash.me.uk

e-book conversion by Matti Gardner
matti@grammaticus.co.uk

Printed and bound in the UK
by the MPG Books Group, Bodmin and King's Lynn.

Foreword

She flung out her arms and pointed to the stage box

ASK many people – as I have asked my students – when and what reading has meant the most to them, and they will often refer you back to the enthusiasms of childhood. Not to the classics so much, but to the literature a child can call its own: the ephemeral comics and magazines which were awaited with such anticipation each week. Their pre-eminence may be passing with the wane of print culture; but look in any newsagent or supermarket today and you will still see a huge array of colourful and eye-catching periodical publication, each with its own band of fond devotees. This may be the last outpost of that which is printed on paper for popular consumption.

What is the history of this phenomenon? Finding out about the writers and readers of ephemera is notoriously difficult. Julia Jones has had luck and commitment on her side. She was lucky enough to come across an extraordinary archive: the sixteen boxes of material which covered the life of a man who spent all his working life as hack, editor and writer for a host of long forgotten publications. She also had the commitment not just to sort and collate the material, but also to set herself the task of bringing it and all it means to a modern audience. Her book will be of great interest to book historians, as well as all of us who have ever joyfully immersed ourselves in popular literature.

Fifty Years in the Fiction Factory gives us Herbert Allingham's life and work. It also sets Allingham in the context of his times, and gives us valuable insights into his readership. One of Allingham's great gifts was his relationship with his readers: he always respects them. In her turn, Julia Jones pays the same respect to both the readers and the writers of a genre often invisible to later generations. Under her lively pen the history becomes visible and accessible.

This is an important contribution to book history, and a moving memorial to the many anonymous writers who have kept us company in our reading lives.

Jenny Hartley
Professor of English Literature
University of Roehampton

She danced round the little dressing-room in sheer delight

Contents

Foreword		v
Acknowledgements		viii
An Allingham Who's Who		x
Introduction	A Man Who Wrote for the Million, 1867–1936	1
One	Born 1867	12
Two	1867–1874: *The Lights of Home*	20
Three	1874: The *Christian Globe*	32
Four	1875: *Every Mother's Book*	46
Five	1883–1888 *Amateur Scraps*	58
Six	1886: The *New Boy's Paper*	69
Seven	1889: The *London Journal*	83
Eight	1893: Beauty For All	96
Nine	1901: 'The Garden of Glory'	111
Ten	1904: *True Blue*	128
Eleven	1907: *Puck* and the *Jester*	144
Twelve	1908: The *Butterfly*	156
Thirteen	1909: *Driven from Home*	171
Fourteen	1911: *The Girl Outcast*	188
Fifteen	1912: *Mother Love*	202
Sixteen	1914: *Human Nature*	216
Seventeen	1916: The *Happy Home* and *Woman's Weekly*	232
Eighteen	1918: The *People's Journal*	246
Nineteen	1921: The *Kinema Comic*	263
Twenty	1923: 'His most industrious apprentice'	276
Twenty-One	1924–1928: *The Girl He Thought He'd Married*	288
Twenty-Two	1931: The *Family Journal*	302
Twenty-Three	1932: *Driven from Home*, again	316
Twenty-Four	1934: *Married to a Monster*	325
Twenty-Five	1934–1936: *Deserted*	338
Notes & Sources		359
List of Illustrations		374
Index		378

Acknowledgements

I've sometimes wondered whether Joyce Allingham realised quite what she was handing on when she left me her father's business papers. She and Margery shared a theory – expounded by Margery in *The Relay*, her unpublished book about old age – that there can be an unexpected rightness about acts of inheritance. Either the person departing finds the perfect legatee in a someone they might not normally have considered, or the person continuing finds that the item they have inherited is surprisingly invaluable. I've written elsewhere about the ways in which Joyce's bequest has persuaded me to think again about different types of fiction and all that I have learned from Herbert and Margery has helped me write some fiction of my own. But a relay is a team effort and if I hadn't found so many kind friends to help me carry the baton of this legacy, the archive would still be collecting dust and I'd be looking vacant on the starting line.

Jean Seaton was the first to understand the help I needed and Jenny Hartley was the person, above all, who provided it. Other people who offered encouragment or practical support during the research stage included John and Carolyn Daines (Workers' Educational Association), Mark Knight (Roehampton University), Andrea King (Ardingly College), Sarah Gjertsen (*Daily Mail*), Steve Humphries (who put me in touch with Dennis and Irene Gilfeather), Bill Moodie (DC Thomson), Warwick Gould (Institute of English Studies, University of London), Laurel Brake (Birkbeck), Andrew King (Canterbury Christchurch University) and my PhD examiners Joanne Shattock (Leicester University) and Nicola Humble (Roehampton University). The website associated with this book (www.fiftyyearsinthefictionfactory.com) includes my thesis and bibliography as well as my catalogues of Herbert Allingham's work. Thanks to BertieWheen for setting this up and to Jack Thorogood and Heidi Carhart for typing the appendices so neatly in the first place.

It's impossible to undertake a project like this without frequent resource to libraries and it's likewise impossible to visit (most) libraries without feeling gratitude to those who work in them. Currently the skills of the Cambridge University library staff and the kindliness of Nigel Cochrane in the Albert Sloman Library at Essex University are uppermost in my mind but the days spent in the Bodleian Library, the British Library, the National Archives, the Wellcome Trust, the History of Advertising Trust, the St Bride's Printing Library and the London Library were all happy days. I left the Family Records Centre feeling baffled and am correspondingly grateful to Andrea King and Margaret Smith who both, apparently, possess the ability to conjure certificates from the most impenetrable files.

My friends in the Margery Allingham Society have been unfailingly encouraging and I'm grateful to them for persmission to quote from letters in their archive and to use their photographs. Michael Allingham, Hebert's nephew, never knew his uncle but has always done his best to answer my questions about their family. My own family have put up with my obsession for many years and my friends do their best to look interested. Craig Brown pointed me to Dorothy Hobson's book on Crossroads, Simon Heffer put me in touch with the *Daily Mail* archive, John Mullan reassured me that I hadn't filched his ideas on anonymity. When I tried out my ideas on the sales team at Signature Books and my fellow-writers at Authors Electric, I was reassured by their understanding comments. Then there was the wonderful final reading team of Patricia Wheen, Peter Dowden, Pippa Lewis and Jenny Hartley and hours of painstaking, imaginative, admirable work from book designer Megan Trudell.

If I had been writing these acknowledgements c1987 when I was sitting on Joyce Allingham's hearthrug taking my first look inside the boxes, I would have expressed fervent gratitude to Christina Carter, Joyce's friend and Margery's former housekeeper. Christina had known Herbert in the early 1930s and always described him as 'a very pleasant man'. She kept me fuelled with regular cups of tea and thinly sliced ham sandwiches with liberal quantities of mustard. Now that I am typing these final words I am supplied with smoked salmon sandwiches and a glass of white wine by my beloved partner Francis Wheen. What more can I say?

An Allingham Who's Who

Four generations of family members who appear in this book

top to bottom: *Phil, Emmie and Margery Allingham 1918; Joyce Allingham 1916; Emily Jane Hughes (Granny); James Allingham at his desk in Fleet Street*

I **William Allingham** (1803–1874), a man of property, 'James Galantry' in *Dance of the Years*. Married Elizabeth Jane 'Jinny' Jackson (1822–1872), 'Jinny Timson' in *Dance of the Years*. Parents of James, John, Julia, Emily Jane, Frederick, Walter, Percy and Haidée.

II **James William Allingham** (1840–1920), printer, publisher, advertising agent, founder of the *Christian Globe*, 'William Galantry' in *Dance of the Years*. Married Louisa Browning (1838–1920), 'Miss Julia' in *Dance of the Years*. Parents of Will, Herbert, Florence (died in childhood), Arthur, Claude, Alfred, Walter, Philip ('big' Phil), Ernest ('Tod').

Albert John Allingham (1844–1921), publisher, writer, editor, founder of the *Boys World*, *Our Boys' paper* and the *New Boys' Paper*, known professionally as 'Ralph Rollington', 'Tom Galantry' in *Dance of the Years*. Married Eva Smith from USA. Parents of four children including Grace (1873–1960), chorus girl (stage name Nelly Vaughan). Settled at Pope's Hall, Essex.

Emily Jane Allingham(1852–1952), 'Granny', 'Debbie Galantry' in *Dance of the Years*. Married William Walter Hughes, photographer, 'Walter Raven' in *Dance of the Years*. Parents of Phoebe (daughter of Walter Hughes's first marriage), Emily Jane (Em), Maud, Walter (died in WWI), Hilda (died in childhood).

III **Herbert Allingham** (1867–1936), editor and writer, 'Jeffrey' in *Dance of the Years*. Married Emily Jane Hughes (Em) (1879–1964), milliner, writer, housekeeper, 'Belle' in *Dance of the Years*. Parents of Margery, Philip ('young' Phil), Joyce.

Arthur Allingham (graphic artist). Married Florence Fisher. She was a friend of Lilian Carter (née Robinson) and introduced Margery Allingham to her future husband, Pip Youngman Carter. Florence also undertook Herbert Allingham's typing and other clerical work.

Claude Allingham was an occasional actor and writer.

Phil and **Ernest Allingham** managed the JC Francis advertising agency. Tod (the youngest brother) continued to work in advertising until his death in 1958. He managed the 'Bisto' account.

Maud Hughes (1881–1961), editor, founder of the *Picture Show*. Married Edward Wood, journalist.

IV **Margery Allingham** (1904–1966), writer. married Pip Youngman Carter (1904–1969), editor, artist and writer, son of Lilian Carter.

Philip Allingham (1906–1969), fortune-teller, grafter, author of *Cheapjack* (1934). Married Francesca Esposito (1906–1980), 'Madame Francesca'.

Joyce Allingham (1913–2003), served in WRNS, amateur photographer, administrator, benefactor.

top to bottom: *Emily Hughes and Herbert Allingham, engagement photo 1902; Maud Hughes; Phil and Herbert Allingham at Blackpool 1935*

'Merry & Bright will always delight.
One penny every Thursday'

Introduction
A Man who Wrote for the Million, 1867–1936

'"Who are you?" she demanded'

'THIS chap Anon,' says Michael Flanders in the monologue 'Greensleeves', 'is writing some perfectly lovely... Nobody seems to know who his agent is.'

Herbert Allingham, the hero of this biography, is a verifiable person: a son, husband, father, employee, taxpayer, friend. A handful of family photographs have survived, a few scattered references to his personal qualities: his kindness, tolerance, dislike of boredom, love of the music halls, enjoyment of chess, addiction to cigarettes. Nothing more than will survive of any of us. Or, almost nothing more... Allingham was also one of the uncounted number of writers and artists whose work earns no esteem. For most of his working life he was professionally anonymous; one of the hundreds of un-named or pseudonymous authors whose creations filled the comics and story papers over a period that we should call the Great Age of Print. Sometimes he was Herbert St Clair, David Pitt, Tess Allan-Wood, Houdini, Fatty Arbuckle,

Norma Talmadge, Sessue Hayakawa, Larry Semon, Victoria Strong. More frequently he was acknowledged only as 'the author of...' or as 'A Famous Author' – no name supplied.

Adult readers may look back with nostalgia to the papers they read as children – *Film Fun* perhaps, *Comic Cuts*, *Roy of the Rovers*, the *Dandy*, the *Beano*. Few, if any, know the names of either the writers or the artists who provided such dependable pleasure. The creators didn't matter; it was the excitement, the wish-fulfilment and the jokes that pulled pennies out of pockets week after week. Allingham represents the anonymous writers of a previous generation when the comic and story papers were not for children but for young working adults and the older members of their families. His first serial was published in 1886 when he was eighteen years old. He died in 1936 after fifty years earning his living by producing mass-market fiction as well as working as a hands-on editor and advertising copy-writer. Many of his business files – typescripts, diaries, account books and letters from editors – were preserved by his elder daughter Margery, a celebrated detective novelist and her father's 'most industrious apprentice'.

Herbert Allingham's working life covers a period when the ability to read was spreading throughout all classes, from the younger to the older generations and from men to women. Paper was the characteristic material of the second half of the nineteenth century as iron had been during the industrial revolution. Technological innovations combined with changes in the social and economic circumstances of people's lives to make print the dominating medium throughout society as it has never been before or since. Today, when both entertainment and news media seem to be fragmenting at a bewildering rate, it may seem restful to return to the years immediately before and after 1900. For writers like Allingham, however, the commercial world of print was anything but restful. It was dynamic and exciting, hard and precarious.

Allingham and his editors took their customers seriously. 'I get my living by studying the common people,' he wrote to his most influential employer, Lord Northcliffe, 'as you once did.' As an author he had no direct contact with readers (that was jealously mediated by his editors) but achieved success through his responsiveness to changes in the public mood, his commitment to work and his respect for the hard lives of others. His long-running serial stories dramatise issues such as poverty, insecurity and powerlessness – the facts of life for many of his readers. Yet the stories are colourful and exciting, as most people's lives were not.

Allingham's audience was huge; some of the papers which published his stories sold 250,000 to 500,000 copies a week. After which they were swapped and shared – even in the street. An Ealing Comedy film, *Hue and Cry*, written by TEB Clarke, a close friend of Margery Allingham, offers a glimpse of street-reading. These young readers assume that their weekly adventure story is a tale of true happenings; they are correspondingly dismayed to discover an elderly author in his dressing gown and skull-cap, sitting in a book-lined room, making it up. A nice twist to the film proves eventually that the readers are right. The fictional incidents are true, though not quite in the way they expected.

I'd love to think that 'Tibby' Clarke had Herbert Allingham in mind as he created the reclusive author in *Hue and Cry*. In the late 1920s and early 1930s Clarke had worked for *Answers*. This was the founding publication within the Amalgamated Press, the company that subsequently became

Fleetway Publications and IPC magazines. In the late nineteenth and early twentieth century the AP was an expanding, ground-breaking enterprise. The millions of pennies and halfpennies spent on *Answers, Comic Cuts, Forget-me-Not* and the lesser mass-market magazines in which Allingham's stories were published were the accumulating capital for the largest periodical publishing company in the world. They facilitated the foundation of the *Daily Mail*, the purchase of the *Times* and a dominating voice for a few powerful people in twentieth century news and politics. Allingham's first story for *Answers* was published in 1893, just five years after its foundation by Alfred and Harold Harmsworth and he worked consistently for the AP from 1907 onwards. He would have met Clarke at Margery and her husband Pip Youngman Carter's Essex parties, probably around the time that Clarke published his autobiographical *Jeremy's England* – an account of his travels round the country as 'Mr *Answers*'. The screen presentation of the *Hue and Cry* author, however, suggests a reference to Allingham's younger contemporary, 'Frank Richards' (Charles Hamilton) – a writer so prolific and pseudonymous that George Orwell, famously, could not believe that a single person could have produced so many words over such a lengthy period.

On one level the anonymity of the author removed a barrier between the reader and the reality of the story. On another level it was an editorially imposed strategy. This is an opposite anonymity to the literary device explored by John Mullan in *Anonymity: a Secret History of English Literature* (2007). The anonymity of Allingham, Richards and their peers is the anonymity of the common writer. It is an anonymity that permeates their work far more profoundly than the mere denial of a name. 'Anon' in the age of Greensleeves perhaps had an individual voice – or perhaps not. There were different sets of expectations between high culture, the lyrics of the court that could be bound into expensive collections and the attributions guessed at – was this song by the stubbornly independent Sir Thomas Wyatt, the dashing Earl of Surrey or even the King himself? – and the peddlers' ballads of the countryside and street which were passed from hand to hand or transmitted orally. Although Allingham does have a personal voice, it is unlikely to be apparent on first reading. He and his fellow penny-paper writers work though cliché and stereotype, shared narrative formulae that have their roots in folk and fairy tale. His melodramatic fiction was a form of journalism and his serials were never published in book format (other than the 4d volumes in newsagents' 'libraries').

'Like hair-dressing and hotel keeping, publishing is forced to be class-conscious,' wrote Margery Allingham, 'and just as front rank restaurateurs are sometimes known to have smaller cheaper establishments tucked away in the back streets where, under less dignified names, money is made and odds and ends are used up without waste, so sometimes distinguished publishing houses have humbler sisters where less rare but equally filling mental dishes are prepared and distributed.' Margery never despised the way in which her father had earned his living. She had observed him at work since childhood and remembered his study 'lined with an impressive glazed book-case containing volumes which were incomprehensible to me.' Allingham was a Fabian sympathiser and dedicated intellectual. His correspondence with the novelist William McFee shows him engaging energetically with the ideas of Shaw, Chesterton, Wells and Nietzsche. There had been, however, plenty in his study to please a child. 'The shining mahogany cupboards beneath were crammed with the coloured "comics" which were my father's files and my delight. I could look at them if I did not speak, sing or mutter and if I never took one out of the room.'

Her grief was intense when he died. Almost her first action was to pack up all his surviving manuscripts, typescripts, business letters and diaries and store them safely in her attic. There they stayed until Margery herself died and her sister Joyce took the boxes with her when she moved from the big house to a bungalow next door. I met Joyce Allingham when I was seeking permission to write Margery's biography in the mid-1980s. An academic study was already being written and Joyce wasn't certain it would be ethical to allow anyone else to begin work until that was complete. Instead she pulled out their father's archive and suggested we sort through the boxes together. I volunteered to collate manuscripts, typescripts and the clipped-out, toast-coloured pages that carried the weekly instalments of printed story. Allingham's writing life had begun in the decade when paper made from wood pulp took over from the more durable commodity made from rags or esparto and I didn't have to be told that the papers which had published his work were the cheapest of their day. Already they were browning down to match the cardboard that surrounded them, small scraps of paper flaking from the folds and edges, falling like the first leaves of an acidic autumn.

Joyce had wondered whether we might find something republishable in the boxes. I hoped so too. I had recently published a new edition of Margery's *The Oaken Heart* and had been intrigued by a reference to her father. She had been thinking of him in the early summer of 1940. 'I never wished my father alive again before this, since he had a most exasperating life, but at that time, if I could have disturbed his eternal meditation and tweaked his sleeve and said, “Come on. England Scotland and half Ireland are alone in Europe, Churchill’s in charge and we’re just going in,” I think I would have done so.’ The throwaway reference to Herbert Allingham’s life as ‘most exasperating’ was unexpected. Margery’s husband, Pip Youngman Carter, described Allingham as a handsome and scholarly man who wrote ‘with donnish precision’ and whose appearance ‘suggested an eminent theologian rather than a Grub Street hack’. ‘He wrote hard and slowly,’ Margery explained, ‘never once relaxing the enormous care that ensured his success.’ She dedicated her ambitious early novel, *Death of Ghost*, to him and used aspects of his personality for the saintly Canon Avril in her most famous novel, *Tiger in the Smoke*. So why had this man’s life been ‘exasperating’?

If I had hoped to find biographical answers in Allingham’s stories I was disappointed. I couldn’t (then) feel any authorial personality. Instead I found melodrama and repetition. Again and again, it seemed to me, Allingham’s stories opened with a young mother staggering desperately through the howling storm, her infant in her arms, both almost dead with hunger and exhaustion. Time after time, wrongly convicted heroes burst through the windows of some rich usurper in their brief moments of escape from unjust incarceration. Hero and heroine missed each other with the regularity of weathermen; their children were traumatically torn from them, then, miraculously, returned. Villains donned impenetrable disguises, armed themselves with extraordinary poisons and seemed impossible to vanquish until the ultimate instalment – which seemed to me, scanning number after disintegrating number, to be excruciatingly slow in coming.

Allingham's comic writing was easier to enjoy at first sight. I chuckled at his pre-Jeeves butler, 'Gaston Gaters', his pre-Campion adventurer, 'the Duffer' and applauded my personal favourite, 'Plucky Polly Perkins', a sparky teenager who sold sweets and tobacco and defeated the forces of pomposity or injustice on a weekly basis in the halfpenny comic called the *Butterfly*. Nevertheless, as soon as I imagined zipping Polly's adventures together into a book, they seemed thin and slap-sticky. They felt ragged around the edges, inconsistent, as two-dimensional and friable as the paper on which they'd been printed. My anxiety became more acute as my collating progressed and I began to notice serials repeated in different magazines with only the title and main characters' names changed yet the story still presented as 'new'. Was Margery's father a literary cheat? No wonder he scarcely ever put his name to his work, I thought then – ignorantly.

I assured Joyce that some university would appreciate the archive. Its value, I was certain, lay in its relative completeness: my then-final list included a selection of diaries, account books and letters from editors in addition to the manuscripts, type-scripts and the printed stories. Although there were gaps, it was frequently possible to see in some detail what Allingham had been asked to do, what he had done (and under what conditions) and how much he had been paid for doing it. It was surely unique. Joyce rarely forgot unfinished business. Towards the end of her life, perhaps when she realised that she had the cancer which would kill her – as it had killed her sister and brother before – she gave me her father's boxes and asked me to keep them until I found somewhere they would be appreciated. After her death I discovered that she had also left me a small financial legacy. This and a grant from the Arts and

Humanities Funding Council enabled proper research and cataloguing, leading to a PhD thesis *Family Fictions*.

The sixteen boxes I inherited proved far from definitive. Allingham's working life was long and his output extensive. I know that I haven't found everything he wrote. In his lifetime there was no legal requirement on publishers to deposit copies of periodicals that were not registered as newspapers. His readers lacked storage space – no glazed mahogany bookcases for them – they were editorially encouraged to swap and share, and buy again next week. Several cheap weekly papers have vanished entirely despite the best efforts of collectors.

Other of Allingham's stories may have been rendered unrecognisable by his editors or fellow common writers. There were times when urgent need for money forced him to sell his copyrights and relinquish control over his work. Plots could be passed around as tangible entities: devised by one author or editor, 'written up' by someone else, no names attached. While Allingham himself was scrupulous, even pernickety, about ownership, he suspected that there were those who were not. Attribution is further complicated by the explicit understanding that most narratives were being drawn from a common stock. Editors would order a 'convict' story, an 'impersonation' or a 'mother love' story knowing that their requirements would be understood. The ninety-eight full-length serials that I am able to list with confidence (www.fiftyyearsinthefictionfactory.com) were published at least 299 times in various formats (straight reprint, abridgement, re-write, re-format) in at least fifty-eight different periodicals or in newsagents' 'libraries'. Over many years Allingham's words touched very many lives, however fleetingly.

Offering a biography of an author who remains so essentially self-effacing may seem perverse. There are no salacious revelations here, no undiscovered masterpieces. Allingham was an almost exact contemporary of Arnold Bennett. Surely, one might argue, a close investigation of the lives and writings of, say, Bennett, Wells and Gissing coupled with the insights in Jonathan Rose's *The Intellectual Life of the British Working Classes* and a good dollop of social anthropology and Mass Observation is all we need to understand reading habits in the Great Age of Print?

All I can say is that, for me, the investigation of Allingham's working life has been thrilling. Margery and Joyce preserved their father's files because they loved and admired him and believed that his work was worthwhile. The vast majority of working-class readers in the Great Age of Print (and working-class readers were the vast majority) weren't reading to better themselves and didn't read fiction published in book form. For their rare moments of entertainment and escape they read newspapers and disposable serial fiction. This was a market that grew exponentially during Allingham's fifty publishing years. His archive offers us an insider's view of a truly popular art form. As a conventionally educated bookish person I have found this illuminating and... humbling.

The fiction factory has changed and diversified since Allingham died. There are only a handful of magazines which still print fiction in instalments – the *People's Friend*, *My Weekly* and *Woman's Weekly* are the sole survivors from Allingham's day. Generally serial stories are very much more likely to be watched or listened to rather than read. If Herbert Allingham were alive today he'd probably be one of the unacknowledged script-writers on a long-running, low-budget, TV soap. Let's hope that the contributors to *EastEnders* or *The Archers* are even now recording their experience. Because, as

Allingham's prolific older colleague, EH Burrage, asserted, 'We were the men who wrote for the Million and as such were not without our influence in the world.'

'As soon as I tried to turn I saw the packing case above my head tremble'

Chapter One
Born 1867

WHERE to begin the story of a working life? At birth or first employment? Allingham's time in the fiction factory commenced in 1886 when his uncle John Allingham ('Ralph Rollington') published the first instalments of his school serial *Barrington's Fag* and paid him 30 shillings for it. Many working people never forget the thrill of receiving their first pay packet; the defining moment that marks the transition from childhood to adult status. For many writers the first sight of their words in print feels equally significant. So it was for Allingham in 1886.

I have, however, chosen to backdate my account to 1867, the year of his birth. Allingham's family circumstances were immediately relevant to his career. Both his father and uncle earned their livings in the periodical publishing industry and the fortunes (or the lack of fortune) of other family members were directly affected by conditions in the print trade. There were printers, photographers, 'black-and-white' men, advertisement canvassers. For three generations the Allinghams' livelihoods depended on the steady consumption of print by their fellow citizens. 1867 was the year of the Second Reform Act. It was an auspicious year for a future fiction worker to be born.

The Second Reform Act almost doubled the male electorate from 1,057,000 to 1,995,000 in a total population of over twenty million. Not everyone was pleased. 'The only thing we can do is as far as possible to remedy the evil by the most universal measures of education that can be devised. I believe it will be absolutely necessary that you should prevail upon our future masters to learn their letters,' said Robert Lowe, MP for Calne in Wiltshire (pre-1867 electorate 124 voters, abolished 1885). Lowe had already served as the first Secretary of State for Education. 'If it is not efficient it shall be cheap', he said. Now he became Chancellor of the Exchequer in the administration that took the first steps towards compulsory education for all. WE Forster's 1870 Education Act had many loopholes and shortcomings but did establish the national system of school boards. Forty years later, in the years immediately preceding the First World War, Britain finally attained near 100 percent nominal literacy. That would be boom time for Allingham.

The electoral reforms of 1867 had been well overdue. The nineteenth century was a period of unprecedented demographic change and internal migration. From nine million in 1801 the population of England and Wales had grown to thirty-two and a half million by 1901. At the mid-point of this dynamic development, the census of 1851 confirmed that England had become the first country in the world where more people lived in urban than in rural situations. From the perspective of the communication and entertainment industries the importance of that single statistic can hardly be overemphasised. The connections between changes in working-class housing and the development of popular reading seem to me to be profound and, as far as I know, largely unexplored.

William Allingham, Herbert Allingham's grandfather-to-be, was already on the electoral register. He was a south London property investor and private mortgage provider; a man whose actions (according to his great-grand-daughter Margery) were mainly dictated by his anxiety to protect his status as a gentleman. William and his wife Elizabeth Jane (Jinny) had lived in their attractive detached residence in Penton Place, Walworth for over thirty years. William had probably spent all his life south of the Thames. He would have witnessed dramatic change as the population of Greater London increased from just under one million in 1800 to over six and a half million in 1901. The population of the parish of St Mary's Newington, where Herbert Allingham would be born, rose from 14,847 in 1801 to 107,850 in 1881. The fields and market gardens, even the marshlands of Walworth and Kennington, were built over to accommodate these new inhabitants.

William and Jinny's oldest son James and his wife Louisa lived minutes away from Penton Place in a modest terraced house in Penrose Street. Herbert Allingham would be their second child. James was not technically a gentleman. He was a compositor by trade and would be the first member of the Allingham family to set himself out deliberately to profit from the extension of literacy. Meanwhile he and his father were busy making money from the housing boom. William Allingham owned several freehold properties in the neighbourhood as well as leaseholds and shares in the rudimentary building societies of the day. He had helped to finance the subdivision of the Georgian squares and terraces, the in-filling of front gardens, and loss of green space. In the 1871 census James described himself as his father's 'clerk and secretary'.

There's no evidence to confirm whether or not James's

wife, Louisa, Herbert's mother, was literate. She had been born Louisa Browning in 1839, one of the youngest children in a family that consisted mainly of daughters. At the time of the 1841 census the family were living in Gower's Walk in the parish of St Mary, Whitechapel. Then, as now, this area contained some of the poorest families in London. Charles Booth's 1889 *Descriptive Map of London Poverty* shows the east side of Gower's Walk as coloured pink – 'Fairly comfortable. Good ordinary earnings.' The west side of Gower's Walk had been demolished to make space for the Tilbury and Southend Railway goods depot and the area beyond is coloured by Booth dark blue and black – 'Very poor, casual. Chronic want.' 'Lowest class. Vicious, semi-criminal.' When space was needed for railways, slum areas were deliberately chosen for destruction. When Louisa was a child Gower's Walk could have been a street on the brink.

In 1861, three years before her marriage to James, Louisa Browning was living with her unmarried oldest sister, an upholsterer in St-Georges-in-the-East. Their seven-year-old niece was living with them. Booth's map colours their street, Little Turner Street, an uncompromising black and dark blue. For Booth, Little Turner Street was a slum. For Louisa, two decades earlier, who knows? Life for a self-supporting East End household of two unmarried sisters and a child is unlikely to have been easy. Her grand-daughters, Margery and Joyce, remember Louisa as ambitious, uncharitable and snobbish. These unattractive qualities become, perhaps, more three-dimensional if she was privately contrasting the relative success and material comfort of her married life with an earlier struggle for survival.

It was not, of course, true that all working-class people were illiterate before the 1870 Education Act. Most Victorian people were working class and this designation covered a huge range of capability, achievement and lifestyle. James Allingham in his capacity as a compositor was working class and so were the struggling seamstresses in Little Turner Street and their neighbours in 'chronic want'. The circulation of the London-published weekly newspapers in the mid 1860s was over two million, with more than half of the total being the cheap, slightly disreputable Sundays, such as *Lloyd's* and *Reynolds' Weekly News* and the *Illustrated Police News*. Fortunes had already been made by a few early entrepreneurs selling fiction in 'penny dreadful' instalments and there was a scattering of slightly more respectable penny story-papers, such as the *London Journal*, founded in 1841. In Scotland, John Leng, the astute editor-proprietor of the *People's Journal* (1858), was poised to found the *People's Friend* (1869). This is the oldest story-paper still in existence in Britain today and the last survivor of what became, in Herbert Allingham's lifetime, such a welcome form of entertainment for ordinary working people.

Three other children, who would push their newspapers and magazines into almost every home in Britain, were born within a few years of Herbert Allingham: Alfred and Harold Harmsworth (Lords Northcliffe and Rothermere), in 1865 and 1868 respectively, and their competitor, C Arthur Pearson, in 1866. They – and the John Leng and DC Thomson companies of Dundee – were Allingham's future employers and the founders of the huge mass-market publishing corporations that would dominate the twentieth century.

The Great Age of Print was fuelled by more than increasing literacy. From 1865 wages had began to increase at a higher rate than prices and by 1870 most working families were 10 percent better off in absolute terms than they had been in 1850. This didn't of course mean that everyone's lives were happier and easier. The 1870s brought a trade depression and even in the good times, individual families experienced constant insecurity in a society with no welfare system. Loss of health or loss of job could spell crisis for the wage earner and his or her dependants. Even in the good times the physical and emotional strain of family care took a far greater toll than we can easily imagine. Mental illness was not as glaringly apparent as physical degeneration and disease but it certainly existed in the Victorian working-class family. The public asylum came as the end for some unhappy people as the gutter or the workhouse did for others.

The increase in working-class incomes from 1865 was an increase measured only in shillings and pence and may scarcely have been perceptible in many households. There were so many new demands on the family budget. Compulsory elementary education, for instance, was not free. Children were expected to bring in between a penny and fourpence every Monday morning – in some schools as much as sixpence. Their dependency increased under the new educational arrangements and their earning power was deferred. Healthcare was not free and the risk of disease and death remained high for all members of the family. There was no more cholera after 1867 but the diseases associated with under-nourishment and overcrowding continued to flourish. The early 1870s saw an especially bad outbreak of smallpox and the virulency of diphtheria increased throughout the latter part of the century. Rents in urban areas accounted for a far larger proportion of the poorer people's earnings than for the prosperous classes. Only pennies, or better still half pennies, could be spared for entertainment.

'Taxes on Knowledge' – the parliamentary stamp duty on newspapers and extra duties on paper and on advertising that had previously kept periodical prices artificially high – had been withdrawn by the early 1860s and there had been important technical developments which affected the speed and cheapness of print production. Broadly speaking the new technology of the industrial revolution had reached printing considerably later than it had reached the primary manufacturing areas of the British economy. In 1800 the maximum output was 250 sheets per hour for the hand operated, single-sheet presses that were not so very different from their fifteenth-century originals. Since that date, however, press design had been transformed by steam power and new, stronger, construction materials. The techniques and raw materials of papermaking had been revolutionised and innovative processes such as stereotyping speeded productivity still further. 1866 was a landmark year when the Walter Press revolutionised the output of the *Times* newspaper, producing twelve thousand perfected eight-page sections in sixty minutes.

There was one spectre at the feast, one unheeded voice predicting where, in social and economic terms, such commercial acceleration might lead. In 1867 Karl Marx, who was living in Maitland Park, north-west London, finally completed the first volume of *Das Kapital*. Publication took place in Germany and the author would be several years' dead before any English translation was made. His work was noticed, briefly and disparagingly, in two of the London review magazines during 1868 but it made little impression on English consciousness in these early years. Herbert Allingham, Arthur Pearson and the Harmsworth brothers were born and grew up in an Age of Capital. The appearance of *Das Kapital* in the year of Allingham's birth has the spurious neatness of an astrological prediction. Marx's analysis, when applied to the print industry, illuminates the larger economic context, the patterns of growth, accumulation, exploitation and alienation that would invisibly determine this new baby's working life.

'"Can you scrub floors?" she asked eagerly.'

Chapter Two
1867–1874: The Lights of Home

How did Allingham's grandfather, William, acquire the money to invest in south London housing? In 1943 Margery Allingham played with their family history in *Dance of the Years*, her 'who am I?' novel. She pretended that William was 'James Galantry', the legitimate offspring of an elderly landowner and a Gypsy girl. In Margery's story the elderly landowner left 'James Galantry' money in trust and he supplemented this shrewdly, first by trading in horses and then by buying and selling little plots of land. Some of these plots came from the Gypsy mother so their origins, as well as his own, had to be concealed behind a façade of the utmost respectability – far more rigidly respectable that was necessary for anyone who was at ease with their position in society.

Autobiographically, in *The Oaken Heart* (1941), Margery claimed that her great-grandfather 'was born in 1800 and was left ten thousand pounds and the injunction that "no gentleman ever works"'. Who had issued this edict? A parent? A trustee? She does not say. Ten thousand pounds would have been a lot of money bequeathed to a young man born in 1800. Joyce Allingham once said that she thought their great-grandfather might have made his money by patenting some sort of invention. Neither sister was convinced of the literal truth of the Gypsy ancestress but they liked the idea. For Joyce it explained a certain bohemianism that she noticed in herself and some of her relations, and when Margery was writing about their brother Philip's decision to become a fortune-teller she said that he went to join the Gypsies, 'as one of our family has always done'.

Margery felt sorry for William, her great-grandfather. 'The annihilating bondage of never being able to work like anyone else of one's ability without losing something irreparable must have irked him as it would me.' Work, for these younger Allinghams, had become a core value. As Philip Allingham wrote, 'You know how we all feel about earning our livings... to be ourselves, to feel well even, we've got to know that we can pay our way and earn.' That was part of Herbert Allingham's legacy to his children, an idealisation of work that went beyond the pragmatic. It stemmed, ironically, from William Allingham's bequests – or lack of them.

It matters less where William had acquired his money than how he managed it. Margery said that he had 'devoted his considerable powers to laying out his money judiciously and lived like a rich man' but she knew that he hadn't died like one. The ten thousand pounds – or whatever it had originally been – was not enough to maintain himself, his wife and their eight children at even a minimal level of middle-class respectability and still have enough to enable all those children to live in idleness as adults. William bought printing apprenticeships for the two oldest boys and possibly the third. The two older daughters were educated as young ladies: Julia learned the piano as her mother Jinny had done and Emily Jane spent some time at school in Germany. Both of them were sufficiently good readers to be kept reading the *Times* to their father 'all day' if he required it.

They were not, however, so ladylike that they couldn't cope with changes of circumstance. Julia took charge of the household after their mother died. Then, after their father also died, she supplemented the family income by giving piano lessons until she married the 'keeper of a refreshment bar'. She had a family of her own and continued to give her younger siblings a home for as long as they needed one – which in the case of Haidée, the youngest daughter (born in 1867, the same year as her nephew Herbert), seems to have been for the rest of her life. When Emily Jane's marriage to a photographer failed, leaving her destitute with a stepdaughter and four young children, she was able to work as a domestic servant.

Emily Jane was Margery's maternal grandmother and was living with Margery in the 1940s when both *The Oaken Heart* and *Dance of the Years* were written. She evidently enjoyed talking about her childhood and leaves a brightly coloured glimpse of the Victorian Allinghams. Consider Margery's description of 'James Galantry's' (William Allingham's) house, for instance: 'It was in Penton Place, just off the Walworth Road, then in its youth and a highly select thoroughfare. It was not very big, eight or nine rooms at the most, but very elegant with double doors to throw the two parlours into one. It had two little gardens; a paved one in front with figures and dwarf shrubs, and a long one at the back, containing a mulberry tree, a pear tree and a syringa with a seat round it.'

This – and further scattered details such as the bluebirds on the main bedroom wallpaper – has the vividness and specificity of a very old lady remembering the details that struck her as a child. The house is characterised by its 'comfortable respectability' and anchors the main character into social acceptability.

How grand was it really? There is a revealing moment when the *Dance of the Years* narrator mentions that 'the servants had not yet been engaged'. The employment of three servants constituted an accepted minimum for middle-class respectability. The 1841 census return for William Allingham's actual household in Penton Place lists only a single fifteen-year-old maid. There are no live-in servants mentioned in either the 1851 or 1861 census. As the house in Penton Place was not large (even in fiction) it would have been much cheaper and more sensible – though not so socially smart – to engage staff who came in by the day. The nineteenth-century Walworth Road did not remain a 'select thoroughfare' for long and living as a 'landed proprietor' (William Allingham's census designation) on the borders of Walworth and Kennington did not imply social exclusivity. In 1851, for instance, William and Jinny's neighbours were a 'labourer in garden' and a post office clerk.

James and Louisa Allingham's house, 18 Penrose Street, where Herbert, his older brother and younger sister were born, was even further removed from its representation in fiction. *Dance of the Years* describes 'William Galantry' (James Allingham) bringing his bride back to 'the large, ivy covered house inconsequentially named Laurel Lodge in the decent suburb of Shepherds Bush'. A version of this house did exist in reality but not until the 1880s and not in south London. Herbert Allingham's birthplace in Penrose Street was in the leafier part of Walworth but had recently been disturbed by the construction of the railway, which ran on high arches over the street and the surrounding area to the Elephant and Castle. The immediate neighbours were families headed by a clerk, a gardener, a compositor and a retired builder. A few of the households had a single live-in servant; others took lodgers. The widow and her two grown-up children who shared Number 18 with James and Louisa recorded the presence of a two-year-old 'child visitor' on the 1871 census. The child's surname differs from her hosts and her birthplace is recorded as Hampstead. The census was taken in the evening and, while the little girl may have been a visitor, it's not impossible that she was one of the many unwanted, orphaned or illegitimate children in Victorian London who were boarded with impecunious widow ladies.

Herbert Allingham's earliest years were spent on geographical and class boundaries. One way out of his birthplace in Penrose Street led to his grandparents' home with the two parlours and those elegant double doors. The other led under the railway arch and across the Walworth Road into East Street. Here there was a new and bustling market and a colony of costermongers and here lived the Larter family, forebears of Michael Collins, author of *The Likes of Us: a Biography of the White Working Class*. Collins's great-grandfather, Henry Larter, was born in 1867, just a few months before Allingham. His father, Will, earned his living making wheels for the costermongers' barrows. Henry Larter would grow up to be a carman, transporting goods between factories in Southwark and Bermondsey, among other semi-casual jobs. Before that he would be convicted for stealing sherbet from a shop in the Elephant and Castle and sent, aged thirteen, to an industrial training ship, *The Shaftesbury*, moored far down the river at East Ham.

Allingham wrote nothing directly about his Walworth childhood. The single surviving moment of insight into his family at home comes via his incomplete diary of 1886. But by then James and Louisa had moved their family west and north, settling eventually in Hammersmith. In 1867, when Allingham was born, the families on the west side of the Walworth Road still had access to the thirteen-acre open space of the Royal Surrey Gardens. There had been a zoo in the Gardens during James Allingham's 1840s childhood, with giraffes. After that, from 1857, there was a music hall, capable of holding up to ten thousand people for high-class concerts or evangelical preaching. In 1872, however, the music hall was demolished and the pleasure grounds sold for building. Neighbourhood historian Mary Boast describes the new Surrey Gardens Estate as built up with narrow tunnel-like streets packed thick with five-storey blocks. It was oppressive and over crowded.

Initially both Allingham families shifted a few streets further west. William Allingham spent the last years of his life in a Georgian house in Kennington Park Road. James and Louisa and their young family moved to Kennington Road in the Borough of Lambeth. But Lambeth too was filling up. George Gissing's novel *Thyrza* (1887) paints a detailed and realistic portrait of the streets between the tree-lined Kennington Road, where the Allinghams lived, and the lively market place in Lambeth Walk.

> The market-night is the sole out-of-door amusement regularly at hand for London working people and the only one, in truth, for which they show any real capacity. Everywhere was laughter and the interchange of good fellowship. Women sauntered the length of the street and back again for the pleasure of picking out the best and cheapest bundle of rhubarb, or lettuce, the biggest and hardest cabbage, the most appetising rasher: they compared notes and bantered with each other on purchases. The hot air reeked with odours. From stalls where whelks were sold rose the pungency of vinegar; decaying vegetables

trodden under foot blended their putridness with the musty smell of second hand garments: the grocers' shops were aromatic: above all was distinguishable the acrid exhalation from the shops where fried fish and potatoes hissed in boiling grease. There Lambeth's supper was preparing, to be eaten on the spot, or taken away wrapped in newspaper. [...] The people were of the very various classes that subdivide the great proletarian order. Children of the gutter and sexless haunters of the street corner elbowed comfortable artisans and their wives; there were bareheaded hoidens from the obscurest courts and work girls whose self-respect was proof against all the squalor and vileness hourly surrounding them.

Herbert Allingham's fiction was written for 'work girls'. Gissing's heroine, 'Thyrza', buys and reads exactly the type of penny story paper that Allingham would be editing from 1889 just two years after this novel was published. James and Louisa and their family had already moved on – first to Chiswick and then to Hammersmith – but it's clear that Allingham never forgot the scenes of his childhood. When he returns to south London in his stories he does not describe the streetscape in detail, as Gissing does, but sketches it with deftness and confidence. Gissing's readers may have been slumming as they read about the Lambeth Walk. They would have relished every sniff of rotting cabbage leaf or glimpse of gutter child. Allingham can trust his audience to know the type of locality he means and not despise it. A sketch is all he needs; more would slow the story's pace.

The Lights of Home (1910) was one of Allingham's earliest successful serials. The hero, Harry, is a young naval officer, the heroine, Lucy, the daughter of a baronet. They have been ejected from their natural habitat, an English manor house, and it takes fifty weekly instalments for them to achieve their return. When the young couple's adventures take them south of the river they are out of their depth: they cannot read the language of the streets.

Saxdell Road is a neighbourhood that has seen better days. The houses are large but faded. Many have long gardens on front of them, all badly kept and littered with rubbish.

At the corner of the road stands the Retreat. This building is even larger than the others and it is more neat and respectable in appearance. Big trees and shrubs in the front garden screen it from the road.

There is nothing in its appearance to indicate that it is any more than a private residence, but *everyone in the neighbourhood knows* it to be Dr Fenn's Private Asylum for the Insane [my italics].

The building is silent; all the blinds are pulled down. Readers would have been willing Harry not to walk up that long garden path, not to ascend those clean stone steps, nor ring that bell, which sounds so far away in the interior of the house with a deep, muffled clang. This is a house where the doors click shut behind you.

Dr Fenn's Private Asylum is connected by a long passage to its hidden annex, a warehouse by the River Thames, dark, rat-infested and with all the apparatus to facilitate a thrilling escape by the heroine. Lucy's child has been left behind, however, and she is forced to return. She is accompanied by two police officers but they are easily fooled by the doctor and Lucy is once again imprisoned. She overcomes the warder, lifts her sleeping baby from her cot, tiptoes into the dark and silent corridor and gazes desperately from the high window.

In the distance, beyond the trees in the garden; she could see the lights of the London street; and could even perceive the people moving restlessly to and fro.

She leaned out of the window, as though to call for help, and that wild thought did for a moment flash through her mind, only to be discarded at once, as she realised the futility of it.

'Oh, to be in that crowded street, poor and penniless, jostled by the passers-by, but free!'

This introduces one of Allingham's main themes – the decency and supportiveness of ordinary people. Lucy and her child do escape and succeed in reaching somewhere not unlike the Lambeth Walk, or perhaps that earlier market place in East Street.

At last, after passing through several dark and almost deserted back streets, she suddenly emerged upon a busy thoroughfare. It was a market centre, and the hawkers' barrows, with their naphtha lamps, lined both sides of the road. It was past midnight but there were still plenty of people about and the whole scene was an animated one.

For the first time Lucy experienced the sensation of being free from pursuit. As she fled through the dark streets, she had felt that someone was on her heels, but here, in the blaze of light, and amidst this noisy, laughing, good-tempered crowd, she felt somehow safe.

She falls asleep on an upturned box and when she wakes, cold and weepy, she meets Sal, a coster girl. '"Hello!" she said cheerfully, "Having a doss on the cheap, ain't you?"' Lucy is inclined to give in to self-pity but Sal has no sympathy with lady-like vapours.

'Don't grizzle, mate! That won't do no good. What's up with the nipper? Ain't it well?'

'I think she is hungry,' said Lucy helplessly, while the corners of her mouth twitched pathetically.

'Hungry! Well you're a rummy sort of mother, you are! You got hands, ain't you? Why don't you work? Or if you can't work, why don't you beg? You got a tongue, ain't you? If it comes to that, I reckon I'd do a bit of stealing afore I'd see a nipper of mine starve! You bet I would! What ho!'

This stings Lucy into a passionate avowal of her willingness to work, if she only knew how. At which point Sal relents. She makes baby Margery a bed on her barrow and takes both mother and child home for 'a bust-up on fish and taters'. Once they are rested and restored Sal spells out the facts of existence.

'You ain't used to work. I can see that by your hands. But if your man is dead or run away, you'll have to set-to. Now, I wants a girl to help me with the barrer – to help shove it when I've got a load, and to give it an eye when anybody calls me away. Will you take on the job, or are you too much of the lady?'

'I shall be very grateful,' declared Lucy earnestly.

'Right-ho! That's a bargain then. I'll give you a bob a day. There's a decent woman as lives across the landing as will look after the nipper for fourpence a day. That will leave you eightpence for grub. You can sleep here with me.'

I can't immediately recall reading any other early twentieth-century author who thinks to factor in the cost of childcare. Allingham's heroines need to face up to adversity. They also need to work although, if they're as refined as Lucy, they're not always particularly effective. Work is hard to find and hard to keep. Even the coster-girl soon hits a lean patch. Meanwhile she proves to be as canny as she is kind. Dr Fenn from the private asylum may have fooled the police, but he stands no chance with Sal.

'Mad?' enquired Sal in astonishment.

The doctor nodded.

'Yes, poor thing, a very sad case.'

'It isn't true – it isn't true! Oh Sal, believe me, it isn't true!'

'Of course it ain't true,' returned Sal promptly. 'None of your half-larks, old 'un! That's my mate. You leave her alone. D'ye hear? You leave her alone. Leggo, you old sinner, or I'll give you what for!'

Dr Fenn makes the fatal mistake of attempting to push Sal aside.

'What!'

There are many ways of saying 'What!' Sal's way made the word seem like an explosion, and caused Dr Fenn to put up his arm quickly to protect his face.

Sal, however, did not fly at him as he anticipated. On the contrary, she kept outwardly very calm. Then, placing two fingers in her mouth, she blew a shrill, ear-piercing whistle.

Almost instantly there appeared, from goodness knows where, a tall, lean man, with an ugly-looking face, a broken nose, and wearing a dirty yellow scarf round his neck.

He came upon the scene with a queer kind of a glide.

'Bill!' said the girl.

'Wot yer, Sal!'

'See that old toff?'

'Yus.'

'Bash him!'

The asylum keeper flees. He dashes down a blind alley which Sal describes as 'the hottest quarter round here'. Sure enough when he emerges 'his coat was in ribbons; his collar was torn from his throat and his usually mild and benevolent face was distorted with rage and terror.' The week's instalment ends with a characteristic moment of Allingham humour as Dr Fenn is routed and Sal has the last word.

As he went screaming down the street, in a frenzy of terror, with a pack of roughs at his heels, Sal turned to Lucy. 'Did you see him shove me?' she exclaimed indignantly. 'Sorcy old villain! I've half a mind to tell the perlice!'

'Lucy found herself suddenly released and Sal's arms around her.'

Chapter Three
1874: The Christian Globe

William Allingham died in January 1874. By July of the same year his son James had produced the registration issue of a penny paper called the *Christian Glowworm*. From this time onwards seven-year-old Herbert Allingham and his brothers would grow up in a household where copy deadlines, advertising rates, distribution and the price of paper were live issues. James Allingham did not observe the convention that home and work were separate spheres. He liked to talk about his work. Herbert's 1886 diary conveys a sense of bustle when 'Dad' comes home from his office in Fleet Street full of that day's doings. The diary mentions occasional business visitors calling at home and the older boys being required to help entertain them. In the 1870s, when James and Louisa still lived in Kennington, advertisements reveal that the property business was managed from their home address.

William Allingham's financial legacies had made the paper possible. After his death there were no more scruples about it not being respectable to be seen to work: James went at it with a will. He moved his family from Penrose Street to Kennington Road and invested in a printing works across the river in Farringdon Street and Bear Alley, close to the eastern end of Fleet Street. As James had been apprenticed as a compositor, it's likely that he already knew this area well. Now he could describe himself as a 'Printer Master' or 'Printer & Publisher'. The registration issue of the *Christian Glowworm* reads like the production of someone who is filled with energy, knowledge and ideas but is not yet sure which way he should direct them. James draws the attention of 'Pastors of Churches and other friends' to his print production services. He has 'NEW TYPE! NEW MACHINERY!' and can undertake every description of letter-press, copper plate and lithographic printing with book binding on the premises.

The first issue of the *Christian Glowworm* was a modest affair. It was a four-page sheet aimed primarily at the Sunday School and tract market but with a complete page (25 percent of the total space) devoted to patent medicine and similar advertisements with two insertions from property finance providers. The editor announced that he had hopes of achieving a circulation of 40,000 by Christmas. The *Glowworm* was soon re-named the *Christian Globe* (a decision not unconnected with the fact that the current market leader was the *Christian World*) and its circulation began to rise. James Allingham was able to claim 31,000 at Christmas, 57,000 in April, 76,500 in May. His paper, he bragged then, had 'more reading matter than any other Christian penny paper in the world'. By October 1875 the *Christian Globe* was published weekly and had become a limited company with almost 200 shareholders. It was registered as a newspaper and the editor had his sights on a weekly circulation of 100,000. James could now claim, credibly, that it was the second best selling publication of its type. The price remained one penny and advertising still accounted for at least 25 percent of its sixteen pages. The newspaper would survive another forty years, providing occasional or regular employment for various of James Allingham's brothers, sons and daughters-in-law, but it would never again be as successful and exciting as in those early days. James Allingham was a natural entrepreneur: innovative, persuasive, energetic, perhaps not over-scrupulous. By the early 1880s he would be moving on again.

James Allingham's initial sales pitch in the *Christian Glowworm* had been directed towards the Sunday School movement. He offered superior religious tracts for sale. 'Being got up in Book Form, Illustrated and printed on good Toned and Coloured paper, they are more readily taken than the ordinary kind of Tract, and are admirably suited to Sunday school teachers to give the Children to take home to their parents.' These were to be sold by the hundred or thousand at prices determined by the number of pages. Another early idea was to include a weekly Sunday School Question Box.

> Question: Does it not add to the interest of a Sunday School to have lady teachers for boys and gentleman teachers for girls?
>
> Answer: Yes. Mix the sexes all you can, yet not too formally. It is even well to put boys and girls together in the same class, under proper circumstances, instead of treating them as wild beasts of different varieties who must be restrained with bit and bridle lest they come near each other.

This feature failed to catch on. Possibly James hadn't got the tone quite right? In 1874 Sunday Schools and tract distribution societies were big, established markets and big, established markets might not be so easy for a newcomer to break into. The *Christian Globe* eventually dropped its tract advertisements though it continued to promote and occasionally to publish other religiously orientated books, such as collected sermons and pious fiction. Later, both Herbert and his wife, Em, would contribute sentimental Christmas tales with some heart-warming moral attached. James Allingham's *Christian Glowworm* promotion of his pictorial tracts as being 'more readily taken than the ordinary kind' unintentionally anticipates where his longer-term success would lie. They sound like a spiritual form of patent medicine.

The newspaper itself was James Allingham's best idea. In his editorial introduction to that first number of the *Christian Glowworm* he presents it merely as a superior sort of tract – 'for men and women who need to read tract-like matter, but who throw tracts aside'. Then, as he expands on his vision, it becomes abundantly clear that what he really wants to do is to produce something 'popular'. He wants his newspaper to be 'interesting' (a stronger word then than now) and to entertain people. 'Useful, exciting and popular'. He wants to build a successful paper: he shows no desire to preach or convert.

This number of 'The Glowworm' is the first of our new series, and will secure, we trust, the approval of our readers. We rejoice to know that during the last few years papers of this sort have multiplied in England, but in proportion to the immoral and hurtful literature they are still in a minority. Our desire is to furnish a periodical that will be welcome in the houses both of people who are connected with the churches and of those who are not.

We are convinced that many read the trashy and vile papers simply because they will read anything that comes to hand, and that these will as readily read moral and religious literature if it be interesting and they can get it. We shall endeavour to make 'The Glowworm' as good as the best penny serials of the day... We hope occasionally to illustrate our pages by pictures and we promise to do our best to make our paper as useful, exciting and popular as possible. We think we have a strong claim on Christian people for earnest and practical support. A little effort on the part of many will secure for us great prosperity and the more we succeed the better will the paper become.

James Allingham has spotted literacy as a business opportunity and literacy plus righteousness as going one better: 'A little effort on the part of many will secure for us great prosperity.' It's easy to smile at the effrontery of this appeal – James was seeking prosperity for himself, not for a church, a charity or any wider cause – but he was not wrong. Other people did get involved and played a part in the paper's success.

One of the most interesting features of the *Christian Globe* (the paper that developed from the *Glowworm*) is the way that it was funded. The initial capital, James's personal contribution, had come from his father. William Allingham's estate had been valued for probate at just under £4,000. While this did not, technically, make him rich it was a thoroughly useful amount even when divided between seven children. To put it in perspective: advertisements in the *Christian Globe* reveal that a long lease on an eight-roomed house in the area could cost £310, or a villa at Twickenham with eleven rooms (including two WCs) and a large garden 'planted with full-bearing fruit trees' could be had for £480. When the paper became a limited company in November 1875 all James's adult siblings were among its initial investors. Over the ensuing forty years of the paper's life Allingham family events such as marriage and divorce, the prosperity and penury of individuals, the shifting balance between generations, can be traced through the transactions in the *Christian Globe* share registers, preserved in the National Archives.

James's closest associates – the men who were most active in helping him to float the *Christian Globe* as a limited company – were a core group of 'Members'. They were south London businessmen and none had any obvious connection with either evangelical religion or the periodical publishing industry. Most of them subsequently became directors of the company. The largest non-family shareholder was a hop-factor (an occupation that may seem surprising in a periodical promoting temperance). The others included a doctor, a 'commission agent' and Louis-Philippe Noble, described as an ivory turner. Advertisements reveal that Noble was also a property developer owning a number of houses in and off the Walworth Road. The doctor and the hop-factor soon dropped out and sold their shares to other 'commission agents' who became closely associated with the management of the paper.

What exactly did all these commission agents do? Characters from the novels of Arnold Bennett (1867–1931) frequently provide a helpful gloss on James Allingham's wheeler-dealer world. Here's a commission agent encountered by the young Denry Machin in *The Card*: 'Mr Calvert was a little fellow of fifty who had made his money in the mysterious calling of a "commission agent". By reputation he was really very much harder than Denry could ever pretend to be, and indeed Denry had been very much startled by the advent of such a client. Surely if any man in Bursley were capable of unmercifully collecting rents on his own account, Herbert Calvert must be that man!'

The 'mysterious calling'... In *The Uses of Literacy* (a book that is almost an A-Z guide to the world of Herbert Allingham's readers) Richard Hoggart refers to a recognised bookmaker as a commission agent. 'Their street corner betting is a risky business, if they ran an account with a Commission Agent it would not be.' James Allingham would soon move away from editorship towards advertising agency. There were commission agents in this world too.

In the mid-1870s James was carrying on his father's property business, partly because this was his duty as his father's executor but perhaps also on his own account. He and his oldest sister Julia had been left the private mortgage portfolio. Early issues of the *Christian Glowworm/Christian Globe,* inserted from James's home address, advertised 'Money ready to be ADVANCED on Freehold or Leasehold property' and, alternatively, 'ONE HUNDRED ONE POUND SHARES in the Camberwell Advance and Investment Company Ltd FOR SALE [...] in consequence of the owner having urgent need of cash.'

Other property-finance companies used James's business address at 29 Farringdon Street. One of these was the Starr-Bowkett Building Society. 'Why pay rent', ran the Starr-Bowkett marketing campaign, 'when by a small weekly subscription you can become your own landlord?' Unfortunately, it was not quite so simple. A ballot was central to the Starr-Bowkett system, thus inviting accusations of gambling. The resulting 'appropriations', intended to provide the thrifty (and lucky) working man with the lump sum necessary to buy or build a house, could became tradable items in the hands of unscrupulous dealers. Arnold Bennett refers to the 'perils' of the Starr-Bowkett system as well as the 'defalcations' of other secretaries of societies. Richard Starr became briefly notorious.

The businessmen in Margery Allingham's family novel *Dance of the Years* are horribly untrustworthy. 'Counsellor Greatpiece', for example, invested in the *Converted World* newspaper as a form of spiritual money-laundering. Margery appears to be setting the scene for a late Victorian tale of commercial treachery of which Bennett himself could have been proud – or John Galsworthy, another of those 1867 babies. 'William Galantry', James Allingham's fictional avatar, is a supreme hypocrite. He is arrogant, unprincipled and his decision to found his penny paper is nakedly commercial.

> (He) worked out the cost of the printing, the office and the distribution, and soon became fascinated. He saw the venture in its clearest and most material light. To him it appeared as a method of selling low-grade bulk paper at forty times its value, with the added advantage that the more of it one sold the higher the profit became. He saw, too, that it was the ink on the paper which did the selling, so that the only real problem was which words to print with the ink.

Which words to print with the ink? It's a good question. 'William' in the novel has acquired a moribund periodical, which is only read, if at all, for its weekly chess problem. He has also converted to Nonconformity and begun associating with the south London preacher, Charles Haddon Spurgeon. Margery's grandmother, Emily Jane Allingham, James's second sister, remembered Spurgeon only as 'low' but he was a big public figure, especially south of the Thames. In the period from 1857 when the older generation of Allingham brothers and sisters was still living in Penton Place, Spurgeon regularly used the Royal Surrey Gardens Music Hall for sermons that reached an audience of thousands. It must have been a memorable sight. This inspires 'William Galantry'.

> One day, as he watched the crowds thronging the Gardens outside the Surrey Music Hall, and thought of the panting mass of humanity in the aisles, and the eager eyes fixed hopefully upon the vision which the earnest East Anglian evoked, it occurred forcibly,

and even reverently, to William that here was a subject that would appeal to a great many more people than the venerable game of chess.

By 1874 when James founded his *Christian Glowworm*, the Surrey Gardens music hall was gone and Spurgeon was established in the Metropolitan Tabernacle near the Elephant and Castle. These were years of religious revivalism. As many as one and a half million people may have listened to the American evangelists Dwight Lynam Moody and Ira Sankey when they visited London in 1875. Star preachers became celebrities and were chased around the country by shorthand writers attempting to transcribe their pronouncements for the edification of the newspaper-reading faithful. James was quick to grasp the possibilities of photography to enhance this cult of personality and to produce spin-off products, such as portraits, for sale to his readers.

The journalist Hartley Aspden remembered that the *Christian Globe* scored an 1870s evangelical coup when James Allingham signed up the charismatic US preacher, Dr de Witt Talmadge. Talmadge only rarely left his home base in Boston but was a polished self-publicist. His sermons were published in scores of American papers and he claimed to preach every Sunday 'to the largest audience in the world'. He sent James Allingham a photo to accompany his first sermon: 'You ask me for my photograph. Here it is; my wife who knows everything of me worth knowing says it is the best of me yet taken [...] In reference to your paper it surprises me by its cheapness and pleases me by its spirit of pure Evangelism. Let there be light! You are welcome to anything I say or write.'

James Allingham's editorial described Talmadge's sermons as 'flowing warm from his heart'. The American offered emotionalism, star-status and a celebration of domesticity that clearly appealed to *Christian Globe* readers as his sermons appeared weekly from 1875 for almost the next forty years. By 1877 Talmadge's sermons were 'phonographically reported and forwarded in advance'. A regular appeal was printed in the paper beside them: 'Dr Talmadge requests that all readers of his sermons every Sunday morning, between eight and ten o'clock, pray for the Blessing of God on his work.' This plea for endorsement and support, involving the millions of unknown readers, accords with the *Christian Globe*'s presentation of itself as a virtual community, a good people's club.

As well as the Allingham family members and the south London entrepreneurs, James Allingham's newspaper attracted a third group of shareholders. In the initial capitalisation £5 shares had been bought, in ones and twos and tens, by ordinary members of the public from addresses all over the country. Half a dozen Nonconformist ministers (including the Spurgeon brothers) were among those who held a few shares each; the listed occupations of the other small shareholders cover a wide economic and social range.

> Stay-maker, horse-keeper, stationer, bank manager, surgeon, doctor's assistant, civil engineer, solicitor, grocer, groom, ironmonger, shop assistant, clerk, accountant, butter merchant, labourer, warehouseman, registrar of births, governess, newsagent, gardener, upholsterer, chemist, pastry cook, hosier, lodging house keeper, watchmaker, brewer, outfitter, book-keeper, spinster.

There were almost two hundred such investors, approximately a quarter of them women. How normal was it for shop assistants, clerks and labourers to invest £10 or £20 in a business flotation? There is nothing comparable in the other penny paper records that I have been able to consult. In Bennett's *The Card*, the Countess of Chell's groom and coachman possess a few shares each in the Universal Thrift Company, but this is as a reward for services rendered. MJ Daunton, writing on the late nineteenth-century 'sociology of investment', observes that lower middle-class people with a little surplus money tended to invest in property or business premises in their immediate neighbourhood (as William Allingham had done); richer people (assessed at over £5,000 at death) were more wide-ranging in their investments. The majority of small investors in the *Christian Globe* cannot have belonged to this wealthier category. Neither were they, in any modern sense, playing the financial market as most of them (unlike the Allingham family members and the 'commission agent' group) retained their holdings, neither selling nor buying, for the lifetime of the Association.

The obvious implication is that their investments were ethically motivated. They were believers and they wanted to feel part of the enterprise. The word 'Christian' had taken on a new shade of meaning from the late 1860s and 1870s. It denoted a sharing of the new evangelical point of view and moved closer to a marketing term, a lifestyle choice. Evangelical religion itself became less dogmatic, more emotional and sentimental, translating easily into acts of practical philanthropy. As a history of revivalism explains, 'Involvement with a Christian group could provide employment (paid or unpaid), social contacts and entertainment as well as personal spiritual uplift.'

Twenty-five years later, in 1900, the *Christian Globe* paid tribute to its readers:

It is pleasant to think of the many forms of social and religious work which the readers of the *Christian Globe* have assisted during these last twenty-five years. Whenever we have advocated any work of Christian endeavour which seemed to us good, we have been encouraged by the hearty approval and support of our readers. We think the reason for this is that we have entered but little into the religious controversies which vex our age, and have been content to advocate on broad lines the cause of righteousness wherever we have seen it. Finally, we have endeavoured to make the *Christian Globe* essentially a paper for the home circle. It is our desire that every member of the household should find in its pages something to specially interest him or her. It has always seemed to us that the kindly human side of life is the side best worth cultivating. What the world wants today is more sympathy, more love, a keener sense of human brotherhood. To help in some small way towards the cultivation of these good qualities is our aim, and in achieving it we doubt not that we shall continue to receive the assistance of our good friends the readers of the *Christian Globe*.

In *Dance of the Years* Margery presents 'William Galantry's' *Converted World* as a calculated sham.

'It's wonderful, Will. So very clever, my dear. But not religious.'

'Not religious, Mama?'

'No dear,' said Jinny, 'not religious.'

It was all that she could tell him and when he argued with her and pointed out the name of the Almighty in every other paragraph, let alone on every page, she stood her ground helpless and without the means of expression.

But Margery's information was coming from her grandmother, Emily Jane, the person who would have been cast as the hapless victim, if the second volume of the family trilogy had ever been written. Her father, Herbert, might have had a different point of view. He clearly learned a great deal from growing up in this practical publishing household and there is no evidence that he disapproved of his father as a businessman. His scattered diary references to 'Dad' sound affectionate as well as dutiful. As an adult he developed his own career so didn't work as closely with James as two of his younger brothers did. Nevertheless he remained more or less involved with the *Christian Globe* throughout its existence and was ready to hurry to his father's assistence whenever there were particular financial or editorial problems.

Neither James nor Herbert Allingham was religious: neither would have wished to enter into 'the religious controversies which vex our age'. Herbert would have agreed with the writer of the twenty-five year tribute that 'the kindly human side of life is the side best worth cultivating' and the concept of the *Christian Globe* as 'essentially a paper for the home circle' was one which was important throughout his career. There were practical reasons for this. The late-nineteenth-century publishers of mass-market penny papers were compelled to assume that the disposable income within their target households was extremely limited. A single weekly purchase was often all that could be managed. Literacy was still patchy: those who could read read to those who could not. Domestic space was limited so people were forced to sit together, often sharing a single source of light and heat. The *Christian Globe* was one of a number of penny papers where the initial evangelistic impulse was secularised and sweetened into a more general offering. 'Every member of the household should find in its pages something to specially interest him or her.' The illustrated front covers moved away from portraits of celebrity preachers towards more general celebrities – philanthropists or royalty – and then to sentimental pictures, often including children.

The idea of family reading is no longer mainstream in modern society and there are many reasons for this – not least increased light and heat and greater private space within the home. As soon as working families had a little more disposable income the twentieth-century periodical publishing companies realised that it would be more profitable to target different gender, age or interest groups with more narrowly focused products, thus fragmenting the household reading experience. This process can be observed throughout Allingham's writing career as the readership of mixed-age or mixed-gender periodicals was split whenever his employers saw an opportunity to get two separate pennies where only one was spent previously. Capitalistic acumen followed as well as led social change. The experience of the First World War, for instance, was so damaging to families – and to faith – that it was not surprising that religious family periodicals suffered correspondingly. The *Christian Globe* was among the casualties.

'The Adventurers'
A photograph of the young Margery Allingham and her brother Phil used as a Christian Globe *front cover, 1912.*

Chapter Four
1875: Every Mother's Book

SAFE TEETHING!
DO NOT LET YOUR CHILD DIE!
Fenning's Children's Powders Prevent Convulsions,
ARE COOLING AND SOOTHING.
FENNING'S CHILDREN'S POWDERS
For Children Cutting their Teeth, to prevent Convulsions.
Sold in Stamped Boxes at 1s. 1d. *and* 2s. 9d. *(great saving), with full Directions.*
Sent post-free for 15 *stamps. Direct to* Alfred Fenning, *West Cowes, I.W.*
Read FENNING'S EVERY MOTHER'S BOOK, sent post-free for 8 stamps.
EASY TEETHING!

Fenning's advertisement, Christian Glowworm

Little Florence Allingham, Herbert's only sister, died in March 1875. The doctor certified that she had had pertussis (whooping cough) for twenty-one days. She died at home, 137 Kennington Road. Her father, James, was present at the end.

Whooping cough is an intensely distressing illness for both the child and her helpless carers. Intense spasms of coughing may continue for several minutes until the child is blue in the face and all air expelled from the lungs. The whoop comes after the paroxysm as she desperately inhales air before the epiglottis is fully open. She may then be sick. Survivors may sustain permanent lung or brain damage: death comes from complications such as bronchopneumonia and encephalitis. Even today there is no medical treatment against whooping cough as such. Antibiotics may help to ward off complications and, in some cases, slow the development of the illness but the main factors that protect twenty-first-century children are vaccination in the first months of life and, possibly, a more recent reduction in the virulence of the bacteria that cause the illness. When Florence died, aged five, there was medically nothing that James and Louisa or their doctor could have done to prevent such an outcome.

They were not alone, of course. Although overall death rates had begun their slow fall from 21.8 per thousand in 1868 to 18.1 per thousand in 1888 (and thence to 14.8 in 1908 and 11.7 in 1928) young children in the Victorian period were horrifyingly vulnerable. Whooping cough was a major killer. It was also highly infectious with every cough droplet showering those nearby with bacteria. As usual the statistics are grimmest for the poorest and worst-housed of the population but there were many families throughout the income range who suffered the same anguish as James and Louisa. An evangelical paper, such as the *Christian Glowworm,* offered them the consolation of religion:

> Let me sit down with you and take your hand. Let me speak with you as one who has thrice tasted the same sorrow and would gladly share the same joy as Jesus gave with it. [...] You may chide yourself with the reflection if only I had known this and done that, or something else had been different, this sorrow would have been spared me, but no, the Lord came in His own time. He took His own way. He has done all things well.

On a human level the advice to parents not to chide themselves 'if only I had known this and done that' appears reasonable and kindly. Yet, as soon as the *Christian Glowworm* reader turns to the next page, a new message is shouted out.

DO NOT LET YOUR CHILD DIE! READ FENNING'S EVERY MOTHER'S BOOK, sent post-free for eight stamps.

The author, Albert Fenning, a patent medicine manufacturer from the Isle of Wight, was one of James Allingham's most regular advertisers. His *Every Mother's Book* bemoans the annual waste of infant life. 'In London alone almost twenty-five thousand children die every year who have not attained ten years of age. But who is to be blamed for this? The mothers? The doctors? Certainly not their all-wise Creator.'

God having been exculpated, poverty and poor town planning let off without a caution, Fenning blames the doctors. Mothers should make up their minds to do without them. 'Its *theme* shall still be the necessity of yourself becoming your Child's only Doctor – and its object, the safety of the little *earth-angel* that nestles in your bosom and the preservation of the small *loved ones* who lisp you Mother.' Every mother has only to make the resolution 'to trust herself and believe that the same reason which assists her in comprehending difficult *crochet*-patterns will also enable her to understand a few medical facts.' Read *Every Mother's Book* and 'you will then know as much, nay more, about Children's diseases and how to cure them than many of the professed Doctors: and being likewise NURSE will be much better able to save life.'

Unsurprisingly, mothers-as-doctors will need to lay in ample supplies of Fenning's products. 'With common sense, a little more care and *by the means of a few simple, safe, sure and ever-ready remedies,* four out of every five of those fated babies can be saved from such an early, such a premature death' [my italics]. Saving four out of every five is a comparatively modest target by Fenning's standards. Elsewhere in *Every Mother's Book* the claims are even larger. Whooping cough, for instance, can 'always' be cured 'within a few days' by Fenning's Hooping Cough Powders, given three times a day. 'A safe and certain antidote to this injurious disease.' Better still, combine them with Fenning's Fever Curer and Fenning's Lung Healers three times a day, then Fenning's Cooling Powders every night.

'We will with thankfulness conscientiously declare that whenever they have been timely adopted and used as prescribed we have not known *one* case fail among the many thousands who have used them for they have always quickly restored the sick child to perfect health.'

Yet there is no cure for whooping cough. Fenning, whose hatred of doctors and distrust of medical science had presumably immunised him against any understanding of the germ theory of disease (developed by Pasteur in the 1860s), offers parents no advice about the importance of quarantining their other children against the deadly, droplet-spread bacteria. If Louisa Allingham had been following *Every Mother's Book* without taking any additional precautions, Herbert, William, little Arthur and baby Claude Allingham would have been lucky to have survived.

Fenning's Cooling Powders were the mainstay of his business, the cure-all no family should be without. Unlike some notorious Victorian remedies, there was nothing chemically harmful in Fenning's powders. Later analysis proved them to contain 65 percent potassium chlorate and 35 percent powdered liquorice. The cost of the ingredients for sixteen sachets was about one farthing: they were sold for one shilling and three pence. *Every Mother's Book* recommended that they should be used every day or every other day at least. If Louisa had given each of her eight boys a sachet a day, as advised, she would have been spending four shillings and fourpence a week – for ingredients worth one penny. Four and fourpence was little less than the amount very poor families spent on a week's rent. And she would have bought them no medical protection whatsoever.

Fenning's manufacturing costs were minimal: his main expenditure was on the patent stamp, on packaging and, above all, on his advertising campaigns. The second half of the nineteenth century was remarkable for the growth and imaginative excess of its advertising. 'Advertising is to business what steam is to machinery – the great propelling power,' was an often-quoted piece of mid-Victorian business wisdom, used, for instance, above the advertising rates section of James Clarke's *Christian World*, Allingham's main competitor. The abolition of newspaper advertising duty in 1853, together with the removal of the other 'taxes on knowledge', attracted a rapidly increasing proportion of manufacturers' rapidly increasing advertising expenditure towards periodicals. Unlike stunts, posters and mail shots, advertising in periodicals offered the in-built advantages of an instant audience and ready-made distribution systems. In return, advertising revenue provided the steady income that encouraged printers and publishers to invest in new machinery that would enable them to vary their layout, keep their prices down, boost their circulation – and thus make themselves still more attractive to advertisers. Unsurprisingly different types of perioidical attracted different types of advertising. As a general rule, the lower the class of paper (therefore the poorer or less well educated its readers) the more patent medicine advertising they carried. The *Christian Globe* carried a lot.

James Allingham had initially tried marketing his advertising services to 'servants requiring situations and employers requiring assistants' but employment advertising was already well established in the *Christian World*, which remained the best-selling evangelical penny weekly. James Allingham's display rates were always a little cheaper than James Clarke's and his interest in technical innovation meant that the *Christian Globe* was better adapted to accept illustrated advertisements – therefore better adapted to sell things than people. James

Allingham's advertising courted the unsophisticated customer. Poorer families, eating a poor diet, would find it hard to pay a doctor's bill so were more likely to try the various tonics, cough medicines and indigestion remedies so copiously recommended.

'Surely to mislead and rob poor sick and suffering humanity, aided and abetted by a government who imposes a stamp duty, is the most despicable crime one can possibly imagine?' asked the Advertised Remedies Exposure Campaign in 1929. It was not a new thought. In the years between 1868 and 1908 Parliament had passed a series of six Acts designed to expose and suppress the charlatans of the patent medicine world – while, at the same time, it continued to legitimise the trade with official stamps. It has been calculated that in 1908, for instance, the government earned three million pounds in duties and the manufacturers spent a further two million on advertising their products. 'The Press reap a rich harvest from the advertising of proprietary medicines and are not prepared to expose them and so kill the goose that lays the golden egg.' The British Medical Association published its own 'Secret Remedy' exposés in 1909 and 1912 and the Government set up a select committee. HG Wells wrote the gloriously satirical *Tono-Bungay* in 1909 – and Herbert Allingham's closest friend William McFee produced a searing indictment of false advertising in his masterpiece *Casuals of the Sea* (of which more later). But there were no great changes: *Every Mother's Book* continued to be published and to recommend Fenning's patent products until at least 1936.

The Victorians of the 1870s took a surprisingly pragmatic – even cynical – approach to advertising in their religious press. A survey of metropolitan religious papers, published in 1875, ends its admiring analysis of the *Guardian* ('the most influential and ablest of them all'): 'The price is sixpence; and as it has a large circulation for a paper published at so high a price, and has a great number of well-paid advertisements, it is one of the best paying weekly papers in London. I should be surprised if the annual profits of the *Guardian* be much less, if less at all, than from £4,000-£5,000.'

Successful advertising agent Henry Sell, who had begun his Fleet Street career at the *Christian World*, went further and highlighted the causal link between effective advertising and religious papers:

> An important fact not always or even generally appreciated is that, though the Advertisement and Editorial columns are entirely dissociated, yet the latter lend the former an unconscious influence which should be borne in mind by the Advertiser, and should guide him in his selection of papers nearly as much as circulation. This is probably the explanation of the extraordinarily successful results of advertising in the religious papers, as it is obvious that such papers do exert *an almost personal influence* on the majority of their readers [my italics].

Good newspaper and magazine editors work hard to promote a feeling of ownership and involvement from their readers and James Allingham had clearly been successful in this. Too successful perhaps? ES Turner, author of *The Shocking History of Victorian Advertising,* convicts the 'so-called religious' press of a variety of malpractices including the advertising of abortifacients, the promotion of financial scams, money-lending and baby-farming. Advertising in the *Christian Globe* under James Allingham's editorship presents a somewhat murky picture. Advertising and editorial columns were not 'entirely dissociated' – as Sell (what a good name) assumed. Sometimes they contradicted one another – as in the proximity of the Fenning's DO NOT LET YOUR CHILD DIE! advertisment and the advocacy of Christian resignation – but that is part of the heterogeneous nature of newspapers and magazines. James began to intersperse advertisements throughout his editorial pages and also to use advertorials (columns that look like articles and are only at the end revealed as advertisement). Other advertisments were very wordy and made lavish use of narrative and personal testimony – thus blurring the boundaries further. Later it would be James's son Herbert who was often employed to write the copy for this style of advertisment.

I have not seen abortifacients advertised in the *Christian Globe* though 'Mrs Labbatt's Female Pills' – a blend of pennyroyal and steel wool 'guaranteed to clear any distressing obstruction' – are occasionally to be found in the *London Journal*, for which James was later the advertising agent and Herbert Allingham the editor. The *Christian Globe* includes some slightly shaky property finance offers and occasional announcements from other financial promoters but I would hesitate to condemn them definitely as scams. Some small ads may come from money lenders and I have noticed two – but only two – which made me wonder about the notorious baby-farmers. 'A respectable married person would take a baby from the birth.' 'Married lady would take entire charge of a child. 5 years for £40.' Did James Allingham consider these advertisements legitimate, or did they simply slip through?

James Greenwood, the journalist who exposed the scandal of the baby-farmers' advertisements, was a friend of James Allingham's brother, John. He suggested that evaluating cost was the key factor when assessing the genuineness of any advertisement of this sort. When an unplanned pregnancy could completely lose a woman her livelihood, as well as her good name, illegitimate children were frequently boarded out – with relatives, with childless couples, with women, perhaps widows, in need of livelihood and occupation. Naturally these children would have expenses and the parent, usually the mother, would be expected to contribute.

The first advertisement makes no mention of payment: was this a purely altruistic offer by the 'respectable married person' or would there have been a private financial negotiation? In the second, £40 would have been a large sum to have paid to the 'married lady' in advance but seems little to cover a child's expenses over five years – about four shillings and fourpence a week – enough to keep the Allingham boys in daily cooling powders or rent a small slum room. Would there have been a refund if the child had happened to die? The children of Herbert Allingham's fictional characters are frequently taken from them and placed in grim, semi-criminal locations, often with some misleading title, such as the House of Hope – and usually in south London.

Editorially, the *Christian Globe*'s attitude to children was notably benign. Although it placed a conventionally high value on obedience, it spoke out against corporal punishments, such as the use of the cane in schools, and against fear-inflicting punishments, such as shutting children in dark cupboards. It insisted that children should be cherished as their time on earth might be short and was always an eager supporter of Dr Barnardo, of National Refuges for Homeless Children, and of the London Society for the Prevention of Cruelty to Children. 'How to make children lovely?' asks the *Christian Globe* 'Family Circle' column rhetorically. 'There is just one way: that is to surround them day and night with an atmosphere of love.'

The *Christian Globe* was a kindly paper. As well as

commenting on church and national affairs, its leader columns and miscellanies embraced a variety of causes: it was against vivisection and white veal, in favour of shelters for cabmen and education for canal folk, indignant about the treatment of native Americans and Hindu wives, and increasingly concerned, in a socialistic way, about the relation of Labour and Capital.

Herbert Allingham's Fabian-sympathising leader columns of 1909 suited it well. He may have contributed many more leaders over the preceding years but there are no records or diaries for this period and the columns themselves are conventionally anonymous. In times of industrial strife the *Christian Globe* took the side of the workers, but reluctantly, wishing that both parties would respect the other's point of view. The *Christian Globe*'s political stance was Liberal-Labour and central concern was with improving the quality of life on earth, not in the hereafter – which could have been a moral justification for advertising, if the paper's management sincerely believed in the value of the products advertised. Joyce Allingham remembers her grandfather James cursing the inefficacy of the indigestion remedies he promoted and it is impossible to believe that he felt personally convinced by the wildly exaggerated claims of Albert Fenning and all the other quacks whose advertisements he displayed. Advertising was, and still is, part of the periodical publishing business. James was, above all, a businessman.

During the 1880s there were some attempts towards greater caution in acceptance of advertisements. The Religious Tract Society, for instance, publishers of the *Boy's Own Paper* (1879), had a policy which forbade advertisements for certain items, such as firearms. James Allingham's brother John, who founded a boys' weekly paper in the same year, happily advertised air rifles and catapults until he sold it to a more scrupulous company in

1886 – when such advertisements promptly ceased and the paper, soon afterwards, folded. The main changes in the advertising world, however, were concerned with the ethics of business practice rather than the censoring of individual products. By 1883 James Allingham had given up describing himself as a 'printer and publisher' and called himself an 'advertisement canvasser'. He set up an advertising agency in partnership with one of the *Christian Globe* shareholders, James Caradoc Francis, a 'commission agent' from Walthamstow. The profession of advertising agent was relatively new. 'He has sprung into existence almost in the life of a single generation,' wrote W Stead Junior in *The Art of Advertising* (1899). 'The advertising agent is the nerve centre of modern industry... He keeps as it were his finger on the commercial pulse of the world, counts its beats and adjusts the method and quantity of advertising accordingly.'

When not checking the global commercial pulse, the job of an agent, like James Allingham and JC Francis, was to buy space for their clients' advertisements in newspapers and magazines. If the agent already owned the periodical from which they were purchasing the space there was an obvious conflict of interest. This was known as 'farming' and was increasingly deplored. James needed to put some distance between himself and the *Christian Globe*. His shareholding at the *Christian Globe* Newspaper Association was sold and a new firm, AC Bradley, took over as the paper's printers. James's Fleet Street office address changed and he moved house from Turnham Green, Chiswick to 365 Goldhawk Road, Hammersmith. No records of the JC Francis Agency survive and Francis himself went under. He succumbed to depression in 1909 and was discovered dead one morning in the company office, having cut his throat. James Allingham issued brisk press releases and weathered the crisis with particular help from two of his sons, 'big' Phil and Herbert.

The dissociation between James and his newspaper was more apparent than real. His *Christian Globe* shares were soon back in the family and the advertising display spaces (including the regular Fenning's spot) were filled very much as before, though the property advertising had ceased. Additionally the JC Francis agency took over the advertising for all the other periodicals printed and published by AC Bradley Ltd. The role of the agent continued to develop until even small agencies began, routinely, to do more than locate suitable space. They planned marketing campaigns and supplied artwork and copy-writing services. The JC Francis agency survived the demise of the Christian Globe in 1916 and the death of James himself in 1920. His two youngest sons, 'big' Phil and Tod continued running the business. Their brother Herbert was an informal colleague and occasional copy-writer.

Whole page CICFA advertisement written by Herbert Allingham

Chapter Five
1883–1888: Amateur Scraps

Herbert Allingham arrived in Cambridge as a non-collegiate student in 1883. He was fifteen years old. Where, if anywhere, he had previously been to school remains a mystery. The 1871 census shows his older brother, Will, boarding at a small private school in the Kennington Road but there is nothing to show whether Allingham also attended. A randomly filed piece of paper from the Lower Third Form at Chiswick Collegiate Preparatory Department in 1879 may apply to him but has no name attached. All that is certain is that he did not, as his daughters believed, attend Ardingly College in Sussex. Allingham was said to have been 'delicate' as a child and my best guess is that his educational experience may have resembled the character 'Jeffrey' (his character) in Margery's *Dance of the Years* who was always being sent home from school due to ill-health.

Non-collegiate students were, as the term implies, students who were not part of a college. The category had been established in the early 1870s as a gesture towards widening access to the university by reducing the essential living costs.

Life in college cost upwards of £100 a year and the university authorities were realistic about the tendency of undergraduates to encourage one another into extravagance. They were also aware that local traders were more likely to allow young men to run up bills when they were invisibly underwritten by membership of a college. A scheme was drawn up whereby the non-collegiate students would live in approved (and inspected) lodgings, be bound by university rules, pay university dues and have a Censor to record their daily attendance and supervise their well-being.

By the time Allingham arrived in 1883 there were approximately ninety students enrolled under the supervision of a non-collegiate board. They were required to sign on for at least five days of each week for twenty-two weeks' residence during the three university terms: Lent, Easter and Michaelmas. A meeting room had been set up for them in a former furniture shop in the Trumpington Road. There they could pay small extra subscriptions to read the communally purchased newspapers and magazines, take part in occasional debates and join their own boat and cricket clubs. If they were reading for Pass degrees they were compelled to attend certain lectures (to ensure the professors an audience, cynics commented) and some of the colleges invited them to attend their internal courses of instruction for a modest fee. Otherwise the non-collegiate students worked with private coaches towards the various different university examinations and attended any other public lectures that were available.

This was less than ideal. Many of the non-collegiates had not come from public schools: their initial education, like their university education, had been dictated by penury. Access to competent, consistent teaching surely mattered more to this group of students than to most of their college-based contemporaries. The university registers for this period record very few non-collegiate students as possessing the necessary certificates to exempt them from the Previous (or Little-Go) exam. In December 1886, for instance, when Allingham finally passed the Previous, only one non-collegiate student had been exempted from part I of the exam among eighty-nine college-based applicants; two non-collegiates and fifty-nine college students had been excused part II. Allingham (passing in class four) was one of only twenty-two non-collegiate students out of a total of 286 successful candidates. It had taken him three years to reach this point. 'I really must manage it and I will,' he wrote in his diary.

When Allingham reached the next stage, the General exam in Easter 1888, he was one of seven non-collegiates (out of a total 137 students) who passed or were excused. Looking at the BA lists for December 1888 it would appear that whole swathes of the curriculum were beyond the reach of non-collegiate students. There were eight non-collegiate successes in music and the remainder of the eighteen non-collegiate students who obtained degrees did so via theology, modern history, modern languages or part I of the natural sciences. Allingham himself was one of the two successful modern history candidates, albeit in the third class and for a Pass, not an Honours, degree. 'A disorderly collection of fragments of learning' is the way the BA Pass degree is described by the official university historian. In fact, for a non-collegiate student, it was a considerable achievement.

Non-collegiate students were third-class travellers and they knew it. Some of them were managing to keep their university expenditure to as little as £50 a year, half that of the minimum college bill. Most spent £70-£80. Allingham's 1886 diary has an incomplete book list which shows how difficult this could be. Green's *History of the English People* is going to cost him £3 4s 0d, Craik's *History of English Literature* £1 5s 0d, *Introduction to the Literature of Europe* 16s 0d, *History of Greece* £3 12s 0d, *History of Rome* £2 2s 0d and so on. The Censor in charge of the non-collegiates noted that these students were often socially isolated. They did not arrive with a group of friends from public school and lacked both confidence and money. Even when some of the colleges opened their facilities to these outsiders most were too shy to use them. The official university history quotes Sir Maurice Amos, a Trinity man, reminiscing about his experience of Cambridge life in 1891.

> For me, admission as an undergraduate of Trinity was the transition from a rather solitary and very unconventional life to the vivacious world of a great national institution, offering in the fullest measure all that I most desired, the delightful companionship of a great variety of young men of my own age, sports of all kinds, a vivid intellectual life, endless conversation, great libraries, learning in floods; the sweet sense of conventionality, discipline and decorum, symbolised by my blue gown, my surplice in chapel, the bell ringing for chapel, the scrutiny of porters, the unirksome rules about gates and exeats, all of which made me feel at every moment of the day that I was a privileged member of one of the greatest of English Societies.

It seems safe to assume that this was not Allingham's experience. The keepers of the lodging houses where he and his fellow non-collegiate students lived were not allowed to provide their residents with dinners for more than three guests without permission from the Censor. No hired musicians were to be allowed without written permission and no entertainment at all on a Sunday. They were not to give students keys to their outer doors and were obliged to report anyone who went out after 10pm or returned after midnight. The non-collegiates also had to obey all the other statutes of the university, although, given their fundamental need to live economically, the additional prohibitions against involvement in horseracing, gaming, driving a four-in-hand, discharging firearms and putting on entertainments in taverns or public rooms might not have felt too onerous.

The work was hard – or at least Allingham appears to have found it so. It was three years from his arrival in 1883 before he passed the Little-Go exam. Study of Greek and Latin set texts was required as well as Latin and Greek language questions, arithmetic, algebra and Euclid. One paper required study of one of the Gospels in the original Greek, another tested knowledge of Paley's *Evidences of Christianity*. It was hardly surprising that both his daughters believed he had read theology! The General exam, which comprised the second element of the degree, was like the Previous exam but more so – the entire Acts of the Apostles in the original Greek; elementary statics, hydrostatics and trigonometry. Candidates for an Ordinary degree were allowed to specialise only in their last year of study, the point at which Allingham chose modern history.

Did Allingham have any fun at university? Possibly. During his time as an undergraduate the Cambridge authorities did begin to make changes to enhance the experience of the non-collegiate students. From 1885 Allingham and his fellows had some organised lecture courses of their own. The former shop on Trumpington Street where they were obliged to register their attendance was officially purchased by the university, together with buildings on either side and a furniture warehouse at the back. It became Fitzwilliam Hall. Allingham made a few friends and spent small sums such as 11d and 1s 6d playing cards and billiards. He even ran up the occasional debt – the amounts of 6d and 3s are recorded in his diary, as well as a fine for the larger amount of 6s 8d. Best of all he met some girls.

They were Nellie and Lilian Robinson and they were running an Amateur Literary Society. They lived with their widowed mother in Warkworth Road, not far from Parker's Piece, an open grassy area which features occasionally in Allingham's writing as a site for cricket. Warkworth Road and the network of residential streets where Allingham and his fellow non-collegiate students had their lodgings were part of Cambridge's own nineteenth-century urban expansion: unpretentious terraced houses, a brisk walk away from the historic colleges at the city centre. The Society usually had about a dozen members, men and women, some living in Cambridge and some outside. Lilian and Nellie produced and circulated a hand-written monthly magazine, *Amateur Scraps*. They made the rules, solicited contributions, bound the numbers and sent them round the membership before totting up the annual marks of approval and awarding prizes.

First and second prizes were almost always earned by Lilian and Nellie themselves. Their dedication to the project over the three years (1885–1888) from which issues of *Amateur Scraps* have survived suggests that they had time and intellectual capacity that was not otherwise being used. There were women undergraduates in Cambridge by the time Allingham was in residence and they are occasionally mentioned in *Amateur Scraps* – with a cautious interest but no apparent wish to emulate. The Robinson girls claimed equality with their male friends but seemed happy enough to look forward to a domestic future, as companions to their husbands and good Christian mothers to their children.

The Amateur Literary Society grew to a membership of twenty, and then gradually declined. Some of the young men finished their courses and moved on, one to the London Hospital, at least two, probably three, to work as curates. *Amateur Scraps* kept them in contact with their Cambridge existence at the cost of one shilling a year subscription and the postage involved in forwarding each month's number. Towards the end of the surviving run, however, the editors became irritated with those who read but did not contribute: especially if they kept the magazine for more that their allotted two days or, worst of all, mislaid a number. All such were firmly struck off.

The contributions to *Amateur Scraps* were unsigned, except in some of the later numbers where pen names were used. Allingham was 'Clio' in articles or essays: 'Old Growler' for criticism. In June 1885 one of the Robinson sisters provided an essay on novels which Allingham marked with an A of approbation. It included an attack on 'the penny weekly ridiculous papers sold at railway stations or in the poky shops of all large towns.' The essayist expected her reading of fiction to expand her mind and was eager for information about the author. 'We sometimes find that their lives have often been very sad and disappointing, more so in some cases, than that of their most unfortunate hero or heroine.' She expressed gratitude to Fanny Burney 'for setting the example of novel-writing to women' and ended with a defence of love as an eminently suitable subject for books for girls, supporting her argument with verses from Longfellow.

Allingham's friendship with these sisters was a new experience. He had some female cousins and an aunt (Haidée) of his own generation but no one until now with whom he could work in such a congenial venture. Was there flirtation in the air? Years later Lilian Robinson's son, Pip Youngman Carter, wrote of an 'unfulfilled romance' between his mother and Herbert Allingham, a 'near-engagement' even. One of Lilian's closest friends did marry Allingham's next brother Arthur and the family connection led eventually to marriage in the next generation, between Herbert's daughter and Lilian's son.

Herbert wrote to Lilian: 'You and I would not be human if this engagement did not carry our minds back over the years... It so fell out that we both found happiness apart from one another but tonight I like to feel that the qualities that made us sympathise with and understand one another were transmitted to our children and have been the means of bringing them together.'

Allingham's first contribution to *Amateur Scraps* had been a short sentimental serial entitled *Life for Love*. Only one instalment has survived and it is certainly stronger when focusing on the problems of the hero – an impecunious young journalist – than on the personality of the heroine. Alfred 'had chosen a literary career and sought to gain a livelihood by the aid of his pen. None but those who have tried it know what such a life is. How familiar were those short curt notes from editors refusing his sketches, articles and stories.' Alfred and the golden-haired heroine become 'best of friends' but the following number of *Amateur Scraps* is missing so we will never know what happened next.

Herbert Allingham was seventeen when he met the Robinson sisters. When the editor of *Young Folks Paper* rejected his essay on 'The Jew in Shakespeare, Dickens and Scott', which he had submitted to their prestigious Literary Olympics, a regular competitive feature, he gave it instead to

Nellie and Lilian. It's almost surprising that he didn't write for *Amateur Scraps* every month but there was all that studying to be done and he was at least as frequently at home with his family in Hammersmith as he was in his lodgings in Norfolk Street. His contributions are rarely sentimental. He practises writing about character types – such as 'Bores.'

> Poor friends, funny-men, would-be actors, authors, poets etc, collectors for some 'highly charitable purpose' who go about wearing a hungry expression and carrying a memorandum book and a bit of lead pencil, the end of which they ever and anon chew with great avidity as though trying to extract some nourishment therefrom.

Including 'poor friends' in a list of 'bores' is uncharacteristic of Allingham. A protest one year later shows that he has learned better.

> The writer of this article, having first made it impossible for us to mistake who he means, then proceeds to dilate on their peculiarities... He even goes so far as to say that one of these gentlemen required a new pair of trousers and then ventures a sneer at him because his father keeps a shop in the town. This is surely out of place. The Freshman who writes the article... will learn when he has been a little longer in Cambridge that it is not the custom of the 'Varsity to judge a man by the length of his purse or by his position in the social scale... We all know that these two men are eccentric and the present writer has not written these few words in their defence; for he does not number either of them among his personal friends, but what he has written is merely as a protest against that snobbishness and priggishness which of late has endeavoured to make itself seen in the university and which has at last found a place in *Amateur Scraps*.

As time passed the members of the Amateur Literary Society became considerably less inhibited about criticising one another's work. An article from Allingham on the Lyceum Theatre infuriated a fellow contributor.

> Can the London Theatres interest any of us? Is a question that ought to be once and for all answered 'No!' No more than we can interest them from this distance... Does this honourable London-theatre-goer think that we country people are interested in seeing the big name of 'Irving' in big letters? Surely this person is interesting himself on the pretence of interesting us?'

And why not? Allingham was attempting to analyse his own responses to Irving's acting style. He describes himself as 'inexperienced', struggling to understand the greatness of this actor whilst remaining true to his own impressions. Over the last few months he has seen him playing five different parts. He has been overwhelmed by Irving's Mephistopheles; disappointed by his Werner.

> Irving's Shylock I cannot fancy despite all my endeavours to do so. Now and again Irving appeared to exhibit a spark of genius as at the conclusion of the trial scene when all is lost, then the abject despair of the old Jew is very finely expressed; but as a rule he is, to my inexperienced eyes, intolerably dull.

It's not a well-organised piece but it's thoughtful, personal and honest. Allingham loved performance – theatre, music hall, recitation, film. Writing for *Amateur Scraps* also gave him opportunities for quasi-editorial comment.

Frontispiece. The best we have had. Although the water is rather weak.

Sylvia's Mistake. Written in a pretty and unaffected style; but why are our contributors so fond of taking the sad side of life in their stories?

The Rime of the Ancient Tippler. The subject is very slender and trivial but it is written in an easy interesting style; and although Ajax has done better work it is nevertheless quite readable.

The Robinson sisters and their homemade magazine may have been the most valuable component of Allingham's cut-price university education.

Amateur Scraps

Chapter Six: 1886: The New Boys' Paper

The death of Florence in 1875 had left James and Louisa's household boy-heavy. After Florence (1870) had come Arthur (1872) then Claude (1874), who would have been a baby at the time of his sister's fatal illness. There are no more of those suspicious gaps that encourage the family historian to wonder about miscarriages, stillbirths and early deaths. The family was completed by Walter (1876), Albert (1877), Philip (1879) and Ernest (1882). Herbert Allingham would have been seven years old when Florence died. He was her senior by just two years: they must surely have played together, shared a nursery or a perambulator, toddled with their older brother to the Surrey Gardens, Kennington Park or even Lambeth Walk. Yet had it not been for that tell-tale gap, and the evidence of the 1871 census, I would never have guessed that the little girl had existed.

Neither Joyce nor Margery mentioned Florence. For them, their father was defined as being one of eight boys – the eight boys to whom Margery would, years later, dedicate her portrait of a dangerously dysfunctional post-Victorian family. I don't think they knew that their father had ever had a sister. There was certainly no hint of sympathy that their grand-parents had suffered such a loss. Margery wrote harshly in praise (or dispraise?) of Louisa: 'My grandmother had eight sons but when two of them turned out to be little better than imbeciles she didn't worry – there were six good ones.' Joyce told me that James and Louisa deliberately held one or two of the younger boys back to take care of them in their old age because they hadn't had a girl. I thought this was a trifle unkind but when I repeated it to Michael Allingham, son of the youngest son, Ernest, he said, 'Quite likely.' In fact the two youngest boys were shrewd, reasonably successful businessmen. When James and Louisa grew old, they moved to Essex to live near their oldest child, Will. It was the fifth and sixth boys who may have struggled a bit.

All the evidence suggests that Herbert Allingham himself felt defined by being one of a house-full of boys. If this was so, he was in tune with his society. The census of 1861 had shown that 45 percent of the population was under twenty years old and that there was a slightly larger number of boys than girls. Statistically this would not be significant except that the boys loomed so much larger than their sisters in public view. In the period between leaving school and starting a family many of them had some money to spend – even if it was only pennies. With the extension of the franchise, some might be numbered among 'our future masters' and, as the century wore on, even those who would never attain the dignity of a vote mattered increasingly to society as the workers whose labour would maintain the Empire, or as the soldiers and sailors who would defend it. This didn't mean that they were well nourished or well treated, just that they were noticed.

The early mass-market 'trashy and vile' fiction, the penny bloods and dreadfuls that were being marketed from the late

1830s and 1840s were intended mainly for men. Men, even poor men, were more likely than women to have some money available for entertainment. They were also more likely to be able to read. It was not until 1884 that there were, for the first time ever, slightly more women than men able to sign their names in the marriage registers. For most of the nineteenth century, literacy spread more rapidly by age than by gender. With the continuing demographic predominance of young over old and the increasing systemisation of education, each generation visibly outstripped their parents in their ability to read and write. From mid-century the penny-publishers began differentiating their products by age then, much later, by gender. Following this differentiation as it affected Herbert Allingham's career was one of the most unexpected and fascinating by-products of the hours spent cataloguing his stories.

Allingham's first serial story, published 1886, was for the group he then knew best – boys. He wrote it for his uncle, John Allingham, who liked to be known professionally as 'Ralph Rollington'. 'Rollington' had been a boy in the 1850s and vividly remembered the pleasures of one of the first periodicals published especially for boys, Samuel Beeton's *Boy's Own Magazine*:

> I well remember how I sat on one of the old desks in the classroom of the old Academy, with my feet resting on a long form, devouring every line of the story entitled 'The Nine Lives of a Cat', and when the first instalment finished with the loss of the cat's first life, I heaved a sigh and would willingly have sacrificed a week's pocket money to have secured another chapter containing the cat's second life, but unfortunately a whole month had to elapse before another number made its appearance. There is no doubt that there are thousands of British boys who have experienced the same feeling.

But times have changed since then, and weekly papers have quite superseded the old-fashioned Monthly Magazine.

By 1867, when both James and John Allingham were still printers and their father William showed no signs of mortality, the market for boys' papers was being transformed by a new penny weekly, *Boys of England,* edited by Edwin Brett. Brett's surprising achievement was to combine readability with (comparative) respectability. Until 1866 he had been manager of the Newsagents Publishing Company where his low-life tales provoked increasing outrage, culminating in a prosecution under the Obscene Publications Act. In his new incarnation as editor and proprietor of *Boys of England* Brett made the most of this moral panic. His success with *Boys of England* established a pattern whereby each new magazine launched on the market promised something 'pure' and 'healthy' in contrast to the 'pernicious rubbish' supposedly put about by their predecessors. It also unleashed 'one of the most intense periods of competition in the history of juvenile magazines'. Robert Kirkpatrick, a historian of the school story, estimates that more than eighty weekly or monthly boys' periodicals were launched in the next thirty years with, at one point, at least thirty being published simultaneously.

Whoever could publish, did, and wider developments within the industry aided them. Technical progress with stereotyping was particularly significant as the moulds made from typeset stories could be stored for future low-cost reprints – or sold to stave off the creditors. Years later Herbert Allingham's Uncle John ('Ralph Rollington') wrote a memoir of those bohemian days where bankruptcies were commonplace and deals could be made in the street.

> I remember a good many years back, Charles Fox, the publisher, meeting me in Fleet Street. He was carrying a small parcel that appeared exceedingly heavy for its size. 'What on earth have you got there, Charlie?' I queried laughingly. 'Only some old comic electros,' he replied, 'by "Phiz" and I want you to write them up into a comic school story.' I took them home, worked up a plot, and named it *Timothy Teazer's Schooldays*, which duly appeared in the *Boys' Half Holiday.*

Like his older brother James, John Allingham had been apprenticed as a printer but describes himself as being 'of a roving disposition'. Joyce Allingham never knew which of 'wild Uncle John's' stories to believe. She spoke of him as the black sheep of the family, a practical joker with hard-drinking friends, but she was also aware that he played up to his reputation. In *Dance of the Years,* Margery portrayed him as 'Tom', an inveterate prankster and the scourge of his brother's 'good young men'. Other relatives found him merely silly.

Despite their differences of outlook and personality, however, James and John worked unobtrusively together for most of their lives. John was involved in James's *Christian Globe* and, April 1879, he used James's Farringdon Road printing facilities to publish the first number of his own penny weekly, the *Boy's World.* As usual the new paper was to be unlike anything else on the market. It had a masthead motto 'overcome evil with good' and promised that the tendency of its serial stories 'will always be to encourage the practice of uprightness, perseverance, sobriety and reverence for virtue and religion'. John Allingham (as 'Ralph Rollington') filled it with the usual mix of imperial adventure stories, historical romance and tales of school life, usually written by himself. Despite its pious pledges – 'Sixteen pages of pure and healthy literature, beautifully illustrated' – the paper was completely in the standard format, with many of its stories reprinted from previous bankrupt publications. The true contender for the 'pure and healthy' market was the Religious Tract Society's *Boy's Own Paper*, established that same year.

The *Boy's World* ran from 1879–1886, reaching a peak of about 50,000 circulation in 1882 with a companion *Boy's World* Pocket Library published between 1880–1881 and a second weekly paper, *Our Boys' Paper*, running 1880–1883. One of John Allingham's closest observers was among the least impressed. Herbert Allingham clearly preferred the *Boy's Own Paper*. 'Arthur brought the first number of the new volume of the BOP home today. It is a first rate no. The first story opens very well with a remark something like this, "B____ school wanted two slight reforms, one was that all the masters should be dismissed, the other that all the boys should be expelled."'

This was the summer of 1886 and the eighteen-year-old Herbert was home from Cambridge either having failed his first attempt at the Little-Go exam or having been ill. He had a notebook which included some pencil notes taken during a course of theology lectures, a list of textbooks (with notes where they could be bought most cheaply) and a projected alphabetical list of 'Proper Names occurring in the second book of Virgil'. The alphabetical list of names never gets beyond A, the book list remains incomplete and the notebook is then turned upside down to record a few intensely significant months.

Allingham's brothers are also at home. There's plenty of cricket, walks to go fishing at Kew, some rowing at Richmond, a visit to the theatre and an art exhibition for the older boys; tram-rides and outings with parents for the younger. Arthur Allingham, purchaser of the *Boy's Own Paper* was fourteen, the next in age to Herbert. The story that he is about to read is Talbot Baines Reed's serial *A Dog With a Bad Name*. As well as looking forward to the story, Allingham notices the way the *BOP* is being promoted. 'They are advertising widely just now, a new volume begins. They announce stories by first rate writers, Talbot Baines Reed, Jules Verne, Paul Blake, Dr Gordon Stables, AR Hope etc etc.'

Herbert is struggling to motivate himself to study. He's much more interested in the penny publishing world, his own reading, his efforts to develop his writing and his observations of other people.

> While they were all out yesterday and I was sitting at my desk with a splitting headache, my thoughts wandered from one thing to another in that easy manner which is so harmful to the discipline of the mind and so enjoyable to experience. My wandering humour took me to the remembrance of Mr N by which he expressed his opinion that dependants must be treated very roughly to keep them in their places. At the remembrance of this and Mr N's bombastic way of saying it, I could not help being struck by the fact that the lower the man is in the social scale and the smaller the amount of education he possesses, the greater is his contempt for and overbearing insolence towards those lower on the social ladder than himself, whatever may be their education or other good qualities.

I have an uncomfortable feeling that this Mr N is Mr Nowell, the publican who married James Allingham's sister Julia and was therefore obliged to share his home with her dependent siblings. 'I think I might write a short story out of that thought,' muses Allingham. Uncertain, aspirational, perhaps a little priggish – the young Allingham longs to succeed but doubts that this is going to happen on the big stage. He studies the Literary Olympics in James Henderson's *Young Folk's Paper.* He has heard that his Uncle John is considering launching a new boys' paper and isn't sure how he should react. 'He has several blocks on hand and has all the stories written, so he says, and if this is true he may be able to start it. If he does and condescendingly offers to print a story of mine I should like to be able to say I was engaged on the *YFP.*'

His problem is that he doesn't trust his uncle's business sense but can't realistically see himself qualifying for anything more prestigious.

I would have to improve a good deal before I was fit for *YFP.* but anything interesting would do for uncle's paper. Besides it would be practice and something to show, for I should of course do my best to make a good story of it. And even if I found I was not being paid for it, which is very likely, I should not lessen the care expended on it. For I mean always to write my best, whatever may be the subject on hand or the pay expected.

The request came a fortnight later.

A good deal has happened since my last entry. One day Dad asked me if I would write a short sketch for uncle's paper. I said I would see if I had one about me, so he and I looked through my papers. And we came upon my school story. He had read part of it before but now he finished it and liked it so much that he told uncle about it the next day and the following day took it with him to business. The same afternoon (it was last Tuesday) I received a note from him saying that he had shown it to uncle who had read it and said he liked it and who in turn submitted it to Pierce Egan. Who, according

> to uncle, liked it also. Uncle said he would publish it and have it illustrated. [...] The first picture is going to be the ivy scene. Bobby Prowse is going to illustrate it.

The Allinghams' contacts are good. Pierce Egan was the son and grandson of famous popular writers and was at this time employed by CW Bradley & Co. to edit their recently purchased magazine, the *London Journal*. Bobby (Robert) Prowse was one of the best-known illustrators in the penny dreadful market. He had worked regularly for Ralph Rollington's *Boy's World* and appears to have been offering to illustrate stories on spec for the projected paper. His style was dark and melodramatic. Herbert Allingham and his father were soon lobbying for Prowse's replacement by an artist called Phillips, undistinguished but stylistically more refined. The eighteen-year-old talks to his diary as if there were no one els e in whom to confide.

> On Saturday and Sunday last I wrote the cricket match in my story. But am not very well satisfied with it. Besides I am afraid it is a trifle too long. I think I shall be able to make a very decent character out of Barrington but I very much fear Trevor. I am not a wit and I don't quite know how I am to make him say witty things. Platt I think will make a nice character and I am going to introduce an incident as soon as I have done away with the cricket, in which I think I shall be able to unfold the characters of Dacre, Easy, and Norton. They are too much alike at present, especially Dacre and Norton. [...] Of course I think that 'Barrington's Fag' will be a good story (what young author does not think his own work good?) but I can see it lacks knowledge. That is the little bits of instruction with which a good story should be sprinkled are absent. It also lacks description.

In fact its only virtues are, I am afraid, interesting incident and a little (a very little) character drawing. But still, in spite of its faults, I think it will take with the boys. For boys like incident better that they like instruction or description. And it is quite incorrect to imagine that boys don't care for character sketching. On the contrary they soon chuck in a story in which all the characters are puppets.

He's rather a good critic of his own work; living in a houseful of brothers clearly had its advantages. 'Will says the pictures are rubbish but I think the boys will like them.' He knows his audience: unfortunately he also knows the penny paper hierarchy of esteem.

But for all this I would ten thousand times rather see it in a most insignificant part of *YFP.* and get nothing for it, than have it well illustrated in uncle's paper and get a couple of pounds a number. Not that I am likely to get this. Of course I shan't get a penny, nor do I want it. But still I shall feel jolly pleased to see it in print and if the paper is a success (and there is a slight possibility of such a result) I shall feel that I have been awfully lucky in getting it printed.

Herbert Allingham's emotional uncertainty is intensified by his lack of confidence in his uncle. 'I have not much faith in anything uncle takes up.' He was almost immediately proved right.

It seems very probable that uncle's new paper will not make its appearance after all; almost certain that it will not by the advertised date (Monday 27th). Uncle is such a fool; he has no money and goes around borrowing a shilling or two from whom he can. No one will supply the paper and he does not know what to do. He has tried everybody and Dad advised him to go to Hunt. Hunt replied, 'I will give you £4 per week and a third of the profits, only I must take all money in the first place.' And Uncle like a fool refused. Of course if he could do it himself, well and good but he can't. He says he will try and get a partner, I hope he will succeed.

Herbert Allingham, at home and frustrated, provides us with an eloquent vignette of this adventitious, unprofessional, small-scale publishing as Uncle 'goes around borrowing a shilling or two from whom he can'. £4 a week was a respectable editorial salary – why had Rollington turned it down? Finally, however, all seemed well. 'Dad has come home and brings the news that the *New Boys' Paper* will come out on Monday. The paper being procured and the printer having advanced £15 for expenses.' The printer this time was W Burgess of 56 Southwark Street and the *New Boys' Paper* Company found an office in Dr Johnson's House, 17 Gough Square. The *Christian Globe* allocated its entire back page to advertise it. 'The picture is very decent but not A1. May it have every success', wrote Herbert.

Success did not come to the *New Boys' Paper.* John Allingham did not have his brother James's commercial flair and never seems to have grasped that more than start-up funding was needed for a paper to survive in such an intensely competitive market. Carry-on capital was needed to commission new fiction and run energetic marketing campaigns with plenty of prizes. In the past 'Ralph Rollington' had been lavish in his free gift offers but unreliable in delivery. He had no shareholders and papers of this type did not attract significant quantities of advertising. Their prosperity depended on their circulation and circulation was closely linked with the quality of their fiction. 'A boys' paper must have good serials or it will not do,' wrote Herbert Allingham. But his was the only new story in this new paper: all the rest were reprints. Almost as soon as *Barrington's Fag* (by 'Herbert St Clair') had came to an end, Rollington sold the paper to the Aldine Publishing Company. They ran it for less than a year before changing its name to the *British Boys' Paper* and selling it on to the speculative writer-publisher Guy Rayner, in whose ownership it finally expired.

Barrington's Fag is unlike the other, more swashbuckling serials in the *New Boys' Paper.* Its plot is frequently reminiscent of Talbot Baines Reed although it is more frivolous than the Religious Tract Society would have approved. There are scenes of junior mischief-making and sixth-form power struggles, the ragging of masters and resistance to bullies. Episodes include rowing practice, a cricket match, a fight in the woods, joining a theatrical troupe in disguise, saving the headmaster's daughter on her runaway pony, accusations of cheating and a show-down in front of the whole school, when the sadistic replacement headmaster and his toadies are finally ousted. Overarching the forty-four chapters (twenty-one instalments) is the outline of a dramatic intrigue involving a packet of letters sent by the headmaster's elder daughter to her fiancé, who has been unjustly convicted of burglary. For all its faults *Barrington's Fag* is ambitious, readable and quite exciting.

Uncle did pay his young author for his work – '30 s, the first money I have ever earned'. Then, after the sale of the *New Boys' Paper* in 1887, the new owner, Aldine's Charles Perry Brown, offered £25 for the copyright. Herbert Allingham refused to sell. Perhaps he'd already seen enough of the way that other writers' work was hawked about from publisher to publisher as a heap of blurring stereotypes. He dreamed of seeing his story in book form, with his own name on the cover.

The *Christian Globe* had advertised *Barrington's Fag* as 'a true tale of school life' and Joyce Allingham assured me that her father had based the story on his time at Ardingly College in Sussex. Arthur, Walter, Phil and Ernest all attended Ardingly and a later story, *Max the Magnificent* (1907), uses a school named Arlingford which has several features that suggest Ardingly. There is, however, no evidence that Herbert was ever a pupil there – despite an exhaustive search by the school archivist. Nineteenth-century Ardingly was a bargain basement establishment, a Woodard School, founded to offer the public school experience to 'the sons of publicans' at the lowest possible cost (annual fees of £15). Spartan conditions led to some appalling epidemics with several deaths in the early years. Herbert Allingham may have had a fortunate escape.

In later life he never hesitated to take his own children away from any school where they told him they were unhappy. At one moment in this first story, the eighteen-year-old narrator intervenes when a junior boy is facing unjust punishment. 'We are too careless about the emotions of the young: their petty struggles seem small indeed in comparison with the fierce battles we ourselves have to fight in our passage through the world. But really boyhood's hopes and fears, joys and sorrows are just as acutely felt as those of maturer years.'

It's pompous, of course, and unwittingly comic but it's also true and rather touching. Perhaps Allingham did attend some other boarding school before he went to Cambridge: more likely he used his imagination, his reading and the reported experience of his brothers when he constructed this 'true tale of school life'.

Almost twenty years later, in 1905, when Herbert Allingham, a married man and a father, looked at *Barrington's Fag* again, he insisted that the story had been grounded quite genuinely in his emotional experience as a boy. He was writing to Charles Murray, editor of *True Blue* – a penny paper published by the Aldine Press, the same company who had briefly owned the *New Boys' Paper* and had offered him £25 for his copyright.

> My wife tells me you don't care for the 'Fag' – Before deciding will you try it on one or two of the youngsters – office boys for choice? I wrote the story when I was a boy myself and I think it has the boy's point of view – They take themselves very seriously and what seems pompous and priggish to us seems all right to them.'

Allingham's appeal was successful: *Barrington's Fag*, re-titled and lightly rewritten, was republished in *True Blue* in 1905; then again in *Puck* in 1911 and in *Merry & Bright* in 1921. It was a good thing he'd been sufficiently shrewd to retain his reprint rights.

'He hung in this position'

Chapter Seven
1889: The London Journal

LONDON JOURNAL

And Weekly Record of Literature, Science, and Art.

New Series.—No. 216.—Vol. IX.] February 18, 1888. [Price One Penny.

THE most memorable Cambridge scene in Herbert Allingham's fiction is a leaving scene. In 1904, eighteen years after the publication of *Barrington's Fag*, Allingham wrote his second school serial, *A Regular Duffer*, for the Aldine penny paper *True Blue*. Its hero, Will Holt, 'the Duffer', was especially popular and the editor asked for more. *True Blue* readers met him next as the Cambridge undergraduate 'Holt of Emmanuel'. 'Holt of Emmanuel' is no timid non-collegiate student but a young man with 'a certain easy swagger in his walk'. He is, however, short of cash (trouble with the trustees) so has summoned his old school friend, Arthur Merlin, down first-class from London in order to make use of Merlin's £500 inheritance. Holt needs money to rescue an acquaintance called Jorkins, who has taken over his father's jewellery shop in Clerkenwell and has subsequently disappeared. Merlin is not instantly enthusiastic.

'Can't you see that you are spoiling your life for the sake of a silly juggins who is probably in no trouble at all and who, even if he is, is not worth saving?'

'Jorkins is my friend,' replied Holt gravely.

Merlin sprang to his feet impatiently and walked nervously up and down the room.

'Oh, of course,' he cried irritably, 'I know it's no use arguing with you. Well what is the idiotic programme? Suppose I refuse to let you have a penny of my money?'

Over the Duffer's face came the charming smile which Merlin could never resist in the old days

'In that improbable event,' he replied, sweetly, 'I should go to London and accept a situation as a clerk that has been offered to me at eighteen shillings a week, and in the evenings I should pursue my investigations.'

Merlin relents of course.

'Oh Duffer,' he cried, 'You are hopeless. Well we'll have some fun and when our five hundred is spent we'll go into the workhouse together.'

'The workhouse! My dear Merlin, what an unpleasant suggestion! On the contrary when we have spent all our money we will earn some more. Really I begin to hope that my trustees will not relent. It would be rather fun to work for one's living.'

'Not much fun clerking on eighteen shillings a week,' Merlin suggested.

Many readers of *True Blue* would already be clerking on 18 shillings a week. They might long to share the Duffer's insouciant attitude to money, yearn for similar sang-froid and casual disregard for authority. Allingham's young men gallop out of Cambridge, knocking over the university proctor and his 'bulldogs'. 'Forward Merlin!' cried the Duffer. 'There is no time to apologise now. I must write to the good man from town.' Dons and townsfolk try to block their exit but Merlin and the Duffer are saved by a crowd of undergraduates.

The next moment the gallant steed with its double burden was thundering down the lane.

It bore them across Parker's Piece, in and out of the narrow streets beyond and then across the green that borders the River Cam.

They heard behind them a terrific uproar and it was clear that Town and Gown had come to blows but the pursuit was not continued.

'It seems they've had enough of you, Duffer,' said Merlin. 'I fear your 'Varsity career closes today.'

'I fear so,' admitted the Duffer, rather sadly. 'It's been a very happy time; but when duty calls one must not hesitate. Jorkins cries to us for help and he shall not cry in vain.'

Jorkins did not cry for help when Herbert Allingham BA returned from Cambridge but the *London Journal* did. In 1889, aged just twenty-two, Allingham became editor of one of the oldest-established and formerly best-selling penny weeklies. The *London Journal* had been founded in 1845 by George Stiff as the *London Journal and Weekly Record of Literature, Science and Art.* Its earliest readers had included many insecure, newly urbanised, newly educated young people, many of them low-paid clerks (like Jorkins), who needed both guidance and entertainment in their new environment. The *London Journal* was first published by George Vickers in Holywell Street – not a good address – but it was never a gutter paper.

The 'Art' in its title referred to the regular dramatic engravings by Sir John Gilbert and others and 'Science' meant knowledge generally (as it does still, delightfully, in the stacks of the London Library). Fiction, however, was always at the heart of the enterprise, as journalist Henry Vizetelly explained:

> Eventually Stiff worked up the weekly circulation of the *London Journal* to several hundred thousand copies for he allowed nothing to turn him away from his own set purpose – the increasing of the sale of the publication. This was done *not by means of prize competitions and insurance offers after the favourable practice of the present day* but by providing his readers with lengthy and exciting stories, telling how rich and poor babies were wickedly changed in their perambulators by conniving nursemaids, how long lost wills miraculously turned up in the nick of time, and penniless beauty and virtue were led to the hymeneal altar by the wealthy scion of a noble house after they had gained the fair one's affection under some humble disguise [my italics].

Vizetelly was writing his account in 1893 when Allingham was attempting to re-design this venerable paper. Was he offering the young editor criticism, encouragement or some other coded message? His description of classic *London Journal* fiction was accurate. Its readers liked plenty of action and surprise, coincidence and happy endings. The first editor of Stiff's *London Journal* had been GWM Reynolds, author of the sensational *Mysteries of London*. Other early successes included *The Count of Monte Cristo* by Alexandre Dumas and *The Mysteries of Paris* by Eugène Sue. In the 1850s and 1860s the *Journal*'s lead writers were JF Smith and Pierce Egan II. Their 'lengthy and exciting stories' were wildly popular.

> There is a mighty potentate in England and his name is Mr Pierce Egan. Many amongst us fancy that they have a good general idea of what is English literature. They think of Tennyson and Dickens as the most popular of our living authors. It is a fine delusion from which they should be aroused. The works of Pierce Egan are sold by the half million. What living author can compare with him?

Pierce Egan was also the magazine's editor. He was the son of Pierce Egan I, a sporting author from the Regency period, and the father of Pierce Egan III who had commented favourably on Allingham's *Barrington's Fag*. Egan's contemporary, JF Smith, had been even more strikingly successful.

> So cleverly did JF Smith pile on excitement towards the ends of the stories which he wrote for Mr Stiff that the latter told me that the weekly circulation used to increase by as many as fifty thousand when the denouement approached. He surmised that the factory girls of the north, great patrons of the *London Journal*, were in the habit of lending it to one another and, when their curiosity how the story would end was at its greatest height, the borrowers, unable to wait for the *London Journal* to be lent to them, expended their pennies on buying a copy outright.

Minnigrey, Smith's most famous serial, was said to have raised the *London Journal* circulation to 500,000 copies by its October 1852 climax – an unheard-of figure then. Later in the decade Smith deserted the *Journal* for the newly founded firm of Cassell's, who pitched their magazines more explicitly towards a domestic readership. Molly Hughes (born 1867) describes what Cassell's serial fiction meant to her family in the 1870s.

Cassell's Magazine provided stronger meat, far more substantial than we get in the average magazine today. It had to last us a month and I think that every word in it found some reader in the family. When we had all read the portion of the serial story, and very definitely not before, we discussed it endlessly at teatime, how the characters would turn out, who would marry whom. With so little other reading matter to distract us we were able to carry all the details in our heads until the next issue.

The *London Journal* was a weekly rather than a monthly magazine, shared in factories as well as families, but the pleasures would surely have been similar. In the 1850s George Stiff had sold it to WS Johnson who continued to invest heavily in instalment fiction. In one especially shrewd move he purchased the copyrights of all the serial stories written by JF Smith after his desertion to Cassell's. Johnson developed a steady and supportive relationship with his author-editor, Pierce Egan II. 'Give the poor man sensation,' Egan advised. 'Let him sup full of horrors; initiate him in all the mysteries of crime; but always be it remembered that one condition is essential to the success of the dreadful tale, that it should somewhat ostentatiously ally itself with morality.'

Pierce Egan died in 1880 and was succeeded as *London Journal* editor by his son. Sales began to decline. Some commentators attributed this to the third Pierce Egan's lack of the family talent for fiction-writing but it may also have been that the *London Journal* was slow to respond to an intense new competitiveness among the just-respectable penny weeklies. From 1881 George Newnes's *Tit-Bits* offered readers a startlingly original combination of scraps of knowledge, jokes, shorter fiction, advertising and headline-grabbing competitions. *Tit-Bits* was a publishing sensation and was assertively marketed. Did Johnson see the writing on the wall or was the *Journal* simply less attractive to him without his old friend at the helm? In 1883 he sold the magazine to the printer-publishing firm of CW Bradley & Co – together with its wealth of fiction copyrights.

CW Bradley had recently become the printers of the *Christian Globe*; they had also purchased Ralph Rollington's *Boy's World* and *Our Boys' Paper*, briskly closing down the latter. James Allingham's advertising agency, JC Francis, took over management of the *London Journal*'s advertising space. Pierce Egan III, however, remained as editor and sales continued to fall. Frank Jay, a journalist and early penny paper collector, explains what happened next.

> Then, early in 1887, one of the publishers (Mr EJ Blogg), suggested to Mr Bradley an experiment – namely to republish *Minnigrey* in serial form. The proprietors were not in favour of this, but later in the year, as sales continued to decline, it was a case of 'death or glory'. So the decision was come to try JF Smith again. The feature was boomed and in six weeks the sales had jumped by over fifty thousand per week [...] Several of JF Smith's romances were then republished in serial form from 1887 onwards and some of Pierce Egan's at the same time.

James Allingham's partner, JC Francis, wrote a disingenuous letter to the *Star* newspaper in 1890 celebrating the success of the *Minnigrey* experiment but it would eventually become apparent that this was a success that boded ill for the paper.

> Mr CW Bradley was a shrewd man of business and a good employer, but the success he achieved by reprinting Mr JF Smith's

stories made him believe that any old story was better than any new one. It may be said that *The London Journal* was both revived and killed by reprints.

JF Smith, meanwhile, had died in New York, destitute. The copyrights of all his stories belonged to the publishers so there was nothing, no reprint fees, no royalties, to support him in old age.

Allingham's own relationship with the *London Journal* probably began with a short story, contributed in March 1889. *Eileen's Choice* was only his second commercially published work and evidently helped to establish his credentials. Short stories were an accepted means for fiction-writers to build up a relationship with an editor, as well as a way of developing narrative technique.

Just a few years later, in 1893, the famous editor WT Stead, was interviewed on the topic 'How to Become a Journalist'. He identified both inside and outside roads: the sons and daughters of journalists could be 'gradually trained' to help their fathers or mothers ('In that case you would have to learn shorthand and typewriting and pick up French and German') whereas men and women born outside 'the purple' would have to get past the gatekeepers.

> You think you have a gift for writing? Well, you may have, but it does not follow that you have the gift for making people pay you for writing, which is a different gift altogether, and one which has often been very much lacking in some of those who had the greatest gift for the other kind of thing. You must remember that the art of getting into journalism is to get someone who holds the door to let you in, and he will not let you in if you go to him as a beggar and ask him for the sake of charity.

Joyce Allingham believed that James and Louisa had wanted their clever second son to enter the church. But then Joyce also thought that her father had read theology at Cambridge when his 1886 diary reveals that he was distinctly anti-clerical. Margery too played along with the suggestion that Herbert's choice of career had disappointed his parents. In *Dance of the Years*, the character 'Jeffrey' (who stands for Herbert) suddenly 'astonished his relations by throwing up all his preparations for the church'. In fact, from the scraps of evidence that have survived, it would seem extraordinary that anyone who had known Allingham since he was eighteen at least could have assumed he would do anything other than seek a job in journalism. 'Stick to it, old chap,' Uncle John had written after the success of *Barrington's Fag*, 'and you will make a Name.'

When Egan died, later in 1889, Allingham succeeded him. Frank Jay described him as 'a young man, fresh from the University, who made up in enthusiasm what he lacked in experience'. The doors had opened wide for Allingham: no wonder he was enthusiastic. In fact there could scarcely have more challenging time to take responsibility for a penny weekly paper. Alfred and Harold Harmsworth had founded their sensationally successful *Answers to Correspondents* in 1888 and C Arthur Pearson was about to counter with his own *Pearson's Weekly* in 1890. Both men had worked for George Newnes on *Tit-Bits* and their rivalry would determine the shape of mass-market publishing well into the twentieth century. Allingham's exciting new job as an editor would prove a poisoned chalice. It would, however, be a great piece of higher education for a future fiction worker.

One of his attractions to CW Bradley may well have been that he was cheap. Twenty years later, in 1909, when he was forty-one, he appears to be earning £2 10s per week for his editorial work at the *London Journal*, plus £1 10s per week for editorial input to the *Christian Globe*. How much had his 1889 starting salary been? Not a lot, I would guess. He continued living with his family in Goldhawk Road. Perhaps he travelled into Fleet Street with his father. The JC Francis office was at 135 Fleet Street and the *Christian Globe* still at 185. The *London Journal* was just around the corner in New Fetter Lane together with a weekly paper, *Spare Moments,* which was also printed and published by Bradley's and had its advertising managed by the JC Francis agency.

The novelist William McFee wrote to Margery years later recalling 'that terrible old building where the Old Boy was editing *Spare Moments* and the *London Journal* and the *Christian Globe*, wearing a frock coat and a top hat and working in a room like a dustbin while the building shook to the presses downstairs.' If there were presses downstairs this must have been CW Bradley's premises in New Fetter Lane though I don't think Allingham ever edited *Spare Moments* on any regular basis and his input into the *Christian Globe* was limited. McFee was always ready to see his friends as actors in some dramatic scenario. He came to know Allingham well in the later years of his editorship of the *London Journal* (probably from about 1905) and incorporated his observations of Allingham's Fleet Street and City milieu into the action of his own first novel *Casuals of the Sea*.

Allingham soon discovered that his editorial freedom of action was limited. He had a proprietor newly converted to the joys of reprinting old serials for no cost and readers who had been taking the paper for the last fifty years and didn't see why it should change now. Newnes, Harmsworth and Pearson, founders of the exciting new papers could develop their own audiences: Allingham had to be careful not to alienate his.

Not that he would have wished to. Although he did introduce competitions and insurance offers to the *London Journal*, in pale imitation of Newnes and the Harmsworths, these were unimaginative affairs with piffling prizes. At heart Allingham was a traditionalist who believed with Henry Vizetelly that the only sound way of building up circulation and ensuring a paper's health was 'by providing his readers with lengthy and exciting stories'.

His problem was that he was not allowed to commission any new serials. The only fiction he was able to increase were short stories and novelettes – and even these were often cadged from readers. He began writing more short stories himself; selling them first to *Spare Moments* or the *Christian Globe* to supplement his editorial earnings, then reprinting them in the *London Journal* to bulk out his empty pages. In 1893 he even sold a short story to the opposition. The Harmsworth paper, *Answers*, accepted his 'Crime and Capture of Wilton Kelly' but regrettably it's a tale I've so far failed to trace. 'Despairing of ever being able to induce his proprietor to engage new writers, Mr Allingham ultimately wrote a story himself,' said Frank Jay. 'This was a very exciting work which bore the sensational title *A Devil of a Woman*.'

Write about what you know is usually good advice for beginners. Here's the opening of Allingham's first serial story for adults, published in the *London Journal* in 1893:

A devil of a woman! True the phrase is strong, but it describes Madge Milton exactly and that must be my excuse for using it.

She was, I firmly believe, the wickedest woman that ever lived. Added to this she possessed a beauty and a power of fascination that can only be described as devilish. On referring to my diary I find that it is ten years within a day or two that I first met her. In those days

I was on the very lowest rung of freelance journalism, living on a few shillings a week and ready to write anything from a sermon to a penny dreadful by which I might pick up a stray guinea or two. That day, being in very low water indeed, I wrote a puff for Credule, the pill man, and managed to get it inserted in the *Evening Crier.* This obtained me an introduction to the wealthy pill manufacturer. He seemed to take a fancy to me and in the course of an interview at his place in the City, he offered me the job of writing a pamphlet which should set forth in good scientific terms the virtues of his famous pill.

When all that was settled and I was about to leave he suddenly remarked:

'Oh, by the way, Mr Darcy, next Friday we are going to have a little social gathering at my place in Richmond. We shall be very glad to see you if you care to come.'

I was simply bewildered; but before I could reply, the door of the room – Credule's private study – opened and a woman stood on the threshold. A woman, have I said? Surely it was an angel.

Sermons – penny dreadfuls – puffs for pills? Young Mr Darcy clearly frequents the same areas of Fleet Street as the *Christian Globe*, the *New Boys' Paper* and the JC Francis Agency. *A Devil of a Woman* was published anonymously, with an explanatory note from the editor of the *London Journal.*

The writer of the following remarkable narrative assures us that it is strictly true in every particular, and a careful examination of the secret dispatches and private papers which he has submitted to us make it impossible for us to doubt his word. The names of persons and places have been altered and even dates have been slightly changed, as nearly all the actors in this strange drama of modern life are still living and had we not taken this precaution, the liberty, nay the very lives of many people of high station may have been imperilled. Otherwise, the strange, true story of intrigue, crime and passion is given to our readers as it came into our hands from the man who was the chief actor in the events it records.

By the end of that first instalment the angelically beautiful lady has persuaded the innocent young journalist to deliver a hatbox to 'a leading member of the British government'. Inside the hatbox is a brown paper parcel.

I fancy all anticipated a surprise: but for the shock of horror, amazement and disgust which we actually received none of us certainly was prepared. For as the brown paper was unwound there rolled out on the Turkey carpet, and at our very feet, the *ghastly bloodstained head of a man.*

Strictly true in every particular?

'Merlin did not hesitate'

Chapter Eight:
1893: Beauty for all

Years later, in 1932, Allingham's friend FA Wickhart, the founding editor of *Spare Moments*, was still commiserating with him over the absence of any remuneration for *A Devil of a Woman*. 'I remember you writing the story for Bradley without any payment. It was CWB all over. Only when you got him against the wall would he fork out. However the sale of the reprints has been some recompense.'

Allingham had learned early to make sure that his copyrights remained his own property whenever possible. It meant that he could sell as many subsequent serial rights as editors were prepared to buy. Twentieth-century editors tended to approach *A Devil* with caution. Most of them replaced the severed head with a photograph of a dead man – thus obscuring the Salome reference which would have spelled out to the reader that this lady was dangerous, even while the hero was struggling to find excuses for her. 'I could not altogether forget the severed head and the suspicious circumstances surrounding the woman I adored; but I felt in my heart that there must be an explanation somewhere.'

A Devil of a Woman was re-published at least seven times

during Allingham's lifetime. In 1900 *Shurey's Illustrated*, a low class picture paper covering sport and slaughter, had no problems reprinting it in its entirety, bloodstained head and all. They even attached the author's name, Herbert J Allingham BA. In 1905, however, the editor of *Puck* rejected *Devil* as 'too Mephistophelean for our guileless readers' and in 1907 William Anderson, fiction buyer for DC Thomson in Dundee, considered it 'somewhat too sensational to use in any of our weekly papers. We might run it however in our evening paper the *Evening Telegraph and Post* which circulates in the counties of Forfar, Fife and Perth.' Interesting to notice this discrimination about what's unsuitable for a weekly paper yet acceptable in the evenings – and why Forfar, Fife and Perth?

Eight years later, in 1915, Anderson's immediate counterpart, the fiction buyer at John Leng's of Dundee, had no hesitation about running the serial as the lead attraction in their flagship weekly newspaper, the *People's Journal.* This editor used the same ploy as Allingham himself had done – he pretended that it might be true. Even at the story's final appearance, in 1933, in a boys' comic called *Bullseye,* the fiction was being maintained that this melodramatic concoction of betrayal, murder, state secrets and international villainy was a true story from the hero's adventurous past. Readers were invited to 'tense' with Frank Darcy 'as he relates one thrilling event after another in the exact order and way that they occurred thirty years ago in real life'.

Not all readers were convinced, even in 1893. The *London Journal* columnist 'Mab' reported that 'several readers of *A Devil of a Woman* have written to me expressing a doubt as to the existence of criminal secret societies such as the League of the Double Life.' She set them straight. 'It's a matter of fact that both England and the Continent swarm with such societies.'

'Mab' had begun writing for the *London Journal* early in 1893 when Allingham was feeling sufficiently confident to attempt some redesigning of his paper. The lead serial was, as usual, a reprint (*Fair Lilias* by Pierce Egan) but Allingham changed the publication day from Tuesday to Friday, varied the layout, brought in some new typefaces and introduced a 'Bright and Brief' column which disseminated random factoids, such as, 'We have one doctor to every 1,450 of the population... The years of the Eiffel Tower are numbered... One Briton in every 45 is afflicted with red or reddish hair.'

Mab's column was simply entitled 'Gossip'. The writer was (allegedly) female, married, pleasure-loving and reluctant to give her age. Her columns appeared regularly from 1893–1899 and again after a second redesign from 1906–1907. In the first period Mab is often used to discharge regular editorial functions. She sets competitions and awards prizes; answers letters, puffs serials and produces advertorials for Christmas cards or for bargain bundles of dress-making material. In her second incarnation, she expends a high proportion of her space talking about her baby, 'Margery'.

Mab writes as the readers' friend – even when she is busily bamboozling them. During 1894 she was kept busy spinning fictions around the provenance of *A Devil of a Woman*. She tells her friends the readers what happened when she called into the *London Journal* office on her return from holiday. She found the editor:

> ...less busy than usual. He was leaning back in his chair, smoking his pipe and looking contemplatively at a pile of papers on the desk before him.
>
> On seeing me he turned round quickly, and, without even

asking me how I had enjoyed myself, or telling me how well I looked, he plunged into the middle of business. 'Oh, Mab,' says he. 'Is that you? Just read this and tell me what you think of it.' At the same time he passed over to me a thin packet of typewritten manuscript.

I folded it up and told him I would read it some time that evening and let him have my report tomorrow. 'Tomorrow! Nonsense,' retorted my worthy chief, somewhat rudely; for, although he is a nice old gentleman as a rule, he is inclined to be a little hasty at times. 'Nonsense. Read it now. No time like the present.'

So I settled myself down with a sigh of resignation, and took up the precious typewritten stuff, fully expecting to be bored. Well, I must admit that I was not bored in the least. The curious and startling title of the story was enough to catch my attention, and when I began to read I became interested at once. People came in and out – printers' boys and so forth – but I hardly noticed them. The strange narrative unfolded in the pages before me had cast its spell over me.

The editor (this nice-if-a-little-hasty old gent) then told Mab how a well-known French dramatist had told him about a 'perfectly true' story, which was 'still more exciting, more full of dramatic situations, than any of the romances which you have published in your excellent paper over the whole fifty years.' The editor has spent a good deal of money obtaining the manuscript because he fancies 'that it will please the readers'. Some months later Mab meets the mysterious author at a party. By this time he has written a second serial, *The Mouth of Hell or The Adventures of Sir Harry Beldair* (1894–1895).

The Editor had with him the author of *The Adventures of Sir Harry Beldair* and *A Devil of a Woman*. He has recently returned from Morocco and is a very queer person indeed. I had never met him before but we got on admirably. I told him that I liked his latest story but didn't find it quite so exciting as *A Devil of a Woman*. 'Ah!', he replied 'in the first story I was recounting events from my own life, whereas the gentleman whom I call Sir Harry Beldair is merely a friend of mine. But still, go on with the story, you will find excitement enough presently.' [...] He is an extraordinary man and never seems happy unless he is mixed up in queer adventures. Even since his return to England he has managed to get into some mysterious intrigue and our Editor follows him about like a shadow lest his valued contributor should be snapped up by a Russian Nihilist or stabbed in the back by the emissary of an Italian secret society.

As Allingham was the author of both *The Adventures of Sir Harry Beldair* and *A Devil of a Woman,* it was not surprising that the *London Journal* editor was following him about 'like a shadow'. Mab is whetting the readers' appetite for this new serial by pretending that it might all be real, exciting them with the thought that, just around the corner from their own daily lives, is an alternative world of intrigue and Nihilists. Presenting the author as a mysterious adventurer just back from Morocco is rather more fun than letting them know that he's an underpaid young chap from the suburbs who travels to work with his dad.

I'm sure that Allingham wrote Mab. Many of the names in her columns, the activities she enjoys and the places she visits are also to be found in Allingham's family life or in his fictions. During the periods he appears most engaged with the paper her columns appear regularly; when he is busy elsewhere, they stop. A scrap of paper survives from late in his *London Journal* period, on which he has jotted down the different types of writing he has undertaken: 'gossip paragraphs etc' are included in the list. Mab's chatty, affectionate persona (she often sends readers her 'best love') helps develop an atmosphere of friendship – which, an editor might hope, would encourage readers to stay loyal to his paper. She is qualitatively unlike Allingham's other columnist, 'Lady Jane', whom he introduced in 1897 to provide specific domestic guidance. Lady Jane embodied the *London Journal's* expert appeal to women readers through her 'Household Hints', 'Toilet Table' and regular 'Woman's World' chat.

Mab urges her 'friends' to write to her – this was market research of course: what features in the paper did they enjoy most; where would their dream holiday take them; what were the facts of their working lives?

As I anticipated, quite a number of my women readers earn their own living. The competition I announced in No. 482 has brought forth some very interesting letters indeed. Pupil-teachers, dressmakers, lace-cleaners, writers, book-binders, telegraph-clerks, manageresses and artists are among the women wage-earners who read my gossip.

'Mary S.' is a dressmaker in a North-country village, and, as her experience is a little out of the common, I give her letter nearly in full. 'I am a dressmaker,' writes my correspondent, 'and I cannot tell you how much I like the work. I often earn from £1 10s to £2 per week. I have two apprentices. I only get five shillings for making a lady's dress and 2s to 3s 6d for a girl's. Nevertheless as I have said, I am making a good living at the work. My husband, by his perilous work in the coal-mine, earns less. The prices paid in Newcastle-on-Tyne for making a dress range from 10s 6d to £1 and more. And, although we in the country only get the small prices I mentioned, we are supposed to keep up to the styles that prevail in the towns. That I still make my occupation pay proves that dressmaking is not a bad trade after all.'

No doubt for a girl who has a taste that way and who possesses ideas as well, dressmaking is a very agreeable and profitable occupation.

The prices named by 'Mary S', however, certainly do astonish me. I had no idea that even in country districts they ranged so low. I am afraid that my correspondent (and her apprentices) must work very hard [...]

Among those who are not satisfied with their present occupations is 'Jenny,' who is a frame-tenter in a cotton mill. 'Jenny' dislikes the close confinement which her work necessitates. Curiously enough she wants to be a dressmaker. I hope she will soon get into some congenial occupation, for, after all, one never does good work if one detests it while one is doing it. 'Jenny' must write and tell me how she gets on.

Mab sent her prize (a copy of JF Smith's *The Will and the Way*) to Mary S, the coal-miner's wife from Lintzgreen, County Durham. She, and the other industrious women who found the time to write in, help us as well as Allingham to visualise some of the magazine's readers and consider its possible appeal. The *London Journal*'s monthly Fashion Supplements, for example, must have been a boon to a village dressmaker, anxiously keeping up with the Newcastle smart set. They contained nothing for her customers' daily needs – the coloured fashion plates are self-consciously Parisian, full of silk and ruffles, unlikely ever to be worn in a North Country mining village – but what a stimulus to dreams!

'Minnie', the heroine of William McFee's *Casuals of the Sea,* is sent out to collect information for 'Mrs Olga Wilfley', a freelance writer of fashion notes for a magazine called *Sunday Words*. They discuss the likely readers:

'They're servants mostly, poor people anyhow, so I suppose they fancy themselves a bit when they read about nice things rich people wear.'

'Yes, and they make up their own things and get ideas from the pictures, I expect.'

Mab has a husband. 'Jack' is introduced, in April 1893, as an amiable domestic prop. He is said to be interested in politics and to have a job in the city. By November of the same year Jack has begun to write Mab's gossip for her occasionally and they vie gently for the readers' attention. In his first contribution Jack affects some bashfulness as well as excitement: 'Besides, I suppose that most of those who read Mab's gossip are ladies. Just fancy that! Here I am told to gossip with some hundreds and thousands of womenfolk all at once.'

Over its fifty-year existence the *London Journal* had moved from being a periodical mostly read by men to one where women were the core readers. There were still men in its audience, however, and the introduction of Jack allowed Allingham to warble happily about matters such as a cricket match between the *London Journal* and *Spare Moments*, in which various of the Allingham brothers distinguished themselves. The inclusion of Jack may have been a small part of a more ethically motivated approach. Several of Allingham's editorial innovations, unobtrusive though they are, seem designed to promote the domestic man as well as recognising the woman who works outside the home. Advice columns and Mab's 'gossip' attempt to interpret men and women to one another within the areas of courtship, marriage and the early years of domestic life and parenthood. This was in line with the *Christian Globe*'s mildly evangelical model of the family, which promoted coupledom at the heart of the household and aspired to friendship and equality between spouses as well as devotion to children.

Allingham's first child, Margery, was born in May 1904

and so would have been in full toddlerhood when the following 'gossip' was contributed by Mab in 1906.

> The other day I took Margery to her first pantomime. Shall I be considered an unnatural parent if I say it was rather a nerve-destroying experience? Margery is a sweet child but restless, also obstinate, likewise easily excited. Moreover she has some peculiar notions. One of them is that if any game is being played she must be invited to take the chief part; consequently, when the curtain went up she expressed a desire to go on the stage [...] As that would have stopped the action of the play I did not care to suggest it to the manager.
>
> Margery grew heated, failing to understand why I, who always do as she tells me, should fail her at this critical moment [...]
>
> In the end she had to be carried out of the theatre protesting angrily and noisily. This attitude of resistance was maintained the whole way home, and not until Jack, acting under my tuition, had made himself ill trying to stand on his head, did the dear child consent to be pacified.

If a reader had believed in the reality of Mab and Jack as a married couple in 1893, it would seem that they'd suffered a long wait before a successful conception and birth. But as Mab herself admitted in November 1906, 'I had no idea that any present reader of the *Journal* remembered my gossip of the '90s.'

Allingham, as editor, had more ways than Mab of getting to know his readers. Earlier issues of the *London Journal* had fulfilled the Science promise of its original title (George Stiff's the *London Journal and Weekly Record of Literature, Science and Art)* by encouraging readers to write in with their requests for information. It was a popular feature, fully utilised by the young urban workers struggling to find their feet in the mid-Victorian cities. Under Allingham's editorship, towards the turn of the century, this nineteenth-century 'Ask Jeeves' was swamped by readers sending photos, letters, locks of their hair, samples of their own or other's handwriting and wanting, apparently, authoritative descriptions of themselves or their friends. Their letters were not printed, only Allingham's replies. Here is a selection from a single issue:

LOVE LADY SHIELD (Newcastle on Tyne) Affectionate, sympathetic, domesticated, weak, yielding and lacking in confidence. You are timid, good-natured, cautious and economical. When you write again, write more fully and we will endeavour to answer you at greater length.

MISS MUGGINS The writer of the enclosed fragment is intelligent, affectionate, warm-hearted, impatient and quick-tempered. That is all we can say about him from so brief a specimen.

A CRAHAM MAIDEN The face is a very pleasant one although it would not be called exactly good looking.

ANXIOUS ALBERT You are straightforward, conscientious, chivalrous, high-principled and with a strong sense of duty.

BLUE-EYED NELL You are decidedly a blonde and delicate greens are the colours which will best suit you.

Of the fifty-eight editorial replies on this sample day, twenty-eight contain personal commentary of this nature. The most common adjectives are 'affectionate', 'sympathetic' and 'warm-hearted'. Readers of the 'Notices to Correspondents' were offered an impression of a wise and understanding editorial presence whose personal benevolence and realism about life was nevertheless underpinned by a clear set of principles. 'RUGBY: Your conduct will not bear investigation. How can you expect us to give you advice?' Mab assured the readers that it was indeed the editor himself who answered their letters. 'His mighty wisdom and his innumerable virtues, not to mention his advanced age, fit him for the task, as I often remind him.' (Allingham would, by this time, have been almost twenty-nine.)

Reading 'Notices to Correspondents' is like hearing one side only of a conversation. Allingham, however, had all those letters, photos, locks of hair. Some of the letter-writers were very young (aged fourteen and fifteen) and many more were in their later teens and twenties (like Gissing's 'Thyrza'). I was surprised when I noticed this as I had assumed the majority would have been older people whose loyalty had been established in the paper's more prosperous days. Editorial language elsewhere certainly gives the impression that Allingham is anxious to retain the paper's 'old friends' as well as making 'many new ones'.

Probably the answer lies in the nature of the domestic magazine as an inter-generational possession. This area of the literary marketplace was booming as literacy levels rose and periodicals became ever more attractive and accessible. The *London Journal*'s 'Notices to Correspondents' might have been especially appealing to the younger family readers as their youthfulness might have made it particularly urgent for them to seek help understanding their own identities. Because they were young they may have been more readily interested in buying and sending cheap portrait photographs of themselves or, as the first board-school-educated generation, they may simply have been more confident in their ability to write letters. The mother from Manchester who hadn't missed a single issue of the *Journal* for fifty-two years didn't write to the editor herself, her son or daughter did it for her.

Usually the editor and his columnists welcomed, indeed

solicited, letters. Replies to letters filled space at no cost and personalised readers to one another – thus building up a sense of community. Nonetheless Allingham may have come to feel that this stream of enquiries from people wanting to be told how blue-eyed and warm-hearted they were, was taking a disproportionate amount of the magazine's public space, and perhaps of his own time. In 1896 he introduced 'Aspasia', dedicated graphologist. Mab went to meet her and described her as 'a mysterious Grecian lady, who now resides in London. [...] She tells a person's character by looking in the eyes, touching the hand, or listening to the voice. In reading character from handwriting her skill is also astonishing.' Readers anxious to have their characters deduced from their handwriting were asked to write her 'a fairly long letter (say two full pages of notepaper) and sign their names in full.'

Aspasia became a permanent expert, contactable through CW Bradley's office and also offering her mysterious gifts to the readers of *Spare Moments*. She may even have brought in extra revenue as she required payment in a steadily increasing quantity of stamps. As her character analyses were presumably little more than an extension of the evaluations Allingham had already been supplying to readers, he could have written her letters himself. 'The Science of Reading Character from Handwriting' (as it was described in Aspasia's advertisements) was just another type of story-telling with the reader predisposed to accept fictions as fact. 'Within a week you will know all about yourself, your virtues and your failings.' I noticed that Aspasia disappeared on a mysterious 'mission' at the same time as Mab went on holiday and the editor was sailing on the Norfolk Broads. They all had to apologise to readers for getting behind with their correspondence.

Allingham would probably have subcontracted Aspasia

if he had been able. Fiction was his preferred way of supplementing his editorial salary but, when time was limited and money needed urgently, his most remunerative activity was not graphology but copy-writing for the JC Francis agency.

THE SECRET
OF A
GOOD
COMPLEXION

BEAUTY FOR ALL

Many think that beauty is not possible for all, that it is but a rare gift of Nature. How great the error of this idea is can be easily proved. Nature is always lavish with her gifts. Take for example your own features, your friend's or even those of strangers, and in the vast majority of these they are perfectly regular, and as far as facial formation and pose – faultless. What then is it that prevents us calling them perfect? What is it keeps you from possessing the beauty you desire? It is the skin and complexion. It is the unsightly SPOTS, PIMPLES, SALLOWNESS, PALLOR, BLACKHEADS, BREAKINGS OUT, SORES and all such disfigurements that mar a face that would otherwise be perfect – without blemish.

All these distressing facial disfigurements are, however, soon removed by David MacQueen's 'Vegetine' pills. This statement is not only made by their discoverer, David MacQueen, but by thousands of the public – men and women – who were formerly sufferers, but thanks to 'Vegetine' pills have now been completely cured. They voluntarily give their testimony that 'Vegetine' pills are the world's great skin and complexion beautifier.

Vegetine cost 1s ½d for a small box or 4s 6d for a large one. I don't know anything about its ingredients – perhaps it contained some vitamin supplement which might actually be beneficial. The column is filled with the testimony of satisfied users. ASHAMED TO BE SEEN – CURED BY ONE BOX – YEARS OF SUFFERING ENDED – MOTHER AND DAUGHTER BENEFIT – OTHER FRIENDS ALSO. Reassurance, collective and individual, is its over-riding message and the basic premise from which it starts is positive and inclusive: nature is lavish, everyone can be lovely – with just a little help. Allingham was the copy-writer.

'The Secret of a Good Complexion' appeared in the *London Journal* issue of 13 December 1896. Next to it was one of Mab's reports of a reader's daily life.

My correspondent is the wife of a steady, industrious workingman. In the summer he earns a pound a week but in the winter his employer deducts a shilling, reducing the weekly income to 19s. There are six children the oldest of whom is eight years and the youngest sixteen months. Against this it must be stated that the family lives rent free and has the produce of the little garden. In the summer all goes well and the husband sometimes earns a shilling or two overtime. But now trade is bad there is no overtime and to make things worse the garden this year has turned out a failure. The potatoes are only like marbles though a few years previously they had been splendid.

My correspondent does not grumble. She only writes to give me a picture of a worker's home in the country as it really is today. But although on every page of her letter there is the spirit of hope and courage one can see that the struggle is a pretty grim one at times. One result of present bad times evidently affects my correspondent and shakes her courage more than any thing else. It appears that in past years she has been able to buy a sixpenny toy for each child at

Christmas time; this year the little ones must go without their toys.

I have only retold in brief EB's story, because I believe it is typical of hundreds of similar simple life-dramas to be found all over the land; and I think it is well if those of us who are apt to grumble if we cannot get every luxury we fancy should get a glimpse occasionally into homes where a shilling or two a week makes all the difference between prosperity and penury.

No boxes of Vegetine for that family, one guesses. Would EB, mother of six children in almost as many years, struggling to feed, clothe, educate a family on 19s a week have been tempted to resort to any of the other remedies advertised more discreetly elsewhere in the *London Journal* had she found herself pregnant again? 'Mrs Labbat's female pills – no irregularity or obstruction can resist them' or 'Towle's Pennyroyal and steel pills, no distressing obstruction can resist them.' The more intimately Allingham came to know his readers, the more clearly he must have realised that BEAUTY FOR ALL was unattainable.

I won't let my children starve

Chapter Nine
1901: 'The Garden of Glory'

In the Christmas Number of the *Journal* I referred briefly to the case of a reader ('EB') who with a brave heart was fighting gallantly against hard times. In doing so I was not appealing for your sympathy and my correspondent made no such appeal. I simply told the story as a bit of real life which I thought contained a lesson for us all. On the Monday, however, following the Saturday on which the story was published, the Editor received the following letter: Dear Sir – If you are aware of the address of your correspondent 'EB' who is mentioned in Gossip in your Christmas number I should be much obliged if you would forward her the enclosed three shillings so that she will be able to give the usual Christmas presents to her children.

It's disingenuous of Mab to deny that her column was not an appeal for sympathy. After reporting the facts of 'EB's life, she had gone on to talk about Christmas presents. 'Better to find out cases like EB's and send your present there than bestow duty gifts on people who do not want them and will not appreciate them.' The sender of the three shillings had clearly taken the hint.

As an editor, James Allingham had made the most of Christmas. One of his most successful innovations had been the *Christian Globe* 'Christmas Hamper', a purely secular supplement to the main paper with a sentimental picture on the cover. Inside were specially commissioned short stories (or 'long completes') family puzzles and Christmas lore. The first instalment of the new year's serial story would usually be included. 'To our readers: If you like our Christmas Hamper order a copy of next Thursday's issue of the *Christian Globe* containing the opening chapters of Annie S Swan's thrilling story of the Indian Mutiny.'

Herbert Allingham (as 'Herbert St Clair') wrote his first 'long complete' for the 1890 Christmas Hamper. This was a tale in three chapters of Gerald, a bored and wealthy young man 'but recently returned from college', who falls in love with the daughter of one of his tenants. The girl and her father are about to be evicted from their home to make way for his projected deer park. He struggles with the idea that he is throwing himself away but eventually asks her to marry him – and is rejected with the spirit of an evangelical Elizabeth Bennett. 'You thought me worthy to be your wife – you who live a useless vegetable, soulless existence: who while possessing wealth, youth, strength and possibly, some ability, by which you might do a man's work in the world and rid it of some of the human wretchedness by which it is oppressed.'

Utterly humiliated he rushes away and she bursts into tears. When young Gerald is next heard of, it is feared he has gone mad. 'He has started some marvellous scheme for doing away with the London slums, elevating the masses, abolishing poverty or something of that sort.' He is once again being robbed right and left just as he was in the days of his hedonism. After a little subterfuge on the part of the girl's father the lovers are reunited and live poor and happy ever after. 'Were all their dreams realised? Well, perhaps not. [...] but there is at least one bright spot in the midst of the darkness where two noble souls are living self-denying lives.'

Self-denial was not necessarily the message readers and advertisers were looking for at Christmas time. In Allingham's subsequent Christmas stories acts of charity were immediately rewarded by prosperity. In 'The Redemption of Richard Deane' (1895) a young artist is jerked out of his egotistical despair by a gallant little crossing sweeper who is struggling to earn sixpence to buy gifts for his brothers and sisters. The artist gives the child his few last coppers then, as soon as he returns to his lodgings, he discovers an envelope containing a commission from the *Pictorial Weekly*. He is on the way to fame and fortune but doesn't forget the 'London Arab'. 'You shall have the finest Christmas you ever heard of. There shall be a pudding so big that it will take two men to carry it, a turkey as large as they grow 'em, mince pies by the dozen and jellies and things by the bucketful.' The boy and the artist go to the shopping arcade together 'and for the next two hours they revelled in the luxury of spending money.'

By the end of the nineteenth century, special Christmas numbers had become commonplace throughout the penny press, providing useful extra work for artists and writers. In 1895 George Newnes's *Tit-Bits* devoted almost its entire Christmas issue to a range of five-guinea competitions. At last Allingham won a prize. His short story 'Our Madge' neatly blends a heart-warming description of charity relieving poverty with his personal love of the theatre. The narrator is another of Allingham's impecunious young journalists. He has spent Christmas Eve at the 'Vivacity' adoring his heroine Madge Meredith, queen of the burlesque. He is hanging around by the stage door, hoping for another glimpse, when he sees the actress accosted by a ragged child. She bundles the child into her carriage and sets off in a direction opposite to her home. The journalist, like any paparazzo of today, hails a cab and follows her. The carriage stops outside 'a gloomy looking house in the dingiest and most poverty-stricken part of Walham Green'.

The journalist waits in the cold until the actress leaves. Then he knocks on the door and pretends to the invalid inside that he 'has' to write an article about Madge Meredith. 'Many stories to her discredit are afloat,' he lies, 'But I admire her greatly, and thought perhaps you could tell me something to her credit? There must be some good in her.' He gets the story he wants and sits up late 'making copy'.

In the morning, as an afterthought, I paid another visit to Walham Green. I was rewarded. The room had been transformed. Holly and mistletoe hid the bareness of the walls, the children were laughing and playing upon the floor amid heaps of toys; a magnificent bowl of chrysanthemums stood on a small table near the invalid's couch. A pleasant faced girl was busy preparing the centre table for what was evidently going to be a very considerable banquet.

Of course Madge was the good fairy who had wrought this startling change. I hurried back to my rooms, altered my copy, and then let the flimsies fly. The result you all know. It was the biggest 'scoop' I ever organised.

That night at the 'Vivacity' almost half the audience arrives carrying chrysanthemums. There's uproar when the actress appears. When she is able to speak, however, almost her first concern is to clear herself from the charge of doing it 'for the ad'. She then capitalises on the public goodwill by appealing for help to provide for her impoverished friend. 'The rest need not take long to tell. The subscription list which Madge headed with £120 grew apace and, as you know, we rushed it up into four figures.'

'Our Madge' offers an insider's take on the manipulation of news. The starving family in Walham Green is a convenient prop to arouse emotion. The actress may have behaved, as she insists, with no thought of extra publicity for herself, but the journalist has seen the whole incident as 'copy' and cares mainly for his column inches.

It was before the days of the new journalism or I should have done even better. As it was, I was satisfied. The 'Daily Telephone' of December 26th gave me two columns, besides a picturesque leader of its own. Madge was immensely popular as it was, and this story of her visit to a fellow-artist who had come upon evil days just suited the 'Telephone'.

Possibly every media generation talks about 'the new journalism' and understands what it means in its own context. Today the phrase means blogging and the 'paperless' paper. Commentators on nineteenth-century periodicals use it when analysing the impact of post-industrial revolution technology on presentation, content, dissemination. It's difficult to agree on a start date for the new journalism amongst the Victorians. Joel Wiener's book *Papers for the Millions: the New Journalism in Britain 1850 – 1914* takes a broad sweep, allowing more than half a century for the process to reach fruition. Kate Jackson, biographer of George Newnes, takes the process back to the developments in the radical and popular press during the 1830s and the expansion of Sunday papers during the 1840s. The phrase itself was first used in May 1887 by Matthew Arnold. He was writing in the *Nineteenth Century*, a magazine that the young Molly Hughes found impossible to get through, but which James Allingham quoted approvingly in the *Christian Globe*. The 'new journalism', said Arnold,

> has much to recommend it [...] it is full of ability, novelty, variety, sensation, sympathy, generous instincts, its one great fault is that it is feather-brained. It throws out assertions at a venture because it wishes them true; does not correct either them or itself, if they are false; and to get at the seat of things as they are, seems to feel no concern whatsoever.

It's quite possible that Herbert Allingham would have read Arnold's article in 1887. Or he could have heard his father comment on any discussion it provoked in the trade. By the time he came to write 'Our Madge' in 1895 Allingham was an editor himself and had a hands-on appreciation of feather-brained new journalism with its emphasis on 'human interest'. 'Our Madge', however, sounds tantalisingly prescient, seeming to anticipate the next major Fleet Street development – the founding of the *Daily Mail* in 1896.

Alfred Harmsworth, the founder of *Answers* (1888), later claimed that he had been working all along to his own 'Schemo Magnifico'. In 1890 he and his brother Harold followed up their initial success with a halfpenny, eight-page weekly, *Comic Cuts*. This was closely followed by *Illustrated Chips*, also a halfpenny. These pricing decisions were highly significant. There was a social gulf between those who could afford a penny for their papers and those for whom only halfpenny purchases were possible. The huge circulations and impressive profits made by the Harmsworth papers came from a more impoverished readership (in relative terms) than had ever previously been regular buyers. By 1892 the weekly circulation of the Harmsworth magazines was over a million and they had dispensed with their original, outside investors.

The following year they became a public limited company, Answers Ltd. Between 1890 and 1894 they had established (among others) *Forget-Me-Not*, the *Wonder*, *Pluck*, the *Union Jack*, the *Marvel*, *Home Sweet Home*, *Home Chat*, the *Sunday Companion*, the *Boys' Friend* and had purchased their first newspaper, the *Evening News* (1894). George Newnes, meanwhile, had developed the *Strand Magazine* (1891), the *Million* (1892) and another evening paper, the *Westminster Gazette* (1893). Arthur Pearson was building more slowly with *Home Notes*, *Pearson's Magazine*, the *Royal Magazine* but solidly – and competitively.

Aspects of the new journalism could be seen throughout these weekly and evening papers but not, as yet, in the dailies. In 1895, when 'Our Madge' was published, the most obvious candidate for Allingham's fictitious *Daily Telephone* would have been the *Daily Telegraph*. Founded in 1855 this had been the first daily newspaper to be sold for one penny and its circulation was still well ahead of competitors at about 250,000. In 1896, however, the situation changed. Alfred and Harold Harmsworth launched the *Daily Mail* – slogan 'a penny newspaper for a halfpenny'. In 1900 Pearson countered with the *Daily Express* and the intense competition that had stimulated the weekly mass-market magazines was played out daily.

Allingham's first success of the twentieth century used rivalry between two down-market daily newspapers as background for a series of six 3,000-word detective stories, *The Achievements of Michael Power*. Once again his protagonist was a journalist but this time he was a much more energetic and knowing character than either the naïve Frank Darcy of

A Devil of a Woman or the unnamed stage-door Johnny of 'Our Madge'. 'We were all smart men at the Daily Record, but beyond a doubt Michael Power was the smartest of the lot. He not only had a wonderful nose for news, but when he got hold of an item he knew how to make the most of it.'

The stories were subtitled *Episodes in the Professional Career of a Newspaper Man* and were published in *Pearson's Weekly* in January 1901. The narrator is cheerfully modern and amoral and there is an atmosphere of excitement, adventure and risk about this new journalistic world. Episode one, the 'Wimbledon Murder Mystery', shows Power convincing his editor to give him space, day after day, to spin out the solution to the murder of a wealthy ship-owner. At first the editor is sarcastic: 'You don't expect that to go into the news page do you? Cut it down to three sticks, cast it in the form of a letter and sign it Sherlock Holmes 2.' Then, when Power begins to suggest that the dead man may have had a shady past, the editor becomes anxious.

Now we of the Record belonged to what was called the new journalism – that is we were more distinguished for enterprise than for scruples; but when Paterson read this production in MS, he caught his breath and looked grave.

'Are you sure this is all right, Mick?' he asked. 'You know it means libel actions and no end of trouble if –'

'There is no "if" replied Power quietly.

Meanwhile our revelations fell like a bombshell upon the country. Our sale went up with a rush. At the clubs everyone agreed that we must know something. Even our rivals were compelled to quote us.

The police visit the newspaper to enquire for the source of their information. The editor assures them that he knows nothing. '"We only use our intelligence," he added, "and follow up clues as they come to light."' The truth was considerably less Sherlockian.

'I had him in my cellar all the time. Ye see it was this way. I was cycling across Wimbledon Common that night and my tyre went wrong. I got off to see what was the matter, when sudden-like there appeared, shambling along the road, a most extraordinary creature [...] Thinking there might be a bit of copy in him I stopped him and nearly got shot for my pains. But I soon made friends, took him home to my place in Barnes, and kept him in my cellar for three months. I had to tell the wife but no-one else knew. I made him pretty comfortable and doled out his story in daily instalments. Oh it was a real fine "scoop".

I burst out laughing. 'What did you do with the man after all?'

'Oh, got him out of the country, with enough to start him afresh in a new land. Paterson paid the piper and glad enough to do it.'

'Well, Mick, I have always held that the one great requisite for the making of a modern journalist is impudence.'

'Yes, impudence and luck,' amended the Irishman, modestly.

A national newspaper abetting a criminal for the sake of a story... oh, shock, horror! In Allingham's next tale, 'The Leadenhall Street Explosion', Power sets up a sting for a rival paper. The narrator's expressions of disapproval fail to convince.

Even in these days of fierce newspaper competition when many things are done that would have been thought *infra dig* twenty years ago, there are certain rules of the game which an English newspaper must observe if it wishes to maintain its position as a responsible organ of public opinion.

We at the Record strained these rules pretty severely every day of the week but we rarely actually broke them.

In the little skirmish which we had with our great Fleet Street rival, the Daily Courier, however, we undoubtedly went too far.

Even Michael Power himself – who conceived and engineered the whole thing – admits – with a grin be it said – that it was not 'in accordance with the high traditions of the British Press.'

The Courier was the only paper we really feared. It not only had any amount of capital behind it and a staff of picked men, but its proprietor was on intimate terms with the leading lights of the Government.

Allingham was writing in a magazine owned by the founder of the *Daily Express*. Was he thinking about the *Daily Mail* when he wrote about the Courier? Even by 1901 Alfred Harmsworth was seen as a man with influence, a man who lunched and spent weekends with politicians such as Lord Rosebery and HH Asquith, George Curzon and Winston Churchill.

Michael Power's trap for the Courier is baited with prejudices that are not unrecognisable today. There has been an explosion in Leadenhall Street. All the evidence suggests that it's a gas explosion but there have been anarchist outrages on the continent and people are jumpy. The Courier chooses the conspiracy theory and indulges itself with some mysterious hints.

We make this suggestion with all reserve, but it is certain that the police themselves are by no means satisfied with the explanation they have supplied to the press and the news-agencies. On the contrary they are pursuing their enquiries into the matter with quite remarkable energy.

Allingham's narrator comments, 'The dear old British public seized on this suggestion with avidity because it had been feeding its mighty mind on nothing else but Continental anarchist plots for the past fortnight.' Michael Power is dispatched by the RECORD to discover what's going on. Instead he plants a false trail of evidence – which succeeds in convincing the COURIER that its suspicions are correct. It harrumphs:

> Now that active anarchism has made its appearance in this country it behoves the authorities to stamp out the hideous thing with merciless rigour. It is not surprising that many people are asking how much longer England is to continue to be the dumping ground for all the human refuse thrown out of other countries.

A long-haired young man is arrested in Paris. The COURIER is triumphant. The RECORD is more triumphant still.

> We should be the last to advocate any interference with the freedom of the press in this country. But the privileges enjoyed carry with them certain responsibilities. We regret that a certain once-responsible London newspaper has allowed itself to forget this fact [...]
>
> Urged on by the sensational and quite unfounded statements of our contemporary the police lost their heads and saw anarchists everywhere. The mistakes they have made would fill a volume but the most ridiculous is that which has culminated in the arrest of a talented young Scotch artist in Paris. [...] Mr Douglas, like many artists, wears his hair long and is somewhat careless in his dress.
>
> By the time these lines are published Mr Douglas will, of course, be at liberty. We think that our friends of the DAILY COURIER – among others – owe him an apology.
>
> Finally we may add for the satisfaction of those who have been

misled by our contemporary's lucubrations: we are happy to be able to state that a closer examination of the *débris* in Leadenhall Street by experts proves beyond question that the catastrophe was due entirely to an explosion of gas.

One word in conclusion. There are few things we value more than legitimate enterprise in journalism, but we hold that to prey upon the public's fears and to create a public scare by the dissemination of false news is unworthy of a responsible English newspaper.

It's all been engineered by Power. The next two stories narrate his 'saving' of the French Republic – using kiss-and-tell trickery; and his crucial achievement of an interview with the German Emperor – through incognito invasion of privacy. The last two are uncomplicated detective tales, though still with the tang of the fictional newsroom about them. '"What's kept out of the papers is often a great deal more interesting than what gets into them," said Michael Power one day.'

It's a good first sentence but marks the end of this series. When 'Michael Power' appears again in Allingham's work (in 1909) he's a slightly grumpy detective running an agency and rather hopelessly in love with his young assistant, Miss Maggie MacFee. He doesn't appear to have any relationship at all with the sparky Irish journalist of 1901. By 1909, however, Allingham was writing for a younger audience where surnames such as 'Power', 'Steel' and 'Dare' were standard issue. 'Michael Power' had become one of Allingham's off-the-peg range of character types.

But that is to anticipate. All six 1901 'Episodes in the Professional Career of a Newspaper Man' carry the author's name and suggest the commencement of a successful career writing light, amusing narratives for villa-dwellers. The other author featured in *Pearson's Weekly* at that same time was Louis Tracy (1863–1928), a popular and prolific creator of patriotic adventure stories, science fiction and romance. There was a big market for what might be called lower middle-brow fiction. Lead serial writers for *Answers* or *Pearson's Weekly* as well as for the *Daily Mail*, *Daily Express* and George Newnes's famous *Strand Magazine* reached millions of people and could earn big money. At this moment Allingham appeared to have his foot in that lucrative door. Why didn't he go any further? There is no editorial correspondence surrounding the Michael Power stories; nothing to indicate whether they were unsolicited offerings accepted ready-written, whether they were sold through a fiction bureau or requested from Allingham by the *Pearson's Weekly* editor. Nor whether he tried anything comparable again and was rejected.

In fact the promising opening to 1901 turned out to be the beginning of the three quietest years – fiction-wise – in Allingham's entire career. The *London Journal* seemed to be running on autopilot. Mab had fallen silent in 1899 and direct editorial intervention was rare – other than a brief outburst in praise of tobacco. 'It is comforting to know that nearly all great authors were addicted to tobacco [...] And with very many modern writers there is the same fondness for the weed which at once soothes and stimulates.' Regular editorial duties, such as replying to readers' letters, continue:

> The college students appear to be a pair of scamps.
>
> The young man's conduct towards you was most ungentlemanly.
>
> You have behaved unhandsomely in the matter.
>
> Forget the man. He appears to be as base as he is silly.
>
> A youth of seventeen and a girl of sixteen are too young to

marry. As the young fellow is only earning a pound a week we should think that his lack of means to support you would itself deter you from eloping with him.

Only rarely does the editor betray impatience. 'You ask too much: employ a solicitor.' Elsewhere he insists that he is happy in the service. 'It is by no means a trouble but rather a pleasure to tender information and advice to those who seek it through the medium of these columns.'

Allingham did produce one other notable short story in 1901. 'The Garden of Glory' was written for the *Christian Globe* 'Christmas Hamper' and is subtitled 'A Christmas Fairy Story of London Life'. It's almost a heart-warmer, but not quite: it's evangelical, certainly; shows a sophisticated understanding of publicity and makes a neat feminist point. In the process it rejects the world of Michael Power and those smart men at the DAILY RECORD. 'The Garden of Glory' is the title of a mysterious bestselling book. 'You will remember that *The Garden of Glory* was something more than the book of the season. Even level-headed critics declared that it was a great book and that its unknown author was a new force in the world's literature.' The author is anonymous and excites widespread curiosity.

One day a group of men, all distinguished in their various callings, were discussing the book in the smoking room of a famous London club. 'It is preposterous that the personality of such a genius should remain hidden any longer,' said one. 'Let us make an attempt to draw him out of his shell.'

They decide to hold a banquet and to send the anonymous author an invitation via his publishers.

The suggestion was carried out. Nearly a hundred men, distinguished in literature, art, science and politics appended their names to the invitation, which was forthwith despatched. In a couple of days came a reply. To the astonishment of most people it was a brief and courteous acceptance.

But the author does not arrive. Instead they receive a request. 'You say you admire my book and through it you admire me [...] Go out into the street and invite the first poor outcast that you see to be your guest for the evening in my place.'

'Preposterous! The man is utterly mad!' growled a dignified pillar of the Church.

'Sold, by Jove!' laughed the clever journalist who had been chiefly instrumental in getting up the affair.

'The eccentricity of genius,' drawled a third.

'What extraordinary insolence!' blurted out one of the most distinguished of England's generals.

Nevertheless they're men of the world. They regain their good humour and decide to do as they have been asked, 'at least it would cause some diversion'. A judge, an artist and a geology professor are sent out and duly find a wretched woman clinging to the Eaton Square railings. There's a ripple of laughter when they bring her into the mansion. Some protests are heard.

Then, suddenly the woman raised her head and the shawl slipped from her shoulders to the ground. In a moment the laughter was hushed. 'The face was the face of a young woman but so pale, so sad, so wan, that every man in the room experienced a strange sensation of guilt.'

The young artist longs to paint her; the statesmanlike host does his best to put her at her ease but she relapses into apathy, showing neither interest nor embarrassment. 'It is to be feared that the rest of the company almost forgot their guest; as the dinner proceeded the constraint which clever men usually feel in one another's company vanished and gave way to amusing talk and hearty and prolonged laughter.' They are shocked when the woman finally speaks.

I will not ask you why you have done this kindness to me – an outcast. I understand that this gathering came together to do honour to another whose place I have taken. He is lucky to have so many friends. You are all successful men; so much I have learned from your chairman's words during dinner. No doubt most of you deserve your success; you have doubtless gained it by many years of arduous toil, by steadfastness of purpose and by many sacrifices. But forgive me if I ask you one question. Now that you have reached the summit and with both hands grasp all that the world can give you – honour, wealth and pride – do you never look back and give a thought to those you have passed on the way? Oh! believe me, there are those who have worked as hard, striven as bravely, and who have fallen by the way. Life's pitiful failures!

In their faces she sees amusement, scorn, bewilderment. Only the artist seems to sympathise. Then she leaves.

When the door was closed on the slight, shabby figure, the distinguished gentlemen left behind stared at one another awkwardly for a moment.

'Can anyone tell me,' murmured the professor at length, 'whether we are the heroes of a romantic accident, or the dupes of a ridiculous plot?'

'What do you think about it?' asked the judge turning to the journalist who was standing by himself frowning in deep thought.

'I think,' he answered slowly, 'that it is curious that none of us ever guessed that the author of *The Garden of Glory* was a woman.'

'And I must ask you, Sir William Joyce, to mind your own business'

Chapter Ten
1904: True Blue

THE young artist followed the outcast woman as she left Eaton Square. He went with her all the way to Limehouse in East London where she introduced him to a boys' club. Boys' clubs, settlements in slum areas and social outreach generally were stuff of life to the philanthropic wing of the *Christian Globe.* Allingham's 1886 diary, for instance, records an afternoon at home in Hammersmith when he was left to take care of a 'Mr Williams of Westminster, Lambeth etc.' who had called unexpectedly to see James. They had a 'rather slow' afternoon watching cricket but the day livened up when 'Dad and the mater' returned.

> Williams with stories about his boys quite amused us all. It appears that he has started a club for boys and it numbers about one hundred and ninety members. The attractions consist of boating, swimming, cricket, football, boxing, fencing, running, parallel and horizontal bar practice. He gives them lectures etc at stated intervals but does not interfere with the management of the club. Making the boys look after it entirely of themselves and any disorder is subdued quite by themselves.

The author of *The Garden of Glory,* who has been so withdrawn at the grand dinner party, livens up when she is once again among her boys. The artist, however, feels uneasy in this 'foreign land'. He knows that he has been wasting his talent as a society portrait painter, though 'earning a lot of money and meeting a number of charming people'. Soon, however, he finds himself 'at the centre of an admiring, if somewhat boisterous, group who watched him while he made ludicrous caricatures for them in a sketch-book'. He accepts a penny hymn sheet and joins in their rendering of 'Hark! the herald angels sing' and, when all the boys have finally disappeared 'down dark lanes and mysterious courts', he finds himself alone again with the young woman.

'I like your friends,' said Clive.

'You will like them better when you know them better. You people who live in Society know very little of real life.'

'You think me very ignorant?'

'Yes, that is it,' said the girl simply. 'You people are not wilfully cruel; you are only ignorant.'

'But I am willing to learn.'

'Then come and live in Limehouse. You are an artist. Come and live among the people, learn to know them as they really are. Then you will do something great.'

'But the life is so sordid, so ugly, so utterly vile!'

The girl looked up at him and her eyes, and her eyes were full of pity.

'How ignorant you are!' she said. 'Will you never understand us? We have our sins and our sorrows but we also have our joys, our ambitions and our hopes!'

Sometime in those very first years of the twentieth century Allingham fell in love. Emily Jane Hughes (Em) was his first cousin, the oldest daughter of James Allingham's second sister, also called Emily Jane. The older Emily Jane became Margery, Philip and Joyce's much loved (though gently mocked) Granny. She spent long periods with them during their childhoods and lived with Margery for at least twelve years before her death. Born 1852, Granny was their main window on the Victorian past, on their great-grandfather William Allingham, on the early years in Kennington and on the foundation of the *Christian Globe*. Herbert Allingham would have had many more sources of information; his own observations, his parents, Aunt Julia Nowell, Uncle John, other aunts, uncles, cousins, family friends. But no account has survived either from him or from Em as to the circumstances in which she was living before their marriage or at what point they discovered that their feelings for one another were more than cousinly. So we are left with what Joyce told as Granny's story, plus Margery's fictional variation of the same in *Dance of the Years*.

According to Joyce, the older Emily Jane had been pushed into marriage by her brother James for his own business ends. Her husband, William Walter Hughes, was a photographer (and a WW Hughes did undertake some photographic assignments for the *Christian Globe*). When Walter and Emily Jane married in 1878 he was a widower with a young daughter Phoebe (born 1875). He was thirty-four, Emily Jane twenty-five, a well-educated but not a clever girl. She had spent some time at school in Godesberg, Germany, a similar establishment perhaps, to that attended by Isabella Beeton and her sisters. Emily Jane was dutiful, devoutly Christian, sweet-natured and had a little money of her own – her share of William Allingham's legacy.

According to Joyce, Walter Hughes was an alcoholic. They had four children together – Em (born 1879), Maud (1883), Walter (1885) and Hilda (1888) – but in the end Emily Jane took the children and left. Joyce didn't know exactly what happened but was convinced that only violence, possibly against the children, would have driven Granny to take such a decisive step.

What happened next is not known either. The registers confirm that Emily's *Christian Globe* shares were gone and Joyce believed the family to have been desperately poor. My impression, from Joyce, was that the children were still quite young when their mother left their father. That would have made the 1890s years of real struggle for Emily Jane. She and her children may well have dropped off the family radar. Both Joyce in conversation and Margery in fiction blamed their other grandparents, James and Louisa, for not helping Granny as much as they should have done, or, in Margery's words, for the sort of charity 'that gives charity its false name'. By the census of 1901 the family had disintegrated. Little Hilda had died, Phoebe was working abroad (possibly as a governess) and neither of the parents is traceable (Walter may have died). Young Walter is working as a servant in an infirmary, Maud is an assistant in a stationer's shop, boarding with her employers, and Em is a milliner's apprentice, also living at her place of work, in her case London's Regent Street. In *Dance of the Years*, Margery's fictional version:

There was an almighty row in the family when Jeffrey married Belle, for after suddenly throwing up all his preparations for the church and taking to painting saleable, if uninspired, illustrations to children's religious books, he had avowed himself a Socialist (a highly unfashionable faith at the time) and then, still abruptly and unexpectedly, had married his music-hall cousin, who, until her success, had been one of his poorest and most despised relations.

Jeffrey – this fictional version of her father – was 'a man in an inescapable muddle'.

Jeffery had been a man who sent his children to exclusive schools and then raved at them for believing the social teachings they learned there; he had been a man who was for ever trying to make friends with working folk only to have them raise their hats to him and turn away uncomfortably; a man who married a woman because she was gloriously vulgar and alive, only to have her leave him for men who were more vulgar and alive than himself.

There are no surviving diaries or letters from this period. Only the contrast in tone of the two 1901 stories, 'the Achievements of Michael Power' and 'the Garden of Glory', offer a way of glimpsing Allingham at about the time he fell in love. He was a low-grade Fleet Street editor with circulation figures to consider, employers and advertisers as well as readers to please. He was also a left-wing idealist, a Fabian, with a genuine, if slightly self-conscious, admiration for 'the common people'. He could be humorous, worldly, slightly cynical or he could be earnest and evangelical. These alternative voices represented alternative possibilities. He was by now thirty-four years old, was still living at home with his parents and had been editing the *London Journal* for twelve years. Margery said that her father 'hated to be bored'.

Em ('Belle' in *Dance of the Years*) was stylish and a bit loud – or so her children thought. She does not look 'vulgar' in her engagement photo but she does look 'gloriously... alive'.

There's lots of her and she has a lovely complexion. Herbert looks serious, supportive and perhaps a little wary. In this first picture to have survived of him, he is already grey. As an editor Allingham had already spent years summing up readers' characters from their photographs. I wonder what he thought of this portrait? Later in her life, and privately, Em would sometimes present herself as fearful, frightened, 'exhausted' by her older daughter's personality. This was not the impression she made generally. In Edwardian terms she was a 'cough-drop', someone who stuck in your throat and made you splutter. It wasn't a compliment but wasn't totally negative either. Sal, the coster-girl in Allingham's *The Lights of Home*, is a cough-drop. So is Babs, the working-class heroine of his later serial, *Human Nature* (1913–1915).

Joyce, Em's youngest child, who disliked her, wondered aloud whether her father had married her mother because he felt sorry for her. They were first cousins yet he had been brought up in relative comfort and she and her family had had to struggle. And there was that suspicion that his father might have been responsible for her mother's bad marriage. Was this a way to make amends? But even Joyce couldn't think that for very long. You don't patronise 'cough-drops' – not if you have any sense – and it seems clear that Allingham married Em because he loved and desired her. He probably liked her cough-drop qualities as well. Most of the time. 'All my dull days came to me before I was married,' he told his friend William McFee. 'Since that time I have often been furiously angry and sometimes driven to the edge of insanity but I have never been dull.'

McFee himself was another stimulant. 'To be frank, my dear Mac,' wrote Allingham in an undated fragment, 'tact and good manners are not your strong points. And a good job too.

I like you as you are and there would be a gap in my life if I ceased to receive your clever and sometimes spiteful letters.' The two men and Em met when McFee was leaving shore life for a career at sea. Their correspondence was initially three-cornered, though later Em dropped out and the two older children, Margery and Phil, joined in. Only McFee's letters have survived. There are a few tantalising scraps from Allingham and from Margery, not a word from Em or Phil. McFee later became a literary celebrity in the United States, outselling Joseph Conrad on occasion and even Edgar Wallace. His letters to Allingham are preserved in the Bieneke Library where the friends decided jointly to sell them in the early 1930s. Allingham's letters should have been included – but somehow they have vanished.

It's especially infuriating when the friends are having a three-way spat on topics such as marriage… A letter from McFee in 1918 (in which he mentions the 'awful expression of smug animalism which is the hall mark of matrimony in our enchanted isle') apparently provokes a tirade from Allingham and a letter from Em as well. He writes back again: 'Well, I expected to get thoroughly basted for my opinion on marriage and here I am, done to a turn! You say my letters wake you up. In a purely pugilistic sense yours "put me to sleep". I am inevitably knocked out, beaten up and otherwise seriously damaged. If my nose doesn't bleed my heart does. What a born optimist you are.'

And he goes on to accuse Allingham of writing about marriage as a local newspaper propagandist writes about war, claiming every reverse as success. But we can only know what McFee says that Allingham (and Em) said – and in the middle of a row who's going to cavil at a little selective quotation? Anyway, for what it's worth, McFee quotes Allingham as having said that 'the right and reasonable motive for getting married is that a man wants a particular girl and can't bear to think of anyone else having her.' In the same letter he cites Em as saying 'most men will go as far as you let them. She's right. They will.' According to McFee both his friends are telling him that 'a man gets married because he wants a girl and the girl wants a home.'

So was that it for Allingham and Em in 1902–1903? Did Allingham, who was probably living quite a celibate life, still at home with his parents and brothers, ask Em to marry him because he was consumed by possessive desire? Did she accept because she yearned for financial security and a home of her own? Possibly. Years later, (again according to McFee) she confided in his (second) wife that sex was 'horrid' and 'men were beasts'. A reported second-hand scrap which makes one feel a bit uneasy when Allingham appears in every other respect to be noticeably un-beastlike. Perhaps that's why McFee felt sufficiently comfortable to report her comment back. (It might also make one wonder, fleetingly, about the nature of the abuse from which Emily Jane had so determinedly removed the four girls in her care.)

Sufficient to say that the cousins married early in 1903 and did not go and devote themselves to good works in Limehouse or any other slum. They moved into a suburban semi-detached villa in Broughton Road, Ealing. In May 1904 their first child, Margery Louise, was born. This event seems to have sent Allingham into a frenzy of writing activity. In 1902 he had produced only one brief, filler story; in 1903 nothing at all, except for his editorial work at the *London Journal* and whatever advertising copy he might have supplied for the JC Francis agency. By 1904 he had completely reorganised his work so he could spend two full days each week writing at home. This meant that he could also admire Margery splashing in her bath, count the number of her dolls, observe her attitude to them and speculate on what might be happening in her mind. 'The more I study children,' writes Mab, 'or, to be honest, the more I study one little child...' Allingham was not a hands-on father to the extent of today's new men but he was both fascinated and personally changed by the experience.

From a biographer's point of view Allingham's decision to work from home means that letters relating to his freelance work have frequently survived – unlike the mass of material that must have poured in daily to the *London Journal* office. The first letters are both rejections. 'Dear Sir,' wrote Frank Girlman of the *Daily Mail* on 16 March:

> If you had kept your story, the first instalment of which I return herewith, to human interest, I fancy that I could have made you an offer for it, but as it is it becomes altogether too wild and improbable for my requirements. I like the way in which you have written it, and I do not see why, if you will remember our talk the other day, you should not write us a really good story. I must impress on you the interest be of humanity and not of wild and improbable schemes.

Allingham did try again and pitched his story at a rather lower level within the hierarchy of the Harmsworth penny papers. He sent four instalments to Charles Sisley, editor of the *Pictorial Magazine*, but received a similar response.

> Dear Sir,
>
> In going through your serial *For Sale – a Woman* I was very surprised to see that the third instalment is very suggestive following as it does on the curtain to the second instalment.

This at once disqualifies the serial for the *Pictorial Magazine* as you know we have to be very particular on these matters.

I think therefore that the best way will be for you to submit some complete stories of 5,000 words each to take the place of the serial. I am returning the four instalments of the serial herewith.

As an editor Allingham had regularly advised his readers 'to begin by writing short stories and so gain experience'. As a newly urgent freelance he found himself obliged to take his own advice. He sold eight short stories to Charles Sisley at the *Pictorial* (or *Penny Pictorial* as it later became) but he hadn't yet given up on his serial. So he tried the opposition. Back, after a few reminders, came a letter from *Pearson's Weekly*:

Dear Sir.

I have now given the subject of your serial very careful consideration, but I regret that I am unable to accept it and I therefore return it herewith.

I must offer you my apologies for the delay in letting you have a definite decision regarding it.

I should be pleased to see any short stories of not more that 3,000 words that you care to send along.

Allingham sold a further seven short stories to *Pearson's* but only one survives, together with only two of the eight sold to the *Pictorial*. Short stories are among the more elusive elements of his work. File copies have not been reliably kept (probably as their resale value was negligible) and several of the magazines in which they were published have not survived, even in the British Library.

One reason that copies are rare among Allingham's

own papers may be that he was composing by hand (as he did throughout his life) and only using a typewriting agency selectively. The cost of typing in 1906 was about one shilling per thousand words. Although Allingham was trying to establish himself with the sorts of magazines, such as those owned by the Harmsworths, that could potentially pay him one or two guineas per thousand words, most of his work at this stage earned considerably less. Ten shillings and six pence per thousand was the norm in the cheaper houses. Sending out uncommissioned stories involved waiting, first for the editorial decision and then for publication. As payment was usually made on publication rather than on acceptance, money expended in advance on typewriting was money trapped in the system. Allingham was aware of the impact of editorial delay on his cash flow and resented it:

> Why doesn't your firm pay more promptly? There are scores of men like myself knocking about Flt St – Here am I with quite a gift for popular fiction and yet I have to stick to journalism for my bread and butter simply because journalism means ready money –
>
> Although I only do fiction 2 days a week I have at the present moment over £50 worth of stuff out – all accepted but not published and therefore not paid for.
>
> One of your papers has had a story of mine 11 months, another has had one 5 months. Is it surprising that we are driven to the cheaper houses where you deliver your copy in the morning and call for the money in the afternoon?

One such 'cheaper house' was the Aldine Press. It was Aldine who had taken over Ralph Rollington's *New Boys' Paper* in 1887 together with much material from earlier failed publications. Charles Perry Brown, the founder of the company, had been among Rollington's circle of acquaintance: Robert Prowse drew for Aldine; EH Burrage, his own company wound up, wrote for Aldine in the early years of the twentieth century as did his brother, AS Burrage. Their main strength was in 3d 'libraries', cheap complete books, published in monthly batches and corresponding to the American 'dime novels' which they regularly reused.

In 1904, however, Aldine was attempting to compete in the area of weekly penny-magazine publishing. Their product, *True Blue,* aimed to appeal to the increasing number of working-class boys and young men abroad (like Allingham's new brother-in-law, Walter Hughes, who had emigrated to Canada) as well as to those at home. Emigration advice was a regular feature and the editor expended an appreciable amount of effort attempting to foster loyalty by encouraging readers to link with one another through the '*True Blue* Trusty Band'. The magazine was a low-budget product. Many of its authors wrote under pseudonyms – as was common in Aldine publications. The more pseudonymity and anonymity in the penny publishing world, the lower the class of paper. An obvious explanation is financial; reprints were cheaper than commissioned originals and it was traditional to omit or disguise authors' names when a story had been previously published elsewhere.

Other reasons for manipulating or reducing the identity of the author were connected with fostering the illusion of the paper. Like many other cash-strapped publications (not least the *London Journal*) *True Blue* attempted to bolster its status by pretending that there were more people writing for it than there were, and that they were more exciting and distinguished than was the case.

'Between ourselves', confided the editor to his readers in December 1904:

> The new serial which will commence in the Christmas number is entitled *A Regular Duffer* and its author is Mr David Pitt. Mr Pitt has not yet been introduced to *True Blue*-ites but he is a writer of worldwide reputation and his tales of school life and adventure have proved some of the most popular ever written. *A Regular Duffer* provides some screaming fun as well as some exciting adventure and it has afforded me more than average pleasure in reading it. I want you to tell your friends about this new yarn of ours and see that they provide themselves each with a copy of our Christmas number next week which contains the opening chapters.
>
> ***
>
> The long-complete which will occupy the front pages of our Christmas number is entitled 'Snowed Up or Christmas at Crag Castle College'. I need hardly say that it is a real rollicking Yuletide tale. With it *another new author*, Mr. Herbert Allingham, makes his bow to *True Blue*-ites and he has given us, for his first, a splendid story [my italics].

Both the stories were by Allingham. 'David Pitt' was not and would never become 'a writer of world-wide reputation'. Nevertheless *A Regular Duffer* did make 'a hit in a small way' as Allingham described it. Eagerly he dug out his 1886 file copy of *Barrington's Fag*, and wrote to a boys' paper editor at Pearson's hoping to re-sell it. The editor was not impressed. 'The principal reason why I am not able to entertain using your tale is because it is apt to be old-fashioned in incident and totally out of keeping with the notions of school tales in the minds of present day youngsters.'

Allingham very rarely argued with editors (common writers knew their place) but he seems to have felt protective about *Barrington's Fag*. 'I doubt whether your policy of insisting that all school stories should be made to one pattern is sound,' he muttered. When he heard from Em that the *True Blue* editor had reacted similarly, he begged for it to be read by actual youngsters. This worked. The editor demanded some re-writing of the early instalments; 'after that I notice that you have settled down more into your stride and have written with great confidence.' Once Allingham began revising he did more than had been asked. Out went most of the 'little bits of instruction' that had seemed so important when he was aged eighteen and in came David Pitt's lead character, 'the Duffer'. 'Curious,' remarked Holt, 'How many grown up people seem to be a bit cranky. I have noticed it so often.'

The Duffer is athletic, resourceful, scholarly but deceptively (infuriatingly) naïve, languid, and eccentric. As a young man Allingham had worried about getting his characters 'to say witty things': in these early years of married life his gift for writing comedy blossomed. Within a week of the newly titled *Captain's Fag* opening in *True Blue*, the editor claimed that 'some hundreds of letters and postcards and even telegrams have reached me bearing winged messages of congratulation and telling of the warm reception Mr Pitt's new tale has met with from every reader young and old.' Soon Will Holt had been transformed into 'Holt of Emmanuel' and was poised for a career in adventurous detection. 'Thus modestly and light-heartedly was launched the firm of Duffer and Co which afterwards became so famous.'

It didn't, of course. Nevertheless readers of Herbert Allingham's daughter Margery may recognise a certain turn of phrase as well as an attitude to characterisation which, for aficionados, raises the question how far the older Allingham's 'Duffer' may have influenced the younger Allingham's 'Albert Campion'. In 1904 what mattered was the existence of Margery as a stimulus to her father's career. Allingham was clearly determined to give his daughter a childhood with dolls and pantomimes, trips to the country and help for her mother in the home. To achieve this he needed to supplement his editorial salary with regular freelance work – weekly serials or commissioned story series, not sporadic acceptances and unpredictable pay. A handwritten fragment survives:

> Dear Murray,
> Send me some money!
> Send me some money!!
> SEND ME SOME MONEY!!!
> Right willingly will I clown and grin for the entertainment of thy juveniles but to do so on an empty belly I flatly refuse.
> Thine more in sorrow than wrath, HJA.

By April 1906 work appeared to be coming in steadily and Em was pregnant with their second child. Allingham was writing in several different styles and dealing with half a dozen different editors. Three long-complete *Duffer, Detective* stories had been published and a fourth written. School stories were also flourishing. He developed a new set of comic characters called *The Frolicsome Five* to add to his 'Dauntless Three', his 'Crag Castle boys' and his 'Boys from St Bede's'. The *True Blue* editor called him to his office to discuss future story lines.

In May 1906 *True Blue* ceased production and Aldine stopped paying – even for the work they'd ordered. Furious,

Allingham appealed to the Society of Authors and managed to shame the company into offering him £6 compensation and confirming that all the commissioned stories were now at his disposal. What was he to do with them?

Agile as a cat Max dashed forwards

Chapter Eleven
1907: Puck and the Jester

Em Allingham began writing in 1906. Allingham both mentored and marketed her work. In October 1906, a month before the birth for their second child, he received a letter from an editor who would 'have pleasure in using Mrs Allingham's tales entitled 'The Wild Convolvulous' and 'The Prince's Wish' at a half guinea each'. The letter continued, courteously, 'I am returning the Santa Claus story because it is a little too early in the season to begin talking of Christmas trees. But it is a pleasant story, and I should be glad to use it but for this objection. Perhaps Mrs Allingham will submit some other stories at her convenience.'

Writing wives and writing mothers were not at all unusual in the common writers' world where productivity and pay were so inexorably linked. There would be writing sisters and writing daughters too. There were other women professionals among Allingham's everyday colleagues. A Mrs Ninnes ran the typewriting agency that he used in Chancery Lane: it would not be long before another of his relatives, Flo Allingham, would take on this task. Allingham employed female journalists as well as freelance female fiction writers on both the *London Journal* and the *Christian Globe* – and was himself employed by women editors. During 1905-1906 he had been writing a melodramatic serial, *The Czar's Chief Spy*, for the penny weekly *Yes and No,* part of the downmarket Shurey's empire. They too often needed chasing for payment and it was frequently Em who would 'happen' to be passing and would call in to collect the cheque. When Em pulled on her gloves and pinned her hat to catch the bus into town she would be expecting either of the two *Yes and No* lady editors to authorise payment.

Casuals of the Sea offers insight into Allingham's world at this time. When McFee was in London he usually took rooms in Clifford's Inn situated in the unobtrusive hinterland behind Fleet Street, the law courts and the Strand. There were lawyers and law students there, of course, and journalist-barristers like FA Wickhart. 'Bachelor girls' – like McFee's fictional creation 'Mrs Olga Wilfley' – could also take rooms in Clifford's Inn.

Mrs Wilfley writes fashion notes for the servant-girl readers of *Sunday Words,* interviews philanthropists about their self-aggrandising projects and provides copy for patent medicine advertisements. 'Minnie', McFee's heroine, comes from the suburbs to type, wash-up, listen and assist for twelve shillings a week – as Mrs Wilfley knows she won't get a qualified woman for less than two pounds. As Minnie sits in Mrs Wilfley's rooms in Clifford's Inn, just a few hundred yards away from James Allingham's office at the *Christian Globe,* she is struggling to concentrate on typing up one of her employer's poorly-written PR interviews. A flashy young advertising clerk arrives.

'I called about a little matter – p'raps you can deal with it.' He took a long envelope out of his breast pocket, drew forth a strip of typed paper and began.

'Come in,' said Minnie and he did so.

'It's on business, I s'pose,' she added.

'That's so. You see,' he put his hat down on the chair and showed her the long strip, 'it's this thing she's done for us on Reaver's Stomach Mixture. It's all right except it don't go into details enough. We want more medical terms, you understand. That's what we want. More medical terms, more realism.'

'Oh,' said Minnie, sapiently. 'I see. I'll tell her.'

'F'rinstance,' went on the young man. 'This bit 'ere,' he indicated the bit with his pencil, 'it wants expanding. She might make another par out o' that, I reckon. Somethink about the gastric juices and the parenchyma. See?'

'Oh yes, I see,' said Minnie again. 'Anything else?'

'Yes. This 'ere,' he indicated another passage lower down. 'Now that's a bit over people's heads that is. You can't put that on the back of toilet rolls, you can't reelly.'

'Back of what?' said Minnie forgetting herself.

When young Minnie goes to lunch she goes somewhere very similar to the ABC tea-room which was, at this time, the most regular meeting place for McFee, Allingham, Em and their other friends and colleagues. 'To her, unused as she was to the great hubbub of the city, the meal in a vast tea-shop was novel, thrilling, stimulating. The café-habit came to her at once, naturally and irresistibly. It abolished the messing with dishes and the smell of cooking.' Em Allingham wasn't much interested in cooking either. Nor, allegedly, in children. Neither McFee's Minnie nor his Mrs Wilfley 'had the slightest propensity for motherhood. In neither of them did the life force direct the imagination towards domestic fecundity and economic ease.' McFee's heroine was quick, self-seeking, single-minded. 'She was one of those people who seem to learn with an economy of failure inexplicable to minds whose interests are more diffused.' And so, according to Margery, was Em. 'She was one of those remarkable women who can always succeed in the thing everyone else is doing and with very much less effort than they. She did not write for as long as the others but she did it and sold the products.'

The tantalisingly sparse glimpses of Herbert and Em Allingham in these early years of marriage and parenthood leave an impression that they were aiming for equality and a working partnership but were, to some extent, forced into their gender-specific roles. When Margery married, twenty-odd years later, friends presented her and her husband with a range of contraceptive devices. Her mother would have had access only to unpleasant (and probably ineffective) abortifacients. Conversely, had Allingham been born at a later date he might have shared more directly in caring for the baby daughter he found so fascinating. As it was the prime responsibility for financing their household was always his: Em's writing remained an occasional extra.

In 1906 he tried once again to modernise the *London Journal* with a new title, new layout and another series of Gossip from Mab but at the paper's heart all he could offer was JF Smith's *Minnigrey* – again. He wrote a string of short stories for his own fiction pages and spent a year struggling to maintain the energetic optimism that the *New London Journal* required. Then, early in 1907, he was persuaded to take on an even more hopeless editorial venture. EJ Blogg, a stationer and one of the directors of the *London Journal* (the same man who had proposed the reprinting of *Minnigrey* in the crisis of 1887), had had another of his fits of retro madness and had attempted a re-launch of Ralph Rollington's *New Boys' Paper.* Arthur Viles, scion of a nineteenth-century penny-dreadful-producing family almost as venerable as the Pierce Egans, had been appointed editor and was filling up the new *New Boys' Paper* with pseudonymous reprints. Viles included Allingham's *Frolicsome Five,* re-possessed from *True Blue,* but the new paper was soon in trouble and Blogg persuaded Allingham to take it over as editor.

In retrospect it was an object lesson in hopelessness and it is a measure of Allingham's innate optimism, or uncharacteristic failure to read the market signs, that he accepted. Perhaps he felt he had no choice. Having identified a shortage of good fiction as one of the *New Boys' Paper's* problems, he immediately ran his own *Max the Magnificent.* 'A very excellent and powerful piece of work and should send the circulation of the *NBP* up to 100,000,' wrote Charles Perry Brown, elderly founder of the Aldine Press. Perry Brown rifled his own store of illustrated tales and sent volumes of old material up to Gough Square for Allingham 'to cut away at'.

He also collected a 'large parcel' of material from American publishers. 'I shall be out in my calculation if you do not make the paper pay,' he wrote encouragingly, but when Allingham asked him for £300 to run an advertising campaign in the *Daily Mail,* he pleaded over-commitment on the stock exchange. He added consolingly, 'You are in much closer touch with your readers. That is a great thing.' Allingham peopled his office with his own stage army, including 'Billy Bard', the poetry editor, a character from one of his 'Crag Castle' school stories. His readers were almost as illusory. In desperation he tried to persuade Peter Keary at Pearson's to come into partnership with him or take over the *NBP* entirely: Keary refused, struggling, not entirely successfully, to hide his amazement at the naivety of this offer.

In 1906 and 1907 the juvenile fiction market was turbulent. Some years earlier, in 1901, the Harmsworths' magazines had been re-organised into a single company, the Amalgamated Press, separating them from the newspaper empire. By 1905 (the year in which Alfred Harmsworth became Lord Northcliffe) the AP was producing six monthly and twenty-eight weekly magazines with a readership numbered in millions. The introduction, in 1904, of a children's comic section within *Puck,* a new weekly paper, had been hugely successful and had encouraged all the AP comic papers to focus more explicitly on youth. Not generally on children, who had no money of their own and whose parents were unlikely to have money to spare for entertainment, but on boys and girls from around school leaving age (twelve) towards the early married years. The nineteenth-century obsession with boys was broadening to a twentieth-century interest in adolescents, defined broadly as early teens to twenties. *Adolescence*, a weighty psychological study published in 1904 by G Stanley Hall, sparked interest and debate whether or not people had actually read it. (A single-volume abridged edition published in 1906 may have helped.)

Allingham had sold a couple of stories to *Puck* in 1905 and the editor had requested more – to include 'plenty of incident'. Nothing Allingham liked better normally but at that period *Puck* didn't pay its contributors fast enough, hence the attraction of *True Blue* whose editor could be badgered into handing over monies owed. Allingham had also sold a long-complete, 'Two

Chums at Oldbridge', to Hamilton Edwards, the editor-in-chief of a string of AP boys' and women's papers. After the collapse of *True Blue* he had offered Edwards his new school serial, *Max the Magnificent,* which had been intended to follow the *Duffer.* This was rejected as 'not strong enough', yet when he offered Edwards a stronger serial, *The Boy Who Won Out,* it caused outrage.

I regret that I am unable to make use of the enclosed story which is not at all on our lines. The drunkenness part is unpardonable in my papers, and I could not possibly allow it to go in. The sort of thing I require is a simple, well-written school yarn with plenty of fun and perhaps a little pathos. Gambling may be introduced occasionally, but it must be very nicely done and the habit condemned [...] I would recommend you to read some of our school serials and get a good idea of their style before making another attempt. The work of Mr Henry St John, Mr John Finnemore, Mr Charles Hamilton and others will form excellent models.

'Dear Sir' (replied Allingham),

I am much obliged to you for your helpful letter of the 23rd.

I was aware that my story '*The Boy Who Won Out*' was entirely different from the school yarns you publish and I only sent it on the chance you might be disposed to make a new departure.

By the way with regard to your objection to the drunkenness episode I am tempted to remind you that the most popular school story ever written contains a chapter dealing with the same subject. I refer to the late Archdeacon Farrar's '*Eric*'. This story is very goody-goody but it has run through thirty-six editions and in chapter eight the hero gets drunk with far less excuse than my hero has for his slip.

My story was an attempt to describe real school life. However I can do the conventional stuff quite well. My *A Regular Duffer*, *The Captain's Fag* and *Max the Magnificent* are all in this line.

There is no record that he ever approached Edwards again.

Puck went into colour in 1906 and raised the presentational stakes across the entire juvenile market. A move to new premises had encouraged re-organisation within the AP and internal competition between increasingly powerful editors was making their business practice ever more aggressive. The company had invested heavily in the latest typesetting and printing machinery and was able to effect massive economies by standardising the layout of whole groups of papers. They were pushing other publishers out of business wholesale. Allingham's near contemporary 'Frank Richards' (real name Charles Hamilton) wrote wistfully of the 'spacious Victorian days' when 'there was room for everybody' before 'the Amalgamated Press overspread the whole horizon like the Genius from the Bottle in the Arabian tale'.

A 1905 letter in Allingham's archive offers a glimpse of the way boys' publishing had changed. In the 1870s and 1880s, Ralph Rollington and colleagues such as Charles Fox, hurrying along with a bundle of 'Phiz' illustrations under his arm, were able to do business in the street or in pubs as well as in their small, ramshackle rooms. Now that publishing was corporate and so many papers and editors had been brought together into the vast edifice of the Amalgamated Press, even finding one's way to the correct office might present a difficulty to the anxious freelance. Frank Atkins, a fellow common writer, is advising Allingham to try his luck with a junior AP editor called Percy Griffith. 'I should go straight in to him with my card and have a chat. His room is on the second floor, same as Mr Back. Go past Back's office, right to the end, turn to the left and go to the end again and you will see the door of his room facing you. He's a very decent little fellow.' Griffith, however, was a particular protegé of Hamilton Edwards and was never keen on Allingham's work.

This was possibly fortunate. Frank Richards (writing autobiographically in the third person) describes what happened when he found himself in Griffith's office – apparently by mistake.

> One day he was asked to call at Carmelite House to see Mr Garrish. How and why he was shown instead into the office of Mr Percy Griffith, he did not know. No doubt someone had pulled the strings. Anyhow, there he found himself, and there he had the happiness – or otherwise – of making the acquaintance of the future editor of *Gem* and *Magnet*. […]
>
> As Frank had called at Carmelite House in the belief that he was to discuss St Jim's with Mr Garrish, he was a little bewildered to find himself discussing a new paper called the *Gem* with a man he had never seen before. It was not much use for him to say anything. Griffith's conversation was largely a one-way traffic. He had little use for interruptions. A nod of assent was all he really needed – if that. A shake of dissent passed unnoticed. He was so accustomed to having his own way that I verily believe it never occurred to him that another man might have another way and want to follow it.

It was Richards's bad luck that the editor from whom he was being poached, HJ Garrish, was an unusually affable and encouraging employer 'who was pleased to express satisfaction in the most agreeable way with never a word to which the most touchy author could have taken exception'. Initially Richards was allowed to write for both editors under different pseudonyms. Then he was told, by Griffith, that the St Jim's series that he was writing for Garrish's *Pluck* was to be amalgamated with the Tom Merry series in Griffith's *Gem*. Griffith soon had Richards organised into writing the whole of the *Gem* and soon the whole of a new paper, the *Magnet*, as well. He was then able to inform other importunate authors, such as Herbert Allingham, that 'for the time being' he was 'unable to consider' any more boys' stories.

AP editorships were being reallocated and departmental boundaries clarified during 1907. Hamilton Edwards's team of Percy Griffith, H Havant and Herbert Hinton took the boys' adventure papers, women's papers and school stories while Harold Garrish, Fred Cordwell and GH Cantle were left with the comics. Letters from Edwards to Lord Northcliffe, preserved in the British Library, allow a glimpse into the seething world of inter-departmental jealousy as Edwards angled to maintain his own standing in his 'Chief's' affections by disparaging his colleagues. Contributors like Allingham and Richards were some distance away from the incomprehensibly bitter rows over seniority, reporting responsibilities and internal advertising, but – as the crucial test of a department's performance was its sales figures, and these were routinely compared with figures achieved in other departments – the pressure to succeed would soon be felt by workers in all areas of a paper's production.

Garrish, who was now responsible for *Puck, Chips, Comic Cuts* and the *Jester*, had noticed Allingham's gift for humour. He welcomed him, flatteringly explained what he wanted and expressed confidence that Allingham would be able to supply. *Comrades True*, Allingham's first contribution to the reorganised group of papers, was published in the *Jester* in the autumn of 1907. Will Holt, ex-Duffer, no longer schoolboy or detective but jungle explorer, is its lead character with Andy Flynn, formerly of Allingham's 'Crag Castle School'. They have been working as clerks but their firm has closed down and they are frankly delighted. 'The world is wide and we are young and strong.' (Among the odd assortment of characters that they meet on their travels is 'Captain McFee of the *Cooing Dove*' who promptly betrays them to their enemies.)

Garrish worked closely with Allingham to ensure the story's suitability:

> Instal of '*Comrades True*' (this is the name I have given your story) that you left with me today will do. Try and work in a little more fun in the dialogue in future. Whenever you see a chance branch out into comic business without of course overdoing it. The coolness of Will is well accentuated. But please don't mention pubs or alcoholic liquors except wine occasionally. Our heroes always keep so fit they never drink. Also don't use foreign terms of address etc such as 'senor'. Keep everything plain English 'Mr.' or 'Sir' etc. [...] You will notice that I am following your yarn very carefully as I think we shall score a success with it.

Allingham sparkled for Garrish – just as Frank Richards felt that he had done. Over the years ahead all the stories (including *Max the Magnificent* and *The Boy Who Won Out*) that had been rejected by Hamilton Edwards and his acolytes would find a place in one or other of Garrish's comics. In January 1909 Allingham made a note in his diary, 'Saw Garrish. His papers doing well. HE's not.' Did he feel just a tiny bit triumphant? Later in that year he would confirm

Garrish's faith in him by producing a story that doubled the circulation of one of his halfpenny papers. Finally Allingham had scored a success. He had found regular work for the next ten years and his own inconspicuous place in Alfred Harmsworth's Schemo Magnifico.

'A yell, long and sustained, broke from the onlookers'

Chapter Twelve
1908: The Butterfly

When Sport Monkimore, the Man with a Million Thousands, secured my services, he made me understand very clearly the nature of my duties.

'Mr Gaters,' he said, with a yawn, at our first interview, 'do you happen to have any brains?'

I smiled and explained that brains were my speciality.

'I'm glad of that, because you'll need 'em if you want to keep your job,' he went on. 'I'm bored; I'm always bored. You've got to amuse me. Think of something.'

Allingham's 'Sport Monkimore' wasn't a satire on his new employers; it was a skittish summer holiday series in one of HJ Garrish's new family of papers. The *Jester* had initially been under the control of Hamilton Edwards's editorial group and had run regular adventures of 'Monk Mortimer – the man with a thousand millions.' Monk was a gung-ho, xenophobic hard man apt to refer to the lower classes, especially if foreign, as 'alien scum', 'whipped curs' and 'human animals'. Later, in 1906, when editorial control of the *Jester* was transferred to Cantle and Garrish, Mortimer was represented more as a Robin Hood figure, righting the wrongs of the (British) poor. Tales of his heroic adventures ran week after week and he was a sufficiently well-established personality to be used in editorial advertisements: 'Rockefeller, Vanderbilt, Monk Mortimer won't need an extra 5s but do you?'

Allingham's parody character was an unashamed drone, lolling around on oriental divans and terrified by a mock-up of the sort of thieves' kitchen that would have had Monk flinging racist insults and spoiling for a fight. The central character and narrator of this six-week series was Sport Monkimore's employee, 'his Trusted Body Servant, Gaston Gaters'. Gaters belongs to the broad comic tradition of servants who are cleverer and more worldly-wise than their employers but know they are required to disguise this: '"I'm not going to do any thinking," says Monkimore, "That's what you're paid for".'

Gaters ensured that his employer was provided with new numbers of the *Jester*, 'price 1d', but even that could not beguile Monkimore indefinitely. 'The Man with a Million Thousands' had much to learn. After Gaters had persuaded him to dress as a highwayman and hold up the Chelmsford coach, then to shoot a tiger skin rug under the impression it had escaped from Bengal, and finally (terrifyingly) to stand for election as a pro-suffrage candidate, Sport could take no more. He pleaded with Gaters to accept ten thousand pounds and leave. 'Don't think I am dissatisfied with you, dear friend. Your ideas are great, colossal, but I need repose Gaston, I need repose.'

Garrish hadn't actually asked Allingham for this short story series; he'd sent him the usual slightly peremptory editorial instruction:

I want you to close up 'Comrades True' in the next instalment as we have a new serial to produce that we cannot delay and we wish to try your three chums in *Puck* in a series of complete stories of three thousand words per week. The *Puck* stories should be refined and the reverse of slangy. Also no mention of strong drink or pubs; more like the old *Boy's Own Paper* type of adventure yarns.

One can imagine how Hamilton Edwards might have reacted if Allingham had chosen to disregard such specific instructions and send instead a burlesque of an existing series. Garrish, however, was delighted. 'Your yarn of Potts is quite excellent. I suppose it is a take off on our "Monk Mortimer, The Man with the Thousand Millions". We had better call the series "Bank Baltimore, The Man with the Million Thousands" so as to bring it home to the readers.' This preparedness to listen to the writer was the quality that made him one of the best editors with whom Allingham had to deal. The unfortunate Frank Richards, in contrast, had to learn to survive 'chin solos' from his new editor, Percy Griffith.

He [Frank Richards] then adopted a conversational method which produced satisfactory results. One of his hobbies was learning verses by heart – another memorising master games of chess. [...] Now on many occasions when Percy talked, Frank, not being required to do so, would sit with an expression of earnest attention on his face, playing Andersen-Kieseritski in his head or inaudibly running over his favourite verses. This device enabled him to keep up quite long conversations without undue fatigue.

Garrish and Allingham were building a rapport if not quite a friendship. 'I am very glad you were able to grasp my idea so well. "The three friends together" is exactly the thing I have been trying to impress on authors for some time past but which you alone have been able to grasp.' The two men were about the same age and seem likely to have shared some important attitudes. Garrish, like Allingham, was an editor who contributed to his own papers. The *Jester* in 1906, for instance, published his long-complete stories 'The Fighting Parson', 'Captain Alice' and 'Thirty Bob a Week'. The first two suggest a benign and hearty evangelicalism not unlike Allingham's 'Garden of Glory' style; the third reveals Garrish's sympathetic awareness of the likely economic condition of his older readers. The hero of 'Thirty Bob a Week' expresses the frustrations of a clerk who has advanced as far as he can from the standard starting wage of 18s. He has reached his mid-twenties and has to face the fact that there is no further opportunity available to him. He meets a 'business girl' but knows he mustn't think of marriage.

> And I am a clerk and I earn thirty bob a week and what's more I haven't the chance of rising higher than that. There's thousands of chaps like me. We go away and dream for a fortnight at Herne Bay or Margate of what we would like to do or like to be: of some girl we would like perhaps to be able, to dare, to look forward to – to asking to be our own one day. But for most of us that can be nothing more than a dream [...]
>
> We are educated up to knowing that we must not look for anything beyond a living wage for oneself [...] I am a thirty bob a week man, subject to a week's notice and when that comes it's Rowton House before me or the workhouse.

Harold Garrish had joined the Harmsworths in 1891 when they ran the Pandora Publishing Company ('dedicated to clean wholesome fun and good drawing'). As well as writing for them (anonymously and under various pseudonyms) he became a sub-editor, editor and eventually a director of the company with responsibility for all its comic papers. He stayed with the AP until his death in 1956 – possibly their longest-serving employee, in an age of long service. In the official history, published in 1925, Garrish is described as 'having a flair for what the public – particularly the younger public – wanted.' 1908–1909 was perhaps a sticky patch in Harold Garrish's successful career.

'He opened his heart to me,' wrote Allingham after an hour-long conversation. 'Is dissatisfied with his own job and firm. Says it is getting too departmental. His Lordship too is fussy and has a prejudice about the comics.' Internal strains within the vast Amalgamated Press were exacerbated by the continual comparisons of sales figures between the editorial groups. Pressure on individual editors could become intense if their papers were seen to flag or lose circulation. Just a couple of weeks after Garrish 'opened his heart' he was instructing Allingham to bring his current serial to a close. 'Wants me to stop *Girl.* He is going to try some light stuff as *Puck* is not going [...] Wants me to submit another light serial.'

In later years Allingham's family would frequently equate his skill in serial writing with his skill in chess. This very early serial, *Girl of My Heart* (1908–1909), has an awkwardness of construction that suggests he was not yet comfortable with twisting and turning according to other people's instructions and departmental sales figures. As he writes in an early episode, 'Imagine a man in the middle of a game of chess with all his intellectual faculties exerted to defeat his opponent. Then imagine, just as the player is about to make a critical move, the appearance of a stranger who heedlessly kicks over the board and scatters the pieces to the ground.' Allingham never became socially close to any of his editors (other than Maud Hughes). There was always a wariness in his dealings with even the most appreciative and congenial of them. He knew they had the power to kick his chessboard to the floor.

In addition to *Puck* and the *Jester*, Garrish's editorial group now managed *Comic Cuts, Chips* and the *Butterfly*. Readers were encouraged to buy one of his 'merry little circle of journals' almost every day: 'Tuesday: ('Nuff said. You've bought *Comic Cuts* already.) Wednesday: Buy the *Butterfly* ½d. The dainty little journal printed on green paper. Thursday: Get *Chips* ½d. Your old favourite. Friday: Purchase *Puck* 1d. The one and only coloured comic paper.'

These 'comics' – or more accurately, comic-and-story papers – were produced to a standardised format except that *Puck* had a few coloured pages as its distinctive feature. Pages of drawing and text were interspersed – encouraging to the less confident readers and to younger as well as older customers. The *Jester* was twice as long as the others, cost 1d, and was described as 'the weekend edition of *Comic Cuts*'. *Chips* was sometimes printed on pink paper, *Comic Cuts* on blue, the *Butterfly* on green.

Between 1907 and 1908 Allingham wrote something for all of them: a detective story in the series 'Martin Steel and his Twelve Lady Detectives' for *Comic Cuts*; an adventure serial featuring three chums and a motorised robot for *Chips*; *Comrades True* and 'Sport Monkimore' for the *Jester;* some short stories and the serial *Girl of My Heart* for *Puck*. Considering that he was still editing and writing serials for the *New London Journal* and the *New Boys' Paper* and continuing to write short stories for other companies (notably W. Newman Flower at Cassell's *Penny Magazine*), his two days a week working from home must have been very fully occupied. Especially with two young children in the house and Em at work on her own occasional tales.

In 1908 Allingham wrote his first serial story for the *Butterfly*, the youngest paper in Garrish's 'family' and the most feminine in personality. Its keynote character was 'Flossie, the up-to-date School Girl'.

> Flossie will enchant you quite
> You will love her at first sight
> A mischief-loving Miss is she
> Buy the *Butterfly* and see...

Flossie had a regular space on the back cover in which she regaled her friend Gertie with the different ways in which she met boys. All the males she met wanted to cuddle her and Flossie was never averse to a squeeze or a kiss despite her disingenuous protests. The *Butterfly* was intended for readers of both sexes and Garrish reminded Allingham that they were not necessarily all youngsters. Many adults enjoyed the comic papers although the target audience, particularly for *Puck* and the *Butterfly,* was the newly identified 'adolescent'. The adventures of flirty, frivolous girls like Flossie were stock features across this family of papers. *The Jester* (aiming at a slightly older, in-work, readership) had 'Pretty Peggy, the Girl Behind the Counter' and 'Kitty, the Chorus Girl'.

The *Lights of London Town,* Allingham's first serial story for the *Butterfly*, ran weekly for several months from 1908. Its success soon threatened to outstrip Allingham's power to supply. Garrish's brief notes are constantly nagging for copy 'We want some more "Lights of London Town" as we are none too well provided.' 'We are right out of "Lights". As the story seems popular I am letting it rip. More Monday please.'

The *Lights of London Town* is a slight, rather charming Dick Whittington story of an orphaned country lad, 'Billy', who makes his eventful way to the city. On arrival in Shoreditch the first person Billy meets is a stage-struck Jewish boy named 'Ikey'. Ikey is certain that he is going to become a great actor and earn a hundred pounds a week. Meanwhile he needs someone to support him while he studies his art. Billy finds a job addressing wrappers for Dredge and Cartwright's Patent Infant Food and the two lads set up home together in Kennington. Several adventures later they have achieved modest success. Billy has a job as an 'outside man' in an advertising agency – £1 a week plus commission on sales – and Ikey has made an unexpected hit with his impersonations of Shylock and Fagin. 'He had not meant the impersonations to be comic but that's how they struck the audience and he was now working them on those lines.' The serial ends with the two boys gazing out across the Thames and talking about the great things they would do in the future. 'And whatever we do, we must stick together,' said Ikey.

If the adolescent readers of the *Butterfly* liked Billy, they liked Allingham's next serial even better. *Plucky Polly Perkins* was one of Allingham's most popular creations and was reprinted at least five times during his life. Her story began in the Christmas double number of 1908 and was subtitled 'a story of Pathos, Fun and Adventure, with a bit of Love-making Thrown In'. 'You will be glad to hear,' wrote the *Butterfly* editor in January 1909, 'that our new chum, Plucky Polly Perkins, has speedily won her way into the hearts of our readers and is quite one of the most popular favourites we have ever had.'

Polly and her brother and sister are the privately educated

children of artistic, middle-class parents. When the story opens the children have been orphaned and are facing destitution. Polly plans to take action. 'What is the use of having an expensive education at Miss Montgomerie's high class establishment for young ladies if I can't clean windows?' she asks her genteel sister.

Polly decides to invest their modest legacies in setting up a sweet shop. When the headmaster of her brother's school, St Bede's, arrives to expostulate – and even to threaten – Polly is unperturbed:

'Can I get you anything, sir?' she said demurely.

'No, my dear young lady, I think not,' he replied pleasantly; 'but there is just a word or two I should like to say, if you will allow me. I am Dr Beverley, Headmaster of St Bede's College.'

'Yes, sir,' answered Polly.

'Your brother is a pupil at the college.'

'Yes.'

'And a very promising pupil. I should be sorry, Miss Perkins, deeply sorry, if he had to leave.'

'So should I,' rejoined Polly calmly; 'but I don't think it will be necessary. Of course the fees are high, but I am doing very well here, and hope to do better when I get my new stock in. You will get your money all right.'

Dr Beverley coughed.

'I was not thinking of that,' he said, a little awkwardly. 'The fact is, my dear young lady,' he went on, 'you have, by opening this shop, upset quite a number of people, and among them the parents of several of my pupils.'

Polly opened her eyes in innocent surprise.

'I am very sorry, but I dare say they will get over it,' she observed presently.

The St Bede's parents are not only upset because of the taint of trade but because they fear, justifiably, that their sons will fall in love with Polly. In illustrations Polly is as curvaceous as Flossie, though she is certainly no flirt. The St Bede's headmaster has come to speak on behalf of one of his more hopelessly smitten pupils. He urges Polly to show 'a little coolness, a little maidenly reserve' but she has her own, more effective, methods:

> 'When he comes to your study tomorrow you can tell him that I am not really cross with him and that if he is a good boy and minds his lessons I will perhaps think about marrying him when he grows up.'
>
> 'My dear young lady!' protested the schoolmaster, at a loss for words.
>
> 'Oh, it's always best to be gentle with them!' explained Polly wisely. 'I've had such a lot of little boys fall in love with me, and I always tell them that. It comforts them and makes them work.'

Polly ends by persuading the headmaster to give her an order for £20 worth of cigars. Her confrontations with figures of authority through the ensuing series are invariably successful. She routs a Major General, slaps a policeman who harasses her for a kiss and, when the workpeople go out on strike, she proves equally able to stand up to a bullying mill-owner or an incensed lynch mob.

Polly is decidedly left of centre. 'Although her father had been an artist she had lived in a working-class neighbourhood all her life and all her sympathies were with the wage-earners.' The years towards the end of the first decade of the twentieth century were a time of social soul-searching and industrial unrest. Tom Mullins, Allingham's fictional mill-owner, is not an out-and-out villain but still a dangerous antagonist. Polly offers this advice to the strikers in her hometown:

> 'If you want to beat Tom Mullins, you'll have to fight shy of the public house and keep your brass in your pockets. It's brass that's going to win this fight, and nothing else. Collect all you can and hold on to it for when the pinch comes. You may lay your life that is what old Tom's doing. He isn't ramping round, and playing the giddy goat generally. He is getting ready for battle and that's what you ought to be doing. Now go home and give your wives all the money you've got left to take care of for you. Then cut down your baccy, and go in and win, and good luck to you.'

More than thirty years after the publication of *Plucky Polly Perkins* in the *Butterfly*, George Orwell analysed what were by then twopenny (rather than penny or halfpenny) boys' weeklies.

> You never walk far through the poor quarter of any big town without coming upon a small newsagent's shop. The general appearance of these shops is always very much the same: a few posters for the *Daily Mail* and the *News of the World* outside, a poky little window with sweet-bottles and packets of Players, and a dark interior smelling of liquorice all-sorts and festooned from floor to ceiling with vilely printed twopenny papers, most of them with lurid cover illustrations in three colours.

'Probably,' Orwell suggested, 'the contents of these shops is the best indication of what the mass of the English people really feel and think.' Do individuals straightforwardly accept what they are offered or are they more intellectually picky; taking what they want, altering what doesn't quite suit, and forgetting or rejecting the rest? Orwell tended to take the gloomy view.

> To what extent people draw their ideas from fiction is debatable. Personally I believe that most people are influenced far more then they would care to admit by novels, serial stories, films and so forth and, from this point of view, the worst books are often the most important as they are usually the ones that are read earliest in life.

He cited the school stories in the *Gem* and the *Magnet* as evidence for the prosecution, but, because he couldn't believe any single author could have been writing such stories weekly over thirty years, he didn't notice how closely they expressed Frank Richards's idiosyncratic personality. Instead he saw political vetting: youngsters in search of a fantasy life were being delivered over 'to people like Lord Camrose' (the then owner of the AP) and indoctrinated with 'the illusions which their future employers think suitable for them'. In these two papers Orwell found snobbery, xenophobia and a refusal to recognise the facts of working-class life – or, indeed, the facts of life.

> Sex is completely taboo [...] Occasionally girls enter the stories, and very rarely there is something approaching a mild flirtation, but it is always entirely in the spirit of clean fun. A boy and a girl enjoy going for bicycle rides together – that is all it ever amounts to. Kissing, for instance, would be regarded as 'soppy'. Even the bad boys are presumed to be completely sexless.

This wasn't the case in Garrish's papers in the earlier years of the twentieth century. Kissing is almost the *raison d'être* for *Butterfly* characters such as Flossie, and when Polly meets

Will Holt, she is as seriously attracted to him as Joe Mullins, the mill-owner's son, is to her. Teenage sexual longing simmers throughout this story and is not always treated as comic. Consummation is postponed – as it would need to be for many readers. Polly cannot choose between her suitors and never will. 'We are all very young and the world is before us... let's agree to meet here in a year's time today and have supper again together.'

In fact she goes into partnership with Maximilian Trent – 'Max the Magnificent' – the comic young dandy from Allingham's *New Boys' Paper* serial. Together they set out in weekly short stories ('Perkins and Co') to right cases of social injustice – sweated labour, slum housing, police stitch-ups, adulterated food, poverty in old age. These stories, and others like them, go some way towards contradicting Orwell's assertion that 'in England, popular imaginative literature is a field that left-wing thought has never begun to enter'. Allingham was writing leading articles for the *Christian Globe* on sweated labour, slum housing, poverty in old age etc at the same time as he offered his light-touch treatments of the same subjects in 'Perkins and Co'. Even in stories that have no overt social message (such as *Miss Maggie MacFee*, the series of girl detective tales he was writing for *Puck*) stray sentences suggest a quality of sympathetic observation that Orwell might have approved, had he been a reader then. 'She had the tired look that is seen on the faces of many girls who work in London and who do not feed well.'

Unlike Frank Richards's evergreen *Gem* and *Magnet*, both *Puck* and the *Butterfly* had changed radically by 1939 when Orwell wrote his essay. Allingham was dead and both papers had been re-designed for young children. The AP had been sold, re-organised, cut back in some areas, developed in others. Nevertheless, both Harold Garrish and Fred Cordwell, the editors for whom Allingham had written on the *Butterfly*, were still active and running comics for adolescent readers of the new generation. Their underlying attitudes and their choice of fiction remained markedly different from the editors of the *Gem* and the *Magnet*. *Plucky Polly Perkins*, for instance, was reprinted (for the fifth time) in Cordwell's *Kinema Comic* in 1931. If Orwell had leafed through the teenage comics instead of the boys' weeklies in those poky little newsagents' shops, he wouldn't have found the left-wing press of his dreams but he might have cheered up a little.

The internal editorial rivalry within the Amalgamated Press was probably a good thing for readers. It preserved some remnants of choice as increasing numbers of independent publishers were forced into liquidation by the Schemo Magnifico. It may also have been fortunate for the comics that Lord Northcliffe, 'the Chief', was becoming less interested in their activities as his personal publishing horizons expanded: 1908 was the year that the Harmsworths decisively outmanoeuvred Arthur Pearson for control of the *Times*. Harold Harmsworth (later Lord Rothermere) was now officially in charge of the Amalgamated Press but he too had more on his mind than the possibility of Fabianism in the *Butterfly*.

All that mattered was readers' financial endorsement of the conflicting products. As Garrish reminded Allingham early in their relationship, 'The proof of popularity lies not with me but with the readers.' The Harmsworth brothers, their directors, editors, sub-editors were obsessed with comparative circulation figures and it's disappointing that so few have survived. Among the Northcliffe papers in the British Library, however, are scrappy internal figures for 1909-1910, when Allingham was writing both *Plucky Polly Perkins* and his first drama-story,

Driven from Home, in the *Butterfly*. These reveal that the *Butterfly*'s sales rose dramatically over the year and overtook those of the *Gem*, which declined. From the first episode of *The Lights of London Town* in June 1907 until the abrupt ending of *The Way of the World* in the First World War paper crisis in March 1917, the *Butterfly* would never be without a weekly story from Allingham.

'Polly made many conquests'

Chapter Twelve
1909: Driven from Home

It was a pitch-black night in November, and the rain fell in torrents on the desolate country road, and lashed the high hedges on either side into a kind of living fury.

Along the narrow lane a shadowy figure staggered blindly.

It was the figure of a woman, slight and frail, and in her arms she carried a shapeless bundle sheltered under her cloak, and hugged it tightly to her bosom.

She made little headway against the merciless storm and her every movement betrayed the fact that she was growing weaker and weaker. At times she would stop and sway giddily, as though about to fall in a heap on the muddy, rain-swept road, but each time she recovered herself as by a desperate effort of will, and pressed blindly on once more.

Suddenly the lane widened out, and the wretched wayfarer, peering into the darkness, could see no hedge at her right hand, but only a vague blackness; and then, in the midst of it, she perceived a light.

This is the first scene of Allingham's *Driven from Home*: 'A Story of a Young Girl's Struggles against the Trials and Temptations of the World.' It opened in the *Butterfly* on

6 November 1909, when *Plucky Polly Perkins* still had a couple of months to run, and was the most powerful agent of its success. As Allingham explained later:

> This was the first of my drama stories. It sent the Butterfly up over 100,000 and owing to this success Sir Harold Harmsworth (Lord R) permitted Mr. Cordwell to start three other papers – the *Favourite Comic*, *Merry & Bright* and *Fun & Fiction*. Each of these papers started with a drama story by me and all ran a year or more. I wrote continuously for all these papers up until about 1916 or 1917 when the paper shortages somewhat disorganised our little fiction factory.

The success of the *Butterfly* brought success to its editorial staff. Until this moment FC (Fred) Cordwell, almost twenty years younger than Garrish and Allingham, had been the *Butterfly*'s sub-editor. From 1909 he took direct responsibility as Garrish turned his attention elsewhere. As editor Cordwell's job was to put himself in the place of a reader.

> I think that *Plucky Polly Perkins* is going along splendidly, but if you could manage to bring her away from the seaside I should be much obliged. It is rather late in the season to be at a summer resort.
>
> Thanks for *Driven from Home*. I have just finished the last instalment and think it a very good curtain. Jack must, of course, escape somehow and take Reuben Price with him. We do not want him to fall into the hands of Reuben Price again if it can be avoided.

He evidently expected that readers would relate these stories to real time ('It is rather late in the season to be at a seaside resort') and also that events within them would be taken seriously ('we do not want him to fall into the hands of Rueben Price again if it can be avoided'). Like Harold Garrish, Fred Cordwell achieved lasting success by understanding and respecting his readers. He had started his career as an office boy on the *Daily Mail* then transferred to the AP where he worked for the rest of his life. He is recognised in the company's official history as 'one of the men who have helped to build up the colossal circulations of publications emanating from the Fleetway House'.

For him, as for Allingham, the success of the *Butterfly* was pivotal. On 7 January 1911, *Driven from Home* reached its romantic end: 'Only one thing belonging to those dark days will we remember and that is our love, my darling – the love that never failed us and never can while life lasts, my dear, dear wife!' Cordwell was quick to reassure customers that there would be plenty more reading pleasure coming their way. 'The *Butterfly* has been so tremendously successful and I have been asked by so many readers to enlarge it and make it a penny, so I am starting a new paper, similar to the *Butterfly*, entitled the *Favorite Comic.*'

In fact Cordwell's first new paper, *Merry & Bright*, printed on the same pale green paper as the *Butterfly*, had already reached the shops. Its lead title was Allingham's new serial *Girl Without a Home.* Another new paper, *Fun & Fiction*, followed early in 1911 leading with Allingham's *His Convict Bride.* The *Favorite Comic*, with Allingham's *The Girl Outcast* as its main attraction, appeared later in that year. All priced at ½d. By 1912 these *Butterfly*-derived papers had split away from *Chips*, *Comic Cuts*, *Puck* and the *Jester* to form an editorial subset of their own with Cordwell in charge. Readers could now follow an alternative weekly timetable: Tuesday, the *Favorite Comic* (½d), Wednesday the *Butterfly* (½d), Thursday

Fun & Fiction (1d), Friday *Merry & Bright* (½d), Saturday the *Dreadnought* (1d). The two penny papers sold less well and were quietly revised. *Fun & Fiction* became the *Firefly* and halved its price: the *Dreadnought* was transferred to Hamilton Edwards's group in the early months of the First World War – though not before it had carried the third reprint of *Max the Magnificent*. Garrish, meanwhile, began reprinting Allingham's earlier school serials one after another in *Puck*. From 1910 continuously to the outbreak of war, a boy or girl who bought (or swapped or shared) all these papers and the *Jester* could have been reading a story by Allingham on four days of every week.

They wouldn't have known this. Allingham was neither named nor given a pseudonym; he was 'the Author of *Driven From Home*', '... of *The Convict Bride*', '... of *The Girl Outcast*' – whichever of his serials the editor judged would exert the strongest pull on readers. George Gissing's Thyrza was startled when she learned authors might be buried in Westminster Abbey. 'In her thoughts of books it had never occurred to her that any special interest could be attached to the people who wrote them; indeed she had perhaps never asked herself how printed matter came into existence.' The comics might set a humorous strip in the editor's office or run a short series about the adventures of 'Adolphus the office boy' but flesh and blood contributors were kept well out of sight. Alan Clark, editor of the *Dictionary of British Comic Artists, Writers and Editors*, believes that this fostered a feeling of inferiority amongst the workers

> ...who created, wrote, drew and edited comics that have become part of the social fabric of the nation [...] a situation not helped by the fact that the majority of the writers and artists were freelancers working at home without even some professional camaraderie to

raise their self esteem. Decades later when some artists were traced and interviewed it emerged that their professional lives were almost unknown to their friends and neighbours who knew little or nothing about what they did for a living.

Perhaps Margery's assertion that her father had had 'a most exasperating life' could be connected with this denial of recognition? In 1909, however, Allingham did not lack professional camaraderie or companionship. In fact he had far too much of both. He was still editing the *New London Journal*, still involved with *Spare Moments* and the unsatisfactory office politics around CW Bradley's businesses, and more than ever required to assist with his father's *Christian Globe*. On 6 January James Allingham summoned him to a meeting:

> Saw Dad, John, Phil, Ernest. Arranged to write Malvery about Soul Market. Dad depressed, John wool-gathering. Phil wants me to be 'advisory editor', Ernest anxious to get to work. The necessity of explaining everything to Penfold seems to be the obstacle in the way of progress. I have undertaken to find serials which means if it is a success I get no thanks, if is a failure I get blamed and in any case I get no money.

After the meeting he spent an hour with Garrish – 'He likes *Polly* immensely. He wants two instalments by Monday.' (This was Wednesday). Then he met George Hearn, a fellow author who filled him in on the latest troubling gossip from Aldine. Arriving at Bradley's he tried to arrange a 'boom' (advertising campaign) for *Spare Moments* only be told there was no money. He tried to get a private word with his brother Phil but was unsuccessful. 'Afraid he is going to the dogs. Looks as though Em and I would have to support the whole family in ten years' time or so unless we too break down. Then the whole lot goes under.' His sister-in-law Maud was staying with them in Ealing, involved in some unsatisfactory affair with his favourite brother. There was 'much talk about Phil' when Allingham finally got home that evening. The next day, unsurprisingly, he had a 'bad head' but wrote 1,000 words of *Polly*, business letters for the *Christian Globe*, then sat up until two in the morning waiting for Maud and Phil to come in. The day after that, the sisters had a row 'More talk about Phil: House rocking with feminine emotions. Work difficult.'

Allingham keeps up the diary for the first four months of 1909 and also keeps up his fiction (*Girl of My Heart, Polly, Maggie MacFee*, 25,000-35,000 words per month); his editorship; his work for the *Christian Globe* (leaders, fronts, notices); his advertising copy (Harlene hair products and something called a 'boilerette'); his and Em's social life (McFee is in town) and his involvement in journalistic shenanigans, family money worries and the emotional troubles of his siblings. 'Had tea with Em, discussed Phil; had tea with Phil, discussed Maud.' His two children are not mentioned. In April Em tells him that they should move out of London to Essex. And later in the year they do. Allingham's diary is never again quite so involved and frantic. Instead it becomes a word count, a record of the dogged hours necessary to keep up three or four consecutive lead serials per week at three to four thousand words per instalment.

Instalment fiction was a viable way to earn a living. There was less busy-ness involved than with short stories or contributions to series; fewer speculative letters and last-minute sendings to the typist; less waiting on editors' replies to see whether their whims or their papers had changed. Best of all, no more ill-defined time-lapses between acceptance and publication, when payment would finally be authorised. Allingham wrote his allotted words, sent them to his editor and accepted any corrections. Then the instalment was published and he was paid. Regular writing meant regular earning – as long as the circulation figures continued satisfactory.

There was little flexibility, however. Allingham was never as fast as his daughter Margery who once, in her hack days, claimed to have dictated twenty thousand words in a sitting to earn herself time to have a week's holiday. Or Frank Richards who wrote an eighteen-thousand word story in a day, 'a tour-de-force he has never repeated or wanted to repeat.' Three or four serials a week had Allingham at full stretch; he could rarely get far enough ahead to take time off. He wrote on family holidays, wrote over Easter, wrote over Christmas even. His editors liked to have at least two or three instalments in hand: when he ran them low on copy, the messages became even more peremptory than usual. '*Justice* is late and *The Steel Clutch* is even worse.' 'We are out of copy and the compositor is waiting.'

This was just-in-time production and there was no room for sickness, holidays or nights on the town. Frank Richards (also writing as 'Martin Clifford') had a passion for opera

> ...and this was not always very good for the typewriter. Often he got home very late [...] late nights generally mean late mornings. Martin and Frank often had to push in order not to be left behind by the machines. As a rule they were lucky. But a cold in the head did it!
>
> Percy's strange and astonishing remedy was a 'substitute author' [...] a story not written by Martin Clifford was put into the *Gem* [...] the 'substitute' story was written round Tom Merry just as if Martin had written it. Unkindest cut of all, it was published under Martin Clifford's name.

A 'substitute author' was the ultimate editorial weapon. Allingham once tried arguing with an unsympathetic editor about rates of pay. He threatened to bring a story to an end unless a promised rise was honoured. The editor merely replied that this would be a nuisance as he'd have to find someone else to carry the story on. Allingham capitulated at once. He had no published name to consider but he had intense pride as a craftsman. Interference in his big, carefully thought-out melodramas would have been intolerable – and fortunately quite difficult because of the scale of the undertaking. The pre-war serial stories regularly ran for nine to twelve months each. *Driven from Home* lasted sixty weeks, *Human Nature* (1913–1916) almost two and a half years. When a story must end prematurely (*Girl of My Heart*, 1908; *The Way of the World*, 1917) they are wrenched to a halt.

The Allinghams moved to a large and decaying ex-rectory in a tiny Essex village, Layer Breton. 'It was a square handsome house of yellow stucco, a typical country rectory of the early nineteenth century,' as McFee recalled. 'There was a small dower house in the rear, stables for horses, but no electricity or plumbing.' Allingham referred to their new home, lightly and passingly, as his 'little fiction factory'. He wrote, Em wrote, brothers and guests wrote – McFee stayed a whole summer working on *Casuals*. Soon Margery would demand a room and a desk of her own.

Looked at positively the fiction factory was a busy, productive place. Considered more sombrely Allingham and his fellow workers had become component parts of a devouring system. The Harmsworth brothers had built an empire where they owned the very trees and the timber mills that provided the pulp for their low-grade paper, as well as controlling the typesetting and printing, the writers and artists, the packers and the newspaper boys. The world of small masters and independent businesses in which Allingham had grown up had been engulfed. He had become part of a total, first-to-last automated process, a factory system as described in *Das Kapital.*

> Besides the factory operatives, the manufacturing workmen and the handicraftsmen, whom it concentrates in large numbers at one spot, and directly commands, capital also sets in motion, by means of invisible threads, another army; that of the workers in the domestic industries, who dwell in the large towns and who are also scattered over the face of the country.

Layer Breton Rectory had become, in Marx's terms, an 'outside department' of the Amalgamated Press. Though technically a freelance, Allingham was selling only to the AP comics. There was no time or creative energy left to him for speculative or un-commissioned work. The 'invisible threads' of capital controlled his daily life, and the financial security of his family.

How did he feel about this? In his first volume of autobiography, *In the First Watch*, McFee recalls (or invents) a conversation which took place at Layer Breton between himself, Allingham and another pulp writer (probably George Hearn). Two 'space-brokers' were also there. These were probably Allingham's brothers, 'Big Phil' and 'Tod'.

> They were sharp jolly Fleet Street men. My host had once been an editor. Many an hour we had all spent in the ABC smoke-room in Fleet Street when I was in from a voyage, talking of foreign parts. [...] They had been full of admiration years before when I suddenly ran away to sea. 'A man's life, old chap!' they assured me patting my

shoulder, as though a writer or an advertising man was by comparison no more than an odalisque in a sultan's harem. [...] It was a purely romantic reaction. They had no intention of following my example. They were doing extremely well in what they seemed to think were feminine occupations. Their incomes varied from five hundred to a thousand a year. They could afford to be romantically nostalgic on my account. [...]

I watched my host's fine fingers rolling a cigarette. He smoked twenty or thirty a day and rolled them himself. He was the first literary man I had ever known. His advice had been to stick to my profession. Writing, he said, was too precarious, too crowded, too confining, too poorly paid, too debilitating. It was not, I gathered, a man's life. [...]

'You see, you chaps?' he said, as though he were demonstrating an earlier argument more completely, 'He's an engineer, a ship's engineer. He can get a job anywhere. He's amphibious. We're earth-borne grubs. He doesn't have to write what some editor thinks the public would like. He doesn't have to write at all if he doesn't feel like it. The usual rules don't apply.'

Driven from Home and the spate of drama-stories now pouring from Allingham's pen were written for other 'earth-borne grubs'. His heroes and heroines are not free spirits. They are as inextricably trapped by fate as their creator – and their readers – are trapped by the 'usual rules'. A glance back to the opening passage of *Driven from Home* at the head of this chapter may give some insight into the methods by which Allingham dramatised helplessness in order to provide his audience with excitement and thus, paradoxically, a sense of escape. The shadowy figure staggering blindly up the storm-lashed road, her sleeping child clasped to her breast, is Mary, the story's twenty-two-year-old heroine. Her husband, Jack, is in prison, falsely accused of murder, and the man who he trusted to protect her, her uncle, is doing his best to force her into a new marriage with a millionaire. She has run away to escape his 'insults' but is friendless, penniless and her child is hungry. She has lost her home. This, in an Allingham story, is the worst thing.

The light gleaming though the blackness is that of a wayside inn. The landlady is first suspicious, then kindly, She offers a simple meal, temporary shelter, but all too soon Mary's wicked uncle discovers her. Simultaneously her husband has escaped from prison. He arrives at the identical inn. Coincidences come as no surprise in a world ruled by fate:

'Jack, Jack – my darling, darling Jack!'

The strong arms closed around her and held her as in a vice, and eager passionate kisses were pressed upon her up-turned face.

'My wife,' murmured the man in broken tones – 'my dear, dear wife!'

The first instalment ends here but the prison warders are closing in. For just a moment, in instalment two, hero, heroine and child are together, the nucleus of a family. 'Love mummy now; love daddy too,' declares the child. Even as he speaks, heavy footsteps are heard in the gravel outside. The hero is desperate:

'Oh, Mary, my beloved!' he groaned in a tone of bitter anguish. 'It is hard – it is hard to bear! I could endure my own cruel fate without flinching; but to leave you – you and the child – to face the world alone, persecuted by that villain and shunned by all! Can we turn nowhere and find a friend in this hour of need? Will no one help me to make one dash for liberty?'

It was then that Jim Gubbins the poacher, who had been bottling up his feelings with the greatest difficulty exploded into excited speech.

'Yes, by gum, I will!' he shouted heartily. 'You shall have a fox's chance for your life.'

Jim, who is at this point a slightly comic irritant of the local gentry, proves resourceful and stalwart for the rest of the story, as does Louise, the lady's maid whom he later marries. He is one of many admirable, idiosyncratic, lower-class characters who can cope in situations where the more refined hero or heroine is at a loss. The heroine of *Driven from Home* also finds help from Monsieur Antoine. He is an impresario – the prototype of several benevolent, eccentric, fairy godfather figures from the world of theatre who can be found throughout Allingham's writing. This may be connected with an optimistic understanding, shared between writer and readers, that the stage is one of the few areas where talent can earn a lucky break irrespective of social class. (One of Allingham's favourite cousins Grace, a low-paid dancer in travelling revues, had already been set up in unmarried rural comfort by a smitten 'stage-door Johnny'.)

Class issues are central to Allingham's fiction. Richard Hoggart's explanation of the working-class view of Them and Us could almost have been written as a gloss on its social understanding. Certain professions are beyond the pale. Millionaire financiers are rarely to be trusted; lawyers are viewed with suspicion; prison warders and policemen are presented with unremitting dislike. Clergymen and doctors practising in the community are usually good but may be ineffectual; doctors in private institutions and doctors interested in experimentation are always sinister. Other professions are more individually varied. The prison governor in *Driven from Home* is self-serving, unimaginative and venal whereas, in *The Lights of Home,* the governor is narrow but decent, concerned to reform some of the prisoners in his charge and aware that the corruptibility of his warders may be due to their low wages.

Allingham's characters are stereotypical but the significance of the stories lies in the way the stereotypes are manoeuvred and varied. Individual characters do not drive the narrative, as they might in a novel, they are cast in pre-determined roles and then manipulated by Fate – in the person of the author. It is not therefore a criticism to observe that they are two-dimensional. It's as if these drama-stories belong to an alternative art-form (something resembling the *commedia dell'arte*, perhaps) which in turn reflects a different understanding of existence. The games that are played with the stereotypes depend on the readers' understanding of each character's possible scope.

Social standing is crucial as it determines the amount of power each character can exercise within the succession of confrontations between might and right that is the essential action. Allingham's hero and heroine, for instance, have invariably been wrenched from their class or their domestic location and have only their individual moral qualities and the kindness of others, to help them survive in a hostile world. The early heroines are likely to possess such attributes as 'innate refinement' and their happy ending always includes improved, or reinstated, social position as well as plenty of money, leisure and the downfall of their enemies. The heroes are usually from wealthy backgrounds whether they know it or not and an important part of the stories' action is their repossession of their rightful inheritance. Deprivation of inheritance is such an insistent theme that it is hard not to connect it with working-class readers' unspoken awareness of social injustice or, at least, their longing for an unexpected piece of luck, financial security or personal recognition.

Stylistically, the opening of *Driven from Home* typifies

many of the qualities of Allingham's drama-stories. There are sharp contrasts in lighting and the language is extreme (the hedges are 'lashed' into a 'living fury'). The depiction of the heroine struggling through the storm is intensely visual – stagey even. Allingham's melodramas frequently open with a storm. His next major serial *Girl Without A Home* (1910), written for *Merry & Bright,* contrasts the tempest outside with the cosy tranquillity of a cottage room where a young mother-to-be sits sewing for her baby. It is an emblematic scene, a haven. But, as soon as the cottage door opens, trouble rushes in on the heroine with the relentlessness of the hurricane.

In one of Harold Garrish's earliest letters of instruction he had reminded Allingham to 'work in a good striking subject for a picture in every number'. Allingham never really needed this prompt. From the first instalment of *Barrington's Fag* in 1886 his literary style excels in dramatic tableaux. Then it had been the schoolboy falling from the treacherous ivy, now it might be the heroine defiantly vulnerable in the dock, a hero grappling with his assailants, a mother and her child cruelly excluded from light and shelter. Allingham's reader is always a viewer, whether or not there is an actual picture on the page.

The plot happenings are as stylised as the settings and the characters. Composition by instalments demands every week that there should be an attention-grabbing opening and a surprising, suspense-inducing curtain. The characters must be manoeuvred into their positions – but, as they are 'in the Grip of Fate' (to use a title that could serve as an Allingham catch-all), this is artistically acceptable.

Over the sixty weeks of *Driven from Home* Jack and Mary achieve only brief moments together. They both spend time in prison; both escape; both are recaptured; both are proved innocent after much delay. They both believe the other dead. The heroine suffers total amnesia, destitution in London and momentary triumph as a singing star. The hero endures partial entombment in an underground vault, and unwilling involvement with a criminal gang. The child is kidnapped twice and almost dies twice. There are two fires, a car crash, a shipwreck, a forced marriage, a trial. The plot is fuelled by betrayals, daring escapes, impenetrable disguises and calamitous coincidences. The villains may seem to have been killed at various points along the way but are never finally disposed of until the penultimate episode. Again and again when they are at the hero's mercy, the heroine persuades him to hold back – and vice versa. Vengeance is not, ultimately, for good characters to dispense in these stories. They are acting within an ethical framework that includes an ultimate trust in some higher power. The hero may rail, the heroine may despair, but they never lose their faith in one another, or in God.

And Providence (in the person of the author) finally pulls them through. The creaking of machinery and the stage-management of events is not necessarily detrimental as long as virtue is rewarded and vice punished at the end. Allingham's long drama stories are based on powerful, easily graspable ideas – to get justice, to be reunited with the beloved, to escape destitution, to protect children, to return home. The plot happenings are melodramatic yet the social understanding is thoroughly realistic. Money means power and 'papers' are the key to proving innocence. Despite their weekly twists and turns Allingham's plot structures are essentially simple, suitable for an audience who would spend over a year following them, while dealing with the business of their daily lives – and possibly reading other serial stories at different points in the week.

Driven from Home established a set of formulae. These

were not unique to Allingham but part of a wider shared understanding between common writers and their readers. If a serial story were being read aloud, or in a crowded setting, the use of conventions would have helped people grasp the story's action and bridge the weekly memory gaps. More importantly readers or listeners would have become experienced at guessing what lay ahead (this was encouraged by editorial queries) and might have discussed their predictions with one another.

But they could not have known until the following week whether their anticipations were right. Unlike users of books they had no physical indications as to whether the last chapter was close at hand or still six months away. From the writer and editor's perspective, composition by formulae offered plenty of scope to close down a story if circulation numbers fell or extend it if sales were good. The fact that so many of *Driven from Home's* incidents are repeated (two fires, two child-illnesses, several re-incarcerations) may indicate that Allingham extended the story beyond its planned dates, though there is no extant correspondence to prove this. His approach to construction is always strategic with a variety of possible exit and re-entry points. Allingham's family described his method of plotting as 'intellectual' and equated it with his lifelong pleasure in playing chess.

Florence Bartle, born in Poplar (London) in 1882, remembered penny novelettes being read out of doors in Victoria Park during her childhood to whatever audience would listen. Youngsters are usually assumed to have read to one another within their street groups and reading in the workplace is also documented. Within families the literate members read to the illiterate. The thought of numbers of people waiting week by week for a particular publication day on which to read or listen to the next instalment of a serial gives a dimension of collective experience to the reception of these stories. If serial story happenings were then told on to others who had missed a particular instalment, it brings them perhaps a little nearer to folk tale or to the same shared cultural understanding as is represented by updating friends with the latest plot developments in a TV soap.

Allingham's drama-stories need to be read authentically – that is with intervals between instalments and in the context of everyday life. Sitting silently in a reference library reading issue after issue of the *Butterfly* with one eye on the clock to complete the task by closing time is rather like playing a year's worth of liturgical chorales in a small room at double speed with the synthesiser set to hip-hop. *Driven from Home* and the quarter century of drama-stories which followed it were published in magazines – that is as journalism, not literature. It was when I began to look at their repeats and reissues over Allingham's long career that I realised both the extent to which the stories were affected by events going on around them and the extent to which they offer a social commentary. Not only are we reading at the wrong speed and in the wrong place to re-capture the original readers' enjoyment, but we are also living the wrong lives.

"Sargeant Sims, I think you will find your man behind that screen," said the baronet smoothly

Chapter Fourteen
1911: The Girl Outcast

HAROLD Garrish reminded Allingham that 'the proof of popularity lies not with me but with the readers' – and, as the weeks passed, those thousands of readers built up towards millions. Perhaps, if we can put the penny and halfpenny story-papers back into their own time it may be possible to see – and even feel – how they worked and why people wanted to buy them.

The time when Allingham's writing really caught the fancy of his audience – from *Plucky Polly Perkins* and *Driven from Home* in 1908–1909, through *The Rod of the Oppressor* (1910), *The Lights of Home* (1910–1911), *The Girl without a Home* (1910–1911), *His Convict Bride* (1911–1912), *The Girl Outcast* (1911–1912) to *Mother Love* (1912–1913) – was a period of intense social awareness and debate. The activities of the suffragettes and the increasing militancy of industrial action made headlines but there was also widespread and thoughtful concern about poverty and its effects on the family. William McFee, for instance, dated his inspiration to write *Casuals* from the Minority Report of the Poor Law Commission (1909) and the Commission's findings were regularly discussed in the columns of the *Christian Globe* – many of which were written by Allingham.

This concern also translated into direct studies of working people's lives. A 1909 Fabian Society lecture, 'The Economic Disintegration of the Family', stimulated Maud Pember Reeves and members of the Fabian Woman's Group to carry out an extended social experiment in precisely the area of south London where Allingham had spent his early childhood. Their observations were published in 1913 in *Round About a Pound a Week*.

Take a tram from Victoria to Vauxhall Station. Get out under the railway arch which faces Vauxhall Bridge and there you will find Kennington Lane. The railway arch roofs in a din which reduces the roar of trains continually passing overhead to a vibrating, muffled rumble. From either end of the arch comes a close procession of trams, motor-buses, brewers' drays, coal lorries, carts filled with unspeakable material for the glue factory and tannery, motor-cars, coster-barrows and people [...]

At the opposite end there is no cross-current. The trams slide away to the right towards the Oval. In front is Kennington Lane, and to the left, at right angles, a narrow street connects with Vauxhall Walk, leading further on into Lambeth Walk, both better known locally as The Walk. Such is the western gateway to the district stretching north to Lambeth Road, south to Lansdowne Road and east to Walworth Road where live the people whose lives form the subject of this book.

They are not the poorest people in the district. Far from it! They are, putting aside the tradesmen whose shops line the big thoroughfares such as Kennington Road or Kennington Park Road, some of the more enviable and settled inhabitants of this part of the world. The poorest people – the riverside casual, the workhouse in-and-out, the bar-room loafer – are anxiously ignored by these respectable persons whose work is permanent, as permanency goes in Lambeth and whose wages range from 18s to 30s a week.

Most of these families were living in one or two rooms, struggling to cook with just a couple of saucepans and, once the number of children began to increase, sleeping three and four to a bed with never enough chairs (or boxes) all to sit down at once. The Fabian women asked some of the mothers to keep accounts – to record the incessant juggling with shillings and pence that they were doing every day of every week to make the wages last. They discovered that eight of the women could not read or write. 'They said it was not thought of much consequence when they were girls but they evidently found it extremely humiliating now.' Three used their husbands when they needed help; the rest relied on their oldest children. Unsurprisingly, books as possessions are not mentioned at all in *Round About a Pound a Week*. Some of the women attended a mothers' meeting where *Little Lord Fauntleroy* was read aloud to them. One woman described how she had felt when her husband took her to the theatre to see a dramatisation of the story.

> It roused her imagination in a way that was astonishing. She questioned, she believed, she accepted. There were people like that! How real and how thrilling! It seemed to take something of the burden of the five boys and a girl from her shoulders [...] Mrs K would like to go again if it could possibly be afforded, but of course it could not.

Round About a Pound a Week is insistent on the absolute absence of spare money for the women and younger children in these frugally managed households. In some households – those of the printers' labourers for instance – only 1½d per head per day can be spent on food for everyone except the breadwinner. In most households it is 2d. The men keep back a shilling or two as spending money for themselves and any adolescent children who have started work may also have few spare pence under their own control. Newspapers are the only reading matter that the Fabian observers see being brought home. Suddenly the Harmsworth policy of flooding the market with halfpenny products makes perfect economic sense. 'Our policy,' wrote Lord Northcliffe to AP managing director, Sir George Sutton,

> was to rain paper after paper on the public and thus raise our prestige and block competition. (You will remember that policy was then regarded as madness by those inside and outside the office, especially when I said that most of our new papers should be issued for coin of the lowest denomination.)

Northcliffe had been right. In households where the weekly income was little more than twenty shillings, the expenditure of a penny rather than a halfpenny on a single item of entertainment might feel uncomfortably extravagant. Purchases of even the most basic items, such as tea, were usually made for minimal amounts to spread the meagre wages safely through the week. Two eight-page papers for a halfpenny each would be far more attractive than a one sixteen-page penny paper – as Cordwell discovered when he established his *Butterfly* group of comics, running Allingham's serials. If more money were spent it would usually be at a weekend, close to payday. A couple with one child, living on 8s 6d a week, allowed themselves a single penny newspaper.

> The newspaper was their Sunday treat and was read through from first column to last by both young people. It chronicled more murders and multiple births than any paper the visitor had ever seen. Mrs T would say, in the course of polite conversation: 'Have you

seen the news – five at a birth?' Then she would produce a picture of three nurses and two doctors each holding a baby and would murmur regretfully: 'They're most of 'em dead.'

Lady Bell, wife of an iron-master in Middlesbrough, North Yorkshire, was profoundly impressed by Charles Booth's pioneering methods of social investigation. *At the Works*, her study of the working people she knew, was published in 1907 and included a detailed study of reading habits in two hundred households. Her total sample was more than a thousand working-men's homes visited over nearly thirty years. Their wages covered a wider range than the groups surveyed by the Fabian women in Kennington but were mainly between twenty and thirty shillings a week. The Middlesbrough houses were larger than the one- and two-room dwellings described by Pember Reeves. The long dull streets were lined with four-roomed cottages, hastily constructed in the second half of the nineteenth century as the town mushroomed after the discovery of iron ore. The families seem larger too. Middlesbrough working people usually married young. There was little choice of employment (almost none for the women) and the birth rate was high, as was infant mortality. Lady Bell's sympathies were, above all, with the exhausted, prematurely aged mothers.

It is sad to see many a young woman who started as a bright, nice-looking girl, struggling at first during these years against constant physical discomfort of every kind and sinking at last into a depressed hopeless acceptance of the conditions around her. One's heart aches at seeing a girl of twenty-four or twenty-five, when she ought to be at her best, most joyous, most hopeful [...] already appearing dulled, discouraged, her form almost shapeless, her looks gone, almost inevitably becoming more of a slattern every day by day from sheer incapacity to keep up with her work.

It was for these women that she wanted entertainment – and they who were least likely to get it.

As might be expected the workman reads, as a rule, more than his wife, not only because his interest on the whole is more likely to be stimulated by intercourse with his fellows widening his horizon, but because he has more definite times of leisure when he feels he is amply justified in sitting down with a book.

From the two hundred households in her reading survey, Lady Bell concluded: 'More than a quarter of the workmen read books as well as newspapers, nearly half of them read the paper only and a quarter do not read at all.' Seventeen women and eight men were found to be unable to read and a further eight men and three woman actively disliked it. The solid majority of these Middlesbrough working families (a hundred and five households) chose to buy cheap fiction or the newspapers.

The reading that comes under the hand of the workman consists chiefly of the newspapers hawked about the street and those supplied by the small composite shops found in the poorer quarters. These shops, which sell various other goods – groceries, haberdashery – put before their public an unfailing supply of daily and weekly newspapers suited to their tastes, and penny novelettes.

Lady Bell noticed boys reading *Comic Cuts* and similar comic illustrated papers 'compared with which *Answers* and *Tit-Bits* are the very aristocracy of the press' and her survey revealed that women read them too. Household 51: 'Wife fond of reading but comic papers only.' Household 5: 'Husband reads newspapers only, particularly racing news. Wife spends much time reading penny dreadfuls.' Household 41: 'Husband reads sporting papers only, wife boys' tales of adventure.' Household 67: 'Mother and son both fond of reading – she tales of adventure, he novels.' Household 50: 'Wife fond of reading exciting novels which husband considers a waste of time.' Allingham was still editing the *New London Journal* in 1907, assisting with the *Christian Globe* and selling his first stories to *Chips*, *Puck*, *Comic Cuts* and the *Jester*. Some of these families would certainly have been among the readers of the new halfpenny comic-and-story papers just a few years later.

Bell's survey reveals, as ever, the variousness of people. There were workers reading theology, history, science or who were trying to teach themselves French or German in their spare time and there were families struggling to make out anything at all. Household 34: 'Husband cannot read but likes pictures and his wife reads to him.' Household 1: 'Husband and wife cannot read. Youngest girl reads the paper to them sometimes but "she has a tiresome temper and will not always go on".' In household 33 the husband 'Is devoted to books, spends all his spare time reading [...] His wife cannot read and refuses to learn though he is most anxious to teach her.' Household 23: 'Neither husband nor wife can read. The wife was bought up by an aunt who would not allow her to go to school. Her boy is going to teach her to read.' Household 21: 'Husband cannot read. He says when he was young he was tongue tied and no trouble was taken with him [...] Wife always reads to him in the evenings but he will listen to nothing but romances.' Bell's respondent number 24 was 'fond of reading "downright exciting stories after his work is done, to get his mind into another groove."' He and respondent 186 probably spoke for the majority. 'This woman asked what she liked to read replied: "something that will take one away from oneself."' Lady Bell concluded:

> It seems undeniable that for the great majority of people reading means recreation, not study [...] And we may well rejoice and not seek anything further, if the working-man, and especially the working-woman, whose daily outlook is more cramped and cheerless than that of the man, should find in reading fiction a stimulus and change of thought.

Respondent 185 was a woman who 'at the age of fifty, made a desperate attempt to learn to read, and, being asked what sort of books she would prefer, said, "Something with a little love and a little murder".' No drama-story of Allingham's lacked love or murder. Yet, while his fiction is escapist, it does have a demonstrable relationship to these readers' daily experience. The home was at the centre of most working people's lives, however over-crowded, under-furnished, inconvenient and insanitary: shelter was a primary need – emotionally as well as practically. As Richard Hoggart wrote in *The Uses of Literacy*, 'Where almost everything else is ruled from outside, is chancy and likely to knock you down when you least expect it, the home is yours and real.' Maud Pember Reeves noted the sacrifices her Kennington mothers made to pay the rent, even when they and their families were almost starving.

To be homeless was a terrifying fear – and was the motive force in many of Allingham's stories. Consider the titles of some of his earliest and most frequently reprinted serials: *Driven from Home*, *The Lights of Home*, *The Girl without a Home*, *The Girl*

Outcast and *Romney Hall* (a home that is lost.) In the meta-narrative of all these stories two young people who love one another and wish to marry, or who are recently married, find their security and happiness cruelly destroyed, without warning or desert. The forces against them are colossal and although the hero and heroine find some help, often in unexpected places, it usually takes them a year of week-by-week struggle before they can re-establish the respectable family life for which they long.

'We forget how terribly near the margin of disaster the man, even the thrifty man walks, who has, in ordinary normal conditions, but just enough to keep himself on', wrote Bell. Allingham concurred: 'The poor live constantly on the edge of a precipice,' he wrote in a leader for the *Christian Globe*: The precipice was there for all those families who had only the sale of their own labour on which to rely. It was there for Allingham as well as for his readers, but for families such as those in the Middlesbrough and Kennington studies, the 'margin of disaster' was very close indeed. They needed escape in their reading. The young couple living on 8s 6d a week who read about murders and multiple births every Sunday, presumably felt better at the end of the day because they were reassured about the relative safety and ordinariness of their own lives. Allingham's drama-stories floodlight the worst that can happen, using the techniques of melodrama and the conventions of fairy tales. They rely on the implicit promise of a happy-ever-after ending.

Readers of Christopher Booker's *Seven Basic Plots* have already had pointed out to them the archetypal characters and patternings that shape narrative as we know and love it – linking *Beowulf* to *Jaws*, the *Odyssey* to *Watership Down*. Because the nuts and bolts of Allingham's serials are so easy to see, it comes as no great surprise to notice that he too uses Booker's categories

'Rags to Riches', 'Voyage and Return', 'Overcoming the Monster.' It is perhaps more instructive to mention what narrative types he does not use – there are no 'dark heroes', for instance, no tragedies or fatal flaws. His stories are never introspective.

Neither are they obviously subtle. Richard Hoggart who was brought up in Hunslet, Leeds, surrounded by the 2d magazines for which Allingham wrote at the end of his life, struggles with the clichéd nature of the writing, particularly the use of stock responses.

> Every reaction has its fixed counter for presentation. I run through the account of a trial: the mouths are 'set', the faces 'tense with excitement'; tremors run down spines; the hero exhibits 'iron control' and faces his captors with a 'stony look'; his watching girlfriend is the victim of an 'agonised heart' as 'suspense thickens in the air'.

Allingham's customers were people who liked their language simple – though the tiny, meanly-spaced type in which his stories were set would never be used for similarly unconfident readers today. It's typographical slum-housing; the less you pay, the less white space you get. Hoggart describes such language as 'picture presentations of the known' and defends it robustly as 'speaking for a solid and relevant way of life.' He also, less felicitously, describes this world as 'limited and simple', 'childish and garish' and a place where 'the springs of the emotions work in great gushings'. Looking back at Lady Bell's description of the dulled, discouraged, hopeless, shapeless young mothers, a bit of garishness and gushing emotion would seem to be no bad thing.

So, was that all that Allingham's narratives achieved? Sat tired men and women down for a while and offered them stylised tableaux of things they already knew? If I point out their resemblance to fairy stories will that be the final nail in the coffin of belittlement? Perhaps not if we follow Marina Warner's complex analysis of fairy tales which have 'family dramas at their heart'. In *From the Beast and the Blonde* she presents fairy stories as being a potent mix of the archetypal and the actual – with a generous dash of 'heroic optimism'. Fairy tales seemed to her to be something more than 'picture presentations of the known'. Yes, they map 'actual volatile experience' (growing up, coping with financial insecurity, bereavement, family break-up, social injustice) but in such a way as to offer the possibility of change; they could 'remake the world in the image of desire'. The emphasis in each re-telling can be seen to shift slightly to address the emotional needs of different audiences.

The Girl Outcast, written to launch the *Favorite Comic* in 1911 and republished a further six times over the next fifteen years, suggests that Allingham was well aware of the fairy-tale aspect of his stories. At the heart of *The Girl Outcast* is the enmity of the dark, alluring, older woman, Sonia, the step-mother, towards the young, blonde Doris. Doris may be lovely but Sonia has 'something of that quality that is called fascination'. Essentially she is the same type as Madge Milton, that 'Devil of a Woman', but here she is locked firmly into a family drama instead of plotting the downfall of nations.

Sonia has recently married Doris's father and has lost no time in coming between parent and child. She engineers the father's absence, then his death. Instead of sending her step-daughter to starve in the wild wood, she throws her out into London, 'the mighty city which rewards the strong but has no mercy for the weak'. Throughout Allingham's work London is used as the trial ground, the dangerous location far removed from the shelter of a true home. Doris, 'inexperienced, gentle and retiring', is found, ragged and unconscious, by a handsome prince – or knight errant at least. He is Jack Travers, 'son of one of the wealthiest men in England'. But, as this is only instalment five, Doris and Jack's troubles have barely begun.

Margery Allingham described the 'pop' adventure form as 'A surprise every tenth page and a shock every twentieth'. Translated into halfpenny comic instalments this means at least one major reversal every four thousand words. Transformation scenes are commonplace. The surface of Allingham's writing – costumes, locations, diction – is sub-Dickensian. Apart from the few great gleaming motorcars the settings of most stories might be a vague half-century earlier than their composition dates. One small shift in perception, however, recasts them in the fantasy world of wicked witches, forests, dungeons, lascivious ogres and fairy godparents. The symbolic elements of Allingham's writing spring into focus and it becomes easy to comprehend the appeal these serials made to their readers. The discovery by the hero or heroine that they are the unacknowledged heirs to a fortune can be read politically – these readers are the dispossessed. It can also be read psychologically – relating to the common fantasy of being a prince or princess in disguise, an assertion of personal importance.

The likeness of Allingham's drama-stories to fairy tale is evident in the conventions they share. Conventions such as the impenetrability of disguise, returns from apparent death and the reversibility of maimings (especially blindness and amnesia) are common to both. These are examples of metamorphosis, the single quality that, for Warner, defines the fairy tale. She speaks of 'this instability of appearances, these sudden swerves of destiny [which] created the first sustaining excitement of such stories' for her as a young reader. These would be excellent phrases with which to describe Allingham's roller-coaster plots – 'sudden swerves of destiny', yes! Stuffier editors would censure Allingham for his 'improbabilities'; in fact they give much of the life to his stories. Whatever can go wrong will go wrong, but the reader can trust the author that all will be well in the end.

Warner suggests that fairy tales were often a way for women to express their resentment at their powerlessness. *The Girl Outcast* was written for youngsters, another relatively powerless group. Sonia is frightening not just because she is a Salome or a witch-queen but because she is an adult. Authority will believe her, not her stepdaughter. As narrator Allingham is on the side of the hero and heroine. He reassures them that their suffering will help them to grow and steps in occasionally to offer advice. *The Girl Outcast* is a rites-of-passage story, a common fairy tale or adventure type. Jack and Doris are occasionally inept, but their bravery and their love for one another enable them to move from situations of dependence to become responsible parents themselves. The editorially added subheading in the *Favorite Comic* changes from 'A Story of the Trials and Tribulations of a Young Girl Alone and Penniless in the Great City of London' to 'The Story of a Young Wife and her Young Husband and of a Wicked Woman who Tried to Separate Them'.

Both plot and language draw heavily on the typology of folk and fairy tale. Sonia, 'lithe and sinous' (that is snaky), calls down the forces of evil on the two young lovers. She is in league with both Baron Sarke, a sinister foreigner with extensive powers to impersonate others, and the even more sinister Dr Cain who specialises in disguise and potion-making. Sonia herself turns from beautiful to hideous and back at least twice in the story – as wicked stepmothers so often do. When her facial disfigurement as 'Mrs Silver' is obliterated for the second time, she reappears looking years younger than her first self and poised to lure other young men to their fate. Doris has her personal Cinderella moment when fairy godfather M Antoine provides transport to the ball and a beautiful dress so she can rescue Jack from a designing brunette just on the stroke of midnight.

Material objects do not change in Allingham's stories. There are no magic lamps but most of the other examples of metamorphosis listed by Warner can be discovered. Doris and Jack's dead child, whose body was found in the ashes of a baby farm, the south London 'House of Hope', is rediscovered as 'Doll', a seven-year-old pickpocket with the pluck to defy Sonia as her mother never could. She tumbles from a peach tree like a 'wild-eyed sprite' or 'a creature out of fairyland'. And, just in case the reader misses the point, there is a short scene when Jack is buying the identity of Tom Tiffin, second footman at the prison governor's mansion.

> 'First rate,' replied Tom Tiffin, as with wonder in his eyes he took the three crisp banknotes and the three sovereigns which Jack pushed over the table towards him. 'By Jove it's like a fairy-tale. Here, landlord, a railway timetable please!'

'"My child," said Madame Clare, "to the young all things are possible. Yes, I can make you beautiful again – If I choose"'

Chapter Fifteen
1912: Mother Love

As soon as one of Allingham's major new serials was underway, the editor would canvass readers' opinions. Rewards were offered – a box of paints, five shillings, ten. When *Human Nature* commenced in the *Butterfly* November 1913 the inducement went up. '£5 – Grand Cash Offer!' was offered for opinions of *Human Nature* written on a postcard. 'Do not imagine that good writing or spelling are necessary. All I want is your honest opinion.' The readers did respond but none of their letters to the editor has survived. There is no evidence that any reader ever wrote to Allingham directly or asked for a letter to be forwarded to him.

When he had been an editor himself it had been very different – all those photos and hand-written descriptions, the readers' queries to be answered and wisdom to be dispensed. Richard Hoggart comments that, despite the size and commercial ethos of the twentieth-century corporations producing the cheap, mass-market magazines, 'the authors and illustrators seem to have a close knowledge of the lives and attitudes of their audience.' Allingham described what this had meant to him at the *London Journal*:

In reading a letter I often try to picture not only the person who wrote it but also the home and surroundings in which it was penned. No doubt I make many grotesque mistakes but I find it helps me if I clothe my shadowy correspondents in some human shape. It enables me to picture my readers as a collection of friends, each with an individuality of his own and not merely as a mob of strangers whose weekly pennies help to pay my salary.

Only positive comments were published but the editor read them all. Just once Allingham let through a portrait of a relentlessly dissatisfied reader.

I have pictured him as a little bent rather pathetic figure hurrying out every Saturday morning to his newsagent. Then, having secured his *Journal,* he creeps back to his garret and devours the newly printed pages. I see the old fellow polishing his glasses and settling down with the gleam of battle in his eyes for an encounter with his imaginary enemy the editor. He makes notes as he reads and when he has finished he seizes a pen and fills a postcard with incoherent abuse. This he does week after week with no encouragement and no reward.

If such a character were introduced into a story, the author would be accused of caricature. The idea of this old scribbler is of course very grotesque, but there is just that touch of pathos about it that would have appealed to Charles Dickens who understood better than any writer how quaint are the devices by which some poor souls seek to bring a little brightness into their dull grey lives.

Nothing like this was included in the Amalgamated Press comics. Positive results were fed back to the readers as well as being used internally. A reader, EW, wrote to the editor of the

Jester to say that *The Lights of Home* was 'the best tale I have ever read'. The editor thanked him publicly and hoped he would write again soon. The editor of *Puck*, who had expended six boxes of paints, thanked all his many readers 'for their valuable letters sent to him regarding the contents of *Puck*. You will be pleased to learn that 'Val Fox', 'Tom-All-Alone' and 'The Smart Girl of the Family' will continue in *Puck* until further notice as a result of your representations.'

Although this was phrased to foster readers' sense of ownership of their paper, and thus their consumer loyalty, the editor's response was disingenuous. *The Smart Girl of the Family* was in fact *Plucky Polly Perkins* to which the paper was already committed through purchase of the second serial rights. It would have been financially disadvantageous (though not impossible) for the editor to pull it if readers' letters had indicated dissatisfaction. These editors were attempting to persuade their audience to like what they were already being offered as well as attempting to find out what they liked.

Survey results were fed back to the author in a generalised form to urge greater productivity. When R Chance of the *Jester* wrote to Allingham in 1911 to update him on readers' views, he was bullish:

> I have found that 'The Lights of Home' is extremely popular with my readers and only last week it attained a high place in a competition. Under the circumstances and considering that the paper is doing well I do not want to finish it up yet, so please continue with it until you hear from me to the contrary.

Allingham was less than delighted. *The Lights of Home* had already been running ten months. Its hero, heroine and villain had each died and been revived several times and he was clearly running out of ideas. Also he had, in the interim, successfully negotiated a pay rise from one to two guineas per thousand words for new AP work. *Lights* was still being paid at the old rate. Evidently he tried suggesting to Chance that his new work on *Lights* should be paid at the new rate or he would follow his own inclinations and bring it to a close. The editor was horrified:

> I could not pay such a price as you suggest for the story which has been running such a length of time. You started the story at the rate of one guinea a thousand and it has always been usual for authors to complete yarns at the original rate.
>
> As you have left the instalments until the last moment – to finish the story up in one instalment would inconvenience me considerably, as it would not give me the slightest chance to make a fresh arrangement. Therefore I should be glad if you could see your way to doing for me another ten or eleven thousand words of this story so that I can start another yarn after it. Otherwise I should be compelled to have the end of the story written by another author, which besides being a difficult task would be a great pity.

Allingham gave in and the serial continued for a full fifty episodes, paid for at the original rate. Exchanges of this sort spell out who really ran the fiction factory.

Readers played their part in endorsing the contents of the papers, but readers who were sufficiently organised and confident to write 'sensible and thoughtful' letters on the chance of winning a box of paints or even £5 were probably a minority group. Arnold Freeman, a social observer, has left an eyewitness observation of some boys who may not have written letters. Freeman's study, *Boy Life and Labour: the Manufacture of Inefficiency* (1914) was based in Birmingham, a city with an exceptionally high number of opportunities for artisan training. Yet even in Birmingham there was little hope of advancement for the unskilled labourer.

Freeman wanted to investigate and demonstrate the waste of talent that occurred when boys left elementary school aged fourteen and went straight out to work. The six or seven shillings a week they could earn in a succession of menial jobs were of instant benefit to the income of their struggling households but there was little guidance or further training available to these boys. Most of them would be turned off from their jobs when they approached their twenties and expected to be paid at a man's rate. After that they could hope only for a lifetime of unskilled, low-paid labour or alternate periods of casual work and unemployment. A *Christian Globe* leader suggests that Allingham shared similar concerns.

Freeman started his survey in 1912 with 134 boys in their seventeenth year, selected because they had attempted four or more jobs since leaving school. He completed with seventy-one, the remainder having either lied about their ages or simply disappeared in the course of the investigation. His survey therefore excluded both what he termed the 'superior' boy, on course for higher-paid and better-class manual work, who tended to remain in a steady, single job, and also the boys employed in such casual ways – street trading, for instance – that they did not use the Labour Exchange. 'The bulk of boys selected are, I believe, typical of the mass of uneducative Boy Labour in Birmingham.'

Freeman visited their homes and met their families where possible. He questioned the boys about their work and education, their tastes and beliefs and asked some of them to keep diaries. He found them lamentably ignorant (as those who research the young so often do) and concluded that picture palaces, music halls, cheap literature, football and their own street culture were their sole sources of pleasure, imaginative stimulus and ideas. 'The senses of the adolescent, now open at their widest, are opened not to Nature and Art, but to cheap and tawdry pantomime; his kindling imagination is not nourished with fine, heroic literature, but with the commonest rubbish in print.'

A significant proportion of this common rubbish was supplied by Allingham. Freeman quotes the literary preferences of six boys as typifying the majority. Their favourite papers were Garrish and Cordwell's comics – *Chips, The Butterfly, Merry & Bright, Dreadnought* – and Percy Griffith's *Gem* and *Magnet*. 'These,' said Freeman, 'can be bought second hand very cheaply indeed; they are freely circulated from one boy to another, and are read to the exclusion of almost all other literature, except perhaps Sporting and Police News in the *Mail*.' He quoted some typical titles and synopses extracted at the time of his survey. They include one of Allingham's most popular serial stories, *Mother Love*, which was running in *Fun & Fiction* during 1912–1913.

'MOTHER LOVE': A PATHETIC STORY WHICH WILL TOUCH THE HEART OF EVERY READER

What will not a mother do for the sake of the child she loves? Mother love has prompted heroic actions which have made the world ring and also mothers have found themselves forced to do things that they would have shrunk from had it not been for the sake of their beloved little ones. This narrative tells in a most striking manner the story of a mother who was forced to offend against the law for the sake of her darlings.

Mother Love was Allingham's take on Mrs Henry Wood's *East Lynne* – the novel that Florence Bell in Middlesbrough identified as 'the book whose name one most often hears from men and women both'. An 'admirable compound,' as she describes it, 'of the goody and the sentimental.' Allingham's versions (of which there would be several) were frequently billed by his editors as 'the new *East Lynne*', or 'the greatest story since *East Lynne*', but show significant differences from the original. There is, for a start, no adultery – the mother transgresses because of her need for money, not sex. Her desperation is for her children. The stepmother figure, and the villains generally, are monstrous. Their wickedness completely outweighs the mother's minor slip enabling her to remain pure and anguished throughout. Like Wood's Lady Isabel Vane she is forever watching over her children in disguise but she is not permanently disfigured. Unlike Lady Isabel, she and her children are finally allowed a happy ending.

Allingham named the child in his first *Mother Love* story Margery. Possibly he endowed her with some of the characteristics of his own daughter – 'a taste for long words, newly learned' for instance. This may have made it easier for him to give full force to the heroine's distress and one can understand the older readers of the comics responding strongly to this 'pathetic story'. But it's an interesting choice for the 'uneducative' boys of Birmingham.

Three of the boys who Freeman describes in detail were regular readers of the *Butterfly* and therefore steady customers for Allingham. At the time of the survey boy HH was reading *Chips* and the *Butterfly* and would therefore have been following Allingham's serial *Ashamed of his Mother* – another tale of maternal self-sacrifice, this time for a clever young hero in a top hat who has won a place in a public school. HH was classified by Freeman in group A of his Class Two, 'Boys apparently destined for unskilled work who were fitted for skilled work':

The home of HH is broken up. His father had, for some years before the birth of this boy, been getting such broken employment and beggarly income that he left home when he knew this fresh burden was coming into his life and died soon after. The mother now lives with a married sister and helps support the household by charring and baby-minding. The boy has been looked after from infancy by kind-hearted neighbours, who suggested that their not having the authority of the boy's father was the cause of HH's instability. However that may be, HH has had a changeful career. There are signs that he wanted to learn, and his jobs have mainly been in the same line of work. He went to evening classes for a short period but abandoned them as too burdensome. He left his first job of errands because he didn't like it; was discharged from a second job of errands because a big waiter was scratched but he declares he didn't do it; he left a third job of errands because he could not learn anything (so he says); he next tried to learn chasing but left through shortage of work; then spoon-polishing and brass-polishing, and again spoon-polishing, leaving in each case for what he thought would be a better job. He is now polishing at a silversmith's, and when I asked him why or how he got this last job, he replied, 'I hadn't got any other. You take the first one that comes round to you.' That seems to express with fair accuracy the purposeless nature of the boy's career and the careers of great numbers of boys like him. He appears to have deteriorated since he left school, is pale and weak-looking and seems feeble in character and intellect. This boy will probably never be fit for good work again.

Freeman foresaw a bleak future for this young *Butterfly* reader and others like him, as they became 'ordinary unskilled workers':

> They will use their hands and not their heads; they will in most cases do work which you or I could learn in as few months or even a few days; they will in most cases take low-skilled jobs in factories, in association with machines or as assistants to skilled workers. Their earnings will in almost all cases be well under 30 s a week and insufficient to maintain themselves and their wives and children in comfort, even in decency! They will inhabit the overcrowded areas that fill the central parts of Birmingham, and perpetuate their own inefficiency in the weak bodies and slow brains of their children.

Even this, according to Freeman, was probably out of reach of the other two young *Butterfly* readers in his survey. Boy MC also enjoyed *Merry & Bright*. He would recently have finished Allingham's *Girl without a Home* and gone on to read his next serial for that paper, *The Girl who Married a Scoundrel*. MC was consigned to Class 3, 'apparently destined for unemployables':

> This boy was at Marston Green Cottage Homes for four and a half years and, though a rough sort of fellow, he was – the Superintendent says – 'a sharp boy in school.' He was in Standard VI at the Elementary School afterwards, and satisfactory in character. In physique he was 'rather poor, undersized.' The whole of MC's family combined could not recollect all of his jobs, but the main ones are:- helping in a shop, errands, power press, polishing, errands, labouring, van, errands. His present job is one of straightening wire out at a large brass factory and he asserts that he means to stick to it. The boy's father was a glass-beveller who died of consumption eight

years ago. MC alleges as the main reason for leaving his jobs that his mother has been poor and didn't bother as long as he brought home the money. This is perhaps true, but as one of his brothers remarked of him, 'He's changed because he likes change,' and this seems to be the most accurate diagnosis of the case. He is not at all dejected but is a merry, irrepressible youth. He seems constitutionally unstable, and irresponsible. His intelligence is low and his physique not good – to say nothing of his smallness.

CW, the third *Butterfly* reader, was placed firmly among the 'wastrels'. All that Freeman learned from the boys in this lowest category only convinced him of 'their worthlessness from an industrial or social point of view':

Concerning CW's jobs I have no reliable record. He himself told me: Tube factory (one year); looking after stables etc (two years); militia (six months); and now casting. The Labour Exchange record gives him two jobs neither of which he mentioned to me. His old school teacher says:- 'He has worked at several places.' His parents told me naively that he has had 'a week here and a week there.'

Of his home his head-teacher says: 'This lad was raised in a caravan under conditions hygienically truly awful. The parents are both densely ignorant, with little moral perception.' The home had been moved from the caravan when I saw it – it moves every few weeks – but it was still just as loathsome as when the teacher had known it. The room I saw looked more like a sea of filth and rags and rubbish than a place where human beings lived. The father was then on remand on a charge of 'receiving'. He says he is a hawker.

CW left school at the bottom of Standard IV; 'Physique good but stamina poor'; his character was as good as might be expected in a boy with such blood in his veins. To-day a glance at his face is sufficient to convince the least observant person that there is a kind of moral rottenness in him. His answers to the many questions I put him confirmed the impression he made upon me. He has just completed six months in the 'Special Reserve,' but found the life too hard for him and is glad to be out of it. But for that six months he would probably be far inferior in physique and capacity to what he is.

It is extraordinary and touching to imagine this boy, in these domestic conditions, or, more likely out in the street, reading flimsy copies of the 'dainty' pale green *Butterfly.* He claimed to enjoy all of the comics – so, in addition to *Ashamed of his Mother* (a drama of moral scruple) which was followed later in 1912 by *Romney Hall* (love and treachery in an ancestral mansion), he could have read Allingham's *His Convict Bride* in *Fun & Fiction*, followed by *Mother Love.* A copy of the *Favorite Comic* would have offered him *The Girl Outcast* (fairy tale romance in London) then *League of the Double Life* (a reprint of *A Devil of a Woman*). *The Girl Without a Home,* which had just finished in *Merry & Bright,* was a story yearning for the restoration of cottage bliss. It was followed by *The Girl Who Married a Scoundrel*, an exciting tale of imposture among the gentry. *Puck* was still running *Chums at Rathgar* (reprint of Allingham's *A Regular Duffer*) and if CW had managed to get hold of a copy of the *Dreadnought* early in 1913 he could have read *Max the Magnificent* as well. The more Allingham you read, the worse your life chances?

This boy said he hated his home and having seen it I can quite believe his statement. He spends his earnings at the Picture Palace, the Music Hall, and loafing about the street with mates and girls. (He has been in the militia and this apparently privileges him to have no fewer than five girls who will walk out with him.) He is intensely interested in football, horse-racing and boxing. He confessed shamelessly to gambling and to other worse vices, that most boys are either guiltless of or silent about. He reads the Comics, *The Gem, Butterfly, Picture Fun, England's Boxing,* the *Sporting Buff* for football and the *Mail* for Police News. He mentioned Crippen, when I asked him for his favourite characters in fiction, and said:- 'There's a fellow I like to read about.' His superficial knowledge of Christianity was above the average, due probably to the length of time spent in his religious instruction in a Roman Catholic school and to the religious services in the Army. He neither knew nor cared about politics; nor about any of the parties or principal current measures (excepting, as always, Votes for Women and the Insurance Act!).

On Freeman's evidence CW had already developed his own tastes. He may have been leading the researcher on a little ('Crippen – there's a fellow I like to read about') but he knew what he enjoyed and the *Butterfly* had a place among his pleasures. Freeman concluded:

> Working-boys are not greatly interested in things of real life. They want sensation, excitement, melodrama; they love romance, no matter how fantastic or far-fetched. Their imaginations are prepared for any flight of fancy; their instincts are all agog for anything that is lurid or weird or bloodthirsty; and the literature that is prepared for them makes the most direct appeal to these boyish instincts. The boy, tired with a real life that presents little enough of romance, finds a vent for all the emotional stirrings that thrill in him, in these sensational 'shockers'.

This is an emotional account in itself and wins respect for the humanity of the researcher as he conveys to us the imaginative vulnerability of these sixteen- and seventeen-year-old boys.

But if Allingham's stories did represent their choice of literature – even in part – then they were not reading 'lurid or weird or bloodthirsty' tales, they were reading stories that dramatise an intense longing for family life and domesticity – with 'lurid and weird' incidentals. Heroines were at the centre of most of Allingham's drama-stories as they and their lovers or husbands (and their babies) battle almost overwhelming odds to be together, to find peace, safety, prosperity.

None of these three boys seems to have had functioning mothers. Did the disguised guardian-angel in *Mother Love* answer a yearning? The other Allingham-derived story in Freeman's list of favourites was *The Girl Who Trusted Him*. 'The story of a girl who trusted and believed in her sweetheart all through the bitter times when it seemed that the world was against him.' Although this particular tale was an Allingham plot written up by his friend Richard Starr because Allingham himself was completely over-committed, that motif of a woman's loving fidelity is his stock in trade from *Driven from Home* on. It's not surprising that it might appeal to the 'boyish instincts', and 'emotional stirrings' of these struggling adolescents. The individual incidents and monstrous villains in Allingham's fiction might qualify them to be described as 'sensational shockers' but what is truly shocking, if the narrative incidents are considered as symbolically significant, is the accuracy with which Allingham's serials depict a world where everything conspires against the attainment of this simple human dream of a home.

Freeman found a few (very few) boys who read 'better-class' literature and used the public libraries. There were also a large number of boys who dropped out in the course of the investigation whose leisure decisions are therefore unknown. The boys whose choices he was able to record had made varied selections from the limited range of periodicals available. All of these boys – the studious, the refusniks, the cinema- and comic-lovers – testify to difference. Even though they had been selected in order to typify 'the mass of uneducative Boy Labour in Birmingham', Freeman's respondents were not a homogenous group. There were no homogenous groups when the masses were encountered severally. These ordinary boys, trapped in industrial and social conditions that seemed to Freeman (and to Allingham) deplorable, were exercising one of the very few freedoms available to them, the tightly limited freedom to choose their entertainment.

'These boys are mostly kind and generous and cheerful; and are capable of heroism and self-sacrifice.' Freeman's study was published early in 1914. It is likely that the boys who were physically fittest of those he met would soon have joined or been conscripted into the army. For many of these youngsters – even CW – the future might be short.

'When at last Tom tore himself away'

Chapter Sixteen
1914: Human Nature

At the outset of the First World War Allingham was, as usual, writing a serial for the *Butterfly*. *Human Nature* had first opened in the *Butterfly* in November 1913. Herbert and Em had had a baby earlier that year – Emily Joyce, a sister for Margery and Phil, and this latest heroine had been given her name. The first half of the serial had told the story of two young people, an inventor and an artist, parted by the machinations of a ruthless financier. By 26 September 1914 the hero and heroine, Jack and Joyce, have overcome their difficulties and are finally married. In a regular serial this should be the end. They set off for their honeymoon through the hop-gardens and harvest fields of Kent.

> 'What a beautiful land England is, Jack!' she said, with a sigh of contentment.
>
> 'Yes dear,' said her husband gravely, 'a land to live in, a land, if need be, to die for.'

They arrive at their new home and sit out after dinner in its lovely garden, revelling in their togetherness. Joyce, however, is prescient:

'Beautiful as it is, it would seem like a prison if you went away and left me here alone.'

Jack pressed her hand with a firm grip. 'But I am not going away. No power on earth can now take me from your side.'

A discreet cough near at hand startled them both.

Formulaically this is neat. Allingham's pre-war serials regularly ended with hero and heroine portrayed in just such a tranquil setting when they had finally earned their right to live happily ever after. These serials had usually begun with an intruder fracturing a couple's domestic contentment (often dispatching one of them to prison). In this case the unwelcome visitor is an emissary from the War Office. He has come to ask Jack, as the inventor of the Kingsley monoplane, whether he is prepared to join the Royal Army Flying Corps:

'That would of course involve active service in the field in the event of war.'

Jack raised his eyebrows.

'War? You don't suggest that there is any possibility of England being involved in war?'

The stranger shrugged his shoulders.

'Oh no, I hope not! But this Servian business is developing rather rapidly. It will most likely blow over but we don't intend to be taken by surprise this time. What I want to know is this. In the event of war can we rely on you for special service with the Kingsley monoplane?'

Joyce had risen to her feet, and stood beside her husband. He turned and looked at her.

She was trembling but the brave look in her eyes gave him courage.

Once more he confronted his visitor.

'Sir,' he said gravely. 'In the event of this country being involved in war, I trust every Englishman would do his part to uphold her honour and repel the invader. At any rate you can rely on me. When England needs me I am ready.'

The next instalment (3 October 1914) brings Jack's call to duty. Allowing time for production (three or four weeks was usual, this may have been exceptional) Allingham must have picked this story up and started it on its new career in the first weeks after war was declared (3 September).

Human Nature ran on from its new beginning, throughout 1915 and into 1916. Allingham's existing narrative formulae seemed to adapt easily to the wartime circumstances. The pre-war story had included an ambiguous foreigner, Julian Marck, undertaking sinister medical research. He was effortlessly diverted to spy status (and membership of the secret 'Society of the Eagle and the Serpent'), ready to steal the vital papers that Jack keeps locked in his study desk (a regular location from *A Devil of a Woman* onwards). There was also Babs, a gallant little cockney girl, dedicated to the protection of the ladylike Joyce. She swiftly becomes a symbol of working-class patriotism and effectiveness, quick to spot a sham and very much more acute than her mistress. When Joyce suggests that they ask the War Office for news of Jack, Bobs is scornful: '"You can go where you like, but it's only wasting time," said Bobs emphatically. "If you want to find Mr. Kingsley you'll have to get as near as you can to the fighting line. He's bound to be where the bloomin' bullets are thickest. He's that sort of mug."'

Bobs takes centre stage in the wartime section of *Human Nature*, effectively displacing Jack and Joyce in instalment after instalment as she foils any number of dastardly German plots by the exercise of her loyalty and shrewdness – qualities which are presented as stereotypically working-class. Bobs expresses Allingham's idealisation of working-class pluck and grit. 'I know the common people,' he wrote to Lord Northcliffe in 1915, 'I get my living from studying them as you once did – and I tell you that if this war lasts ten years, it will not be their courage and resolution that will be the first to slacken.' At the end of the serial it is Bobs who crawls un-noticed across the floor and bounds up to take the final bullet, thus saving all the officer-class characters and finally consigning Julian Marck to a firing squad in the Tower of London. Throughout the story Marck has deceived and evaded the intelligentsia time and again. But he has never fooled Bobs.

When she is featured in the illustrations that accompany the weekly instalments of *Human Nature* Bobs is almost a comic-strip character. She is short, broad and bulgy with a flat hat and often a large umbrella, which she uses as a weapon – rather like Carl Giles's famous 'Grandma' pictured as a child. She has a truculent edge to her heroism that suggests a type of music-hall humour and which is echoed later in Margery Allingham's more famous character, Magersfontein Lugg. Margery was ten at the beginning of the First World War and remembered later how terrified she had felt when she read the propaganda stories of the atrocities in Belgium. 'What gave rise to it I cannot remember, but I did have in my mind, or on paper, a very vivid picture of a baby stuck to a stable door with a bayonet. In my imagination of course it was our stable door and the baby, my sister Joyce, born in 1913.' As I pulled out the soft, decaying pages of the *Butterfly* that Allingham had kept as his file copies, I rather hoped that ten-year-old Margery had read these instalments, sitting in her father's study, and had felt reassured by the gallant Bobs.

Human Nature ran for 124 instalments, longest of all

Allingham's productions. There was, however, a variation in the early parting of the hero and heroine that may, in retrospect, appear significant. For the first time in Allingham's drama-stories, the sundering of the couple included explication of their different roles as male and female. When Jack tells Joyce that he will indeed be in the fighting line within a week,

> Joyce stared at her husband with a look of mingled terror and admiration.
>
> This man who she only knew as an adoring lover, gentle and tender as a woman, was suddenly transformed.
>
> With a thrill of wonder she saw before her *a primitive man, a grim fighting animal with the light of battle in his steady brown eyes.*
>
> She was frightened, but she also experienced another emotion which conquered her fears. There was born within her a fierce determination to be loyal to her man, *to be what he expected her to be*, and not to fail him in this hour of crisis [my italics].

Jack also appreciates the situation in gender terms.

> 'It is you women with your courage who give us courage and nerve us to do and dare. Yours is the harder part and the braver part. We go out to new scenes and new adventures; you have to stay at home, hearing good news and bad news, and, what is worse, no news at all, and all the time you have to keep calm and strong so that the courage of those about you does not fail. If things go badly, as well they may for a time, it is you brave and loyal women who will keep up the spirit of the nation so that in the end, come it soon or late, victory must be ours.'

The outbreak of war raised many people's awareness of their gender-determined roles: soldier/wife or mother, adventurer/nurturer, fighter/sufferer. As Allingham, at forty-six, was too old to be expected to join up and his children were too young, there was no effect on his immediate family but change soon came to the Allingham household, the village and the wider family as the young men went away. In *The Oaken Heart* Margery specifically remembered Layer Breton men, Arthur Fletcher and George Playle, both of whom were wounded. Herbert's next brother, Arthur, a commercial artist, was wounded at the Dardenelles in 1915 and Em's brother, Walter Hughes, returned from Canada in November 1915 only to die at Ypres. Looking back to the village she had known as a child, Margery wrote

> I had a sudden recollection of women and old people all in black, as country people were in those days on a Sunday, standing about in the village street reading enormous casualty lists in very small type that seemed to fill whole pages of the paper; a boy on a bike with not one telegram spelling tragedy but sometimes two or even three at a time; and long sad services in the small church which had been a barn and still smelled of hay.

The Allinghams were outsiders in this little Essex community but they could not have failed to be affected by the suffering so close to home. Of the thousand inhabitants of Layer Breton and neighbouring Birch, 160 persons served in the Army, Navy, Air Force or Nursing Service. Of these, twenty-seven would be killed or die on active service, thirty-seven would be wounded or gassed, three taken prisoner, fourteen invalided or discharged, twelve awarded military or nursing honours and three given commissions. News from the front and the obituaries of the dead were recorded month by month in the parish magazine.

Although Margery described her father in this childhood period as a 'preoccupied' man (as he might well have been with so much work on hand) she received letters, later in life, from people who had worked at the Rectory testifying to the interest Allingham took in their affairs and to his personal kindness.

By 1914 Herbert and Em were on friendly terms with Dr JH Salter, who had delivered baby Joyce. Salter, though in his mid-seventies, was in charge of the local Emergency Committee and relished taking occasional command of the Essex Volunteers. He had already persuaded Allingham to join the local Freemasons, of which he was Worshipful Master: now he enrolled him as an Essex special constable. This meant night duties every other week. Allingham would have been tasked with helping to enforce lighting restrictions, being aware of air raid precautions and the plans for evacuation in the event of an invasion. His certificate of service survives.

The Allinghams also knew the Luard family who were prominent in the local community. One member of the family, Sister Evelyn Luard, from the neighbouring village of Birch, frequently wrote home on behalf of wounded soldiers in her care. One mother replied thanking her for her reassurance but wondering whether she could be told which son Sister Evelyn meant – she had three serving in France at that time. Other families were similarly denuded. Dr Salter's diary records a visit from a local woman who had seven sons at the front. It's not surprising to discover that throughout the 1914–1918 war years there was always an Allingham 'mother love' story running somewhere. The motif of the disguised mother watching invisibly over her suffering children must have gained a new resonance in this time of many partings.

The full effect of the war on families became apparent

gradually. Margery remembered 'the time when war was life and there seemed to have been no beginning and to be no end to the intolerable condition of strain in which our elders struggled irritably'. Layer Breton is only a few miles from the Essex coast and the threat of invasion soon seemed real. Dr Salter made notes.

Five or six submarines observed at the entrance to the Blackwater and an attempt at invasion thought probable. It is believed the submarines put in there being quiet and snug, out of the way of the storm and probably for repairs. They were seen putting out in the morning. Then a gunboat, torpedo boats and mine-finders came and dragged the bottom of the sea. The whole country is alive with soldiers and entrenchments are being dug all across the county.

Salter recorded bombs being dropped on nearby Colchester, Coggeshall and Braintree, a Zeppelin raid on Maldon, more Zeppelins over Southend, Latchingdon, Burnham, a balloon brought down at Tollesbury and raids on London. This disruption was as nothing compared with what would come in the Second World War but such nearness to civilians was still new and shocking. The special constables were trained in aircraft recognition and the correct handling of prisoners. By early 1916 the Essex coast felt like a dangerous place. There were rumoured sightings of Dreadnoughts out to sea, Zeppelins were almost commonplace, invasion alarms more frequent. Returning home to Tolleshunt D'Arcy one fine April day Salter found himself 'held up at the entrance to the village by soldiers with fixed bayonets – their orders being to block all roads. Funny times these!'

In September 1916 the only capture of Germans on English soil took place at Little Wigborough, just four miles from the Allingham's home in Layer Breton. On 23-24 September 1916

Zeppelin L-33 dropped its bombs on the East End of London, causing fires and severe damage and killing eleven people. It was brought down by anti-aircraft on its way home and was set alight by its commander on landing. The crew of twenty-one then surrendered to local Special Constable Edgar Nichols and a couple of others who marched them away to nearby Mersea Island. Earlier that same night many people in Essex had watched the death throes of another Zeppelin which had landed twenty miles away at Billericay, leaving no survivors. Allingham's diary is blank over this period but Dr Salter, looking out of his bedroom window in Tolleshunt D'Arcy, observed it,

> like a bright star to the SW. I saw it suddenly enlarge into a great moon, then a greater and then greater still until it looked like a huge fiery balloon, which then burst and fell slowly to earth taking 20 or 25 seconds to do so. When nearly down it seemed to pause and rain a shower of sparks like a rocket exploding.

Then, to the north east, there were more 'brilliant illuminations' lighting up the sky and all the earth around. The people of Little Wigborough and surrounding villages rushed out to watch the final moments of L-33 and Salter was soon called out to deal with a young man on a motor cycle who had broken his leg chasing after the police as they hurried to the scene. Salter described the Zeppelin close up as 'a huge wreck, like a Crystal Palace without its glass'. People soon began taking pieces of the twisted metal as souvenirs and the events of the night lived long in local memories. When Margery Allingham moved into Dr Salter's house almost twenty years later she found a large lump of Zeppelin in the garage.

The emotional atmosphere of the villages and the Allingham

household changed as the war progressed and there were practical difficulties as well. The Old Rectory was an old house in poor condition and therefore laborious to maintain. It had no water supply and all the water used had to be carted half a mile. A dry earth closet and earthenware urinal had been installed but there was still no bath and lighting was by paraffin. Men like Arthur Fletcher who had worked in the garden had gone away and domestic help in general was not easy to keep. Transport too was an increasing problem, especially in the early months when so many horses were commandeered for the army and the price of hay rocketed. Then there were the fuel shortages.

Allingham's working life was slower to change. The small group of halfpenny comics was not as bellicose as other Harmsworth publications. *Human Nature* included racial stereotypes such as the evil high-placed spy and the ultra-obedient Hun soldiery, but when Julian Marck has duped a group of ordinary German tradespeople into possible sedition, Allingham's London policeman just takes their names and addresses and lets them go with a caution. This fleeting incident is presented by Allingham as an exemplar of proper British behaviour. It is quite unlike the actual, shameful, persecution of German nationals, which has been described as 'an ugly chapter in British history'. Popular newspapers – such as Northcliffe's *Daily Mail*, the circulation of which rose 15 percent in the early days of the war – are held largely responsible for outbreaks of mob violence against inoffensive German shopkeepers, or anyone with German-sounding names. Such attitudes were not reflected in the pages of the *Butterfly* and its companions. At least not while Cordwell was still in charge and Allingham the lead serial writer.

The halfpenny comics concentrated on entertaining rather than exhorting their readers. *Merry & Bright* began a long series of Red Cross adventures and the *Favorite Comic* introduced the weekly adventures of 'Molly Madcap the Merry Munition-Maker'. Allingham rewrote an episode of *His Convict Bride* to include a dramatic courtroom appearance by a wounded VC and attempted to structure part of his serial *The Way of the World (Butterfly* 1916–1917) as a war prequel. A few Tommy jokes found their way onto the cartoon pages but otherwise it was almost as if the war did not exist. Some efforts were made to use contemporary allusions to market the *Firefly*, perceived as the weakest member of the group: 'Never mind if the price of bread has 'gone up' the *Firefly* hasn't. It's still ½d.' 'Wearing Khaki? Then he's entitled to a presentation copy of the *Firefly*, price ½d. Give him one.' But generally, until the spring of 1917, this group of papers continued to offer the mixture as before.

The real-time writing in *Human Nature* was not typical of Allingham's post-1914 contributions. His other big drama-stories were *Justice (Favorite Comic* 1915–1916), *London (Favorite Comic/Merry & Bright* 1916–1917) and *The Steel Clutch (Butterfly* 1916). They are set in fiction-times and in places that make no reference to actuality. Only by reading them with cognisance of surrounding national events (as a contemporary reader naturally would) can one notice how subtly the pre-war formula has adapted in response to new emotions and priorities.

The hero of *Justice*, for instance, relinquishes his blonde and gently-born first love in favour of gutsy, dark-haired, working-class Madge. The villain of *The Steel Clutch* presents himself as a superman demanding the aristocratic and beautiful heiress as his fit mate. His megalomania has a different tinge to previous villains as he frequently refers to his own 'higher intelligence' and makes quasi-philosophical assertions such as 'there is no evil but failure, no good but success'. (It is not a surprise to discover, from McFee's letters, that Allingham had been reading Nietzsche at this time.) Such small changes in the relative positions of plot elements reveal his engagement with the wider world and his journalistic awareness of shifts in the public mood.

As the war dragged on, structural change in the mass-market papers became inevitable. The primary audience for the comic-and-story papers had been young and there had been more boys with halfpennies to spend than there had been girls. Most of the men who volunteered for active service in 1914 and 1915 were also young – men in their late teens and early twenties. When conscription was introduced in 1916 it was usually the young and single who were sent abroad first. Even when the upper age limits were extended, the majority didn't get any older. In *Tommy* Richard Holmes generalises that 'one in four of the men who served were under twenty-five years old in 1914' and by 1918 'half the infantrymen in France are eighteen years old'. There was serving and there was dying. JM Winter calculates that age-related mortality was greatest at age twenty and Juliet Gardiner, describing the 'lost generation', suggests that 'perhaps more than 30 percent of all men aged between twenty to twenty-four in 1914 were killed in the war, and 28 percent of those aged thirteen to nineteen'.

Although, when social class as well as age is taken into account, the middle and upper classes can be shown to have suffered proportionately more than the working class (13.6 percent of officers killed as opposed to 11.7 percent of other ranks) yet in sheer numbers there is no doubt where the weight of casualties fell. Some 45,000 officers died between 1914 and 1918 but so did 677,785 'other ranks'. That represents fifteen times as many individual bereavements for 'the common people' and very much greater financial hardship in real terms for those working-class families who had no security apart from the labour of their most active members. As Van Emden and Humphries remind us, 'Bald figures on casualties, dead, wounded, even the shell-shocked, hide a mostly untold story of massive individual dislocation from family, friends, even society at large.' Over five million men, from England and Wales alone, served in the British Forces in the Great War. Their absence changed the daily lives of those who remained at home in innumerable practical as well as emotional ways.

These absences could not fail to have an impact on the penny and halfpenny paper markets. The data however is complex, as there was differentiation between and within social classes on grounds of physique. 'Their poor physical state probably saved the lives of many industrial workers who simply did not reach the minimum physical standard for military service, let alone combat duty,' comments Winter. So perhaps not as many of those Birmingham teenagers went as might have been expected. Perhaps it was their slightly more integrated contemporaries: those who had joined the boys' clubs, had fathers in steady, craftsman-level work and had been just a little better-nourished through their brief lives to date. Possibly the immediate impact of casualties fell a percentage point or two more heavily on buyers of the *Boy's Own Paper* than on the readers of the *Butterfly* and *Merry & Bright*. We cannot know.

The mass-market publishers concentrated on the home market rather than on readers abroad – though they were as keen to see their products in the trenches as they had been to distribute them across the empire. Lord Northcliffe wrote to Sir George Sutton: 'The sale of our periodicals, both newspapers and magazines, is paramount in France.' His context suggests that by 'paramount' he means dominant or at least ubiquitous. '*Titbits* and *Answers* are purchased by the Red Cross and distributed to the wounded soldiers in large numbers [...] The *London* and the *Red* are to be seen in very, very sad places, I can assure you.' These were market leaders among the penny papers and though Northcliffe does not mention the comics, it is likely that they too were being read by some of those millions of men at arms. *Comic Cuts*, the original and longest-running of all the AP comics, gave its name in trench slang to the daily intelligence reports. ES Turner, who was himself 'a little lad' in the Great War years, and became an authority on boys' papers, speaks of youths 'who, when their hour came, threw aside *Comic Cuts* and *The Magnet*, went over the top and died as virgins'.

There are occasional indications that the boys abroad were still thought of as among the readership of the comic-and-story papers. 'Are you sending a copy of *the Butterfly* to that friend of yours in the trenches?' asks the editor. A reader's comment is inserted under a page of Allingham's *The Steel Clutch*: '"Thrilling to a degree" is the verdict on this serial passed by a reader stationed at Cherbourg.' But such comments are rare. Unlike newspapers, such as the *Christian Globe* or John Leng's *People's Journal*, the comics did not include forms for direct subscription. Subscriptions would anyway have been unlikely to catch on as they required lump sum payments rather than the weekly expenditure of halfpennies. The most usual system whereby a young man in the trenches could continue to receive his *Merry & Bright* or *Butterfly* was by private mail. 'You should include this in your Christmas parcel to your brother in the trenches,' instructs the *Merry & Bright* editor. 'It will make him 'Merry & Bright' too.' Families and friends regularly sent letters and parcels to their relatives at the front and the arrival of the day's post became a part of trench life. The understanding was that whatever came would be shared within the unit – a man's surrogate 'family'. Pictures of dugouts show newspapers and magazines as well as books among the quasi-domestic items. Frank Richards wrote that he was proud 'to know that his writings had been read in the trenches in one war and in the Western Desert in the next.' He described the *Magnet* and the *Gem* in the First World War as 'canaries chirping in an earthquake'.

Early in 1917 the effective blockade of Britain by German submarines reduced supplies of many raw materials – including paper – to crisis levels. Rationing was (belatedly) introduced. The *Christian Globe*, already in financial trouble, could survive no longer and within the Amalgamated Press the chirruping halfpenny comics were among the first to suffer. The *Firefly* (ex-*Fun & Fiction*) was incorporated into the *Butterfly*; the *Favorite Comic* into *Merry & Bright*; prices were put up and, there were no more stories from Allingham. His current *Butterfly* serial, *The Way of the World* stopped abruptly, and after a continuous nine-year run nothing further appeared in that paper until some reprints were used in 1920.

This 'somewhat disorganised my little fiction factory', Allingham wrote later. Fred Cordwell had joined up and the mixed-age, mixed-gender readership had fragmented. Allingham himself, now earning two guineas per thousand words for his work within this group, was probably too expensive in hard times. Perhaps also his serials were less popular? The new editor of the *Butterfly* and *Merry & Bright* preferred fictions that were briefer, more fantastical, more war-like and, apparently, aimed at younger readers.

It seemed to work – from the AP's point of view. Later in the summer of 1917, managing director Sir George Sutton, was able to reassure his chief: 'Business at the AP is very good indeed. This is the holiday week of course when everything is generally up. *Answers* is particularly good, 331,000 and sold out and the ½d papers which were raised to 1d have started to go up for the first time.' This cheerful note serves as a reminder of the extent to which life on the Home Front retained a veneer of normality with seaside holidays being taken even within earshot of the guns across the Channel. The nation came close to starvation in 1917 but the AP's gross receipts managed to show an increase.

'Although Baron Stolly was a famous person in his own country, here he was shut up in a coal cupboard by a little London street-arab'

Chapter Seventeen
1915: The Happy Home and Woman's Weekly

The loss of his main customer was evidently a shock for Allingham. Had it not been for the increased earning power of British women it could have been a financial disaster. His annual income had been high in the years immediately before the war when he was writing so prolifically for the *Butterfly* group as well as continuing to supply leaders and occasional serials for the *Christian Globe* and advertising copy for JC Francis. From £549 in 1909 and £655 in 1910 his earnings had shot up as his rate of pay per thousand words doubled and he accrued more reprint rights to sell. His policy of never parting with copyrights except in extreme need paid off handsomely as the rights to popular serials could be sold several times over. *Mother Love*, the most successful, was sold ten times in his lifetime as well as spawning at least four distinct derivatives, each of which could also be sold repeatedly.

In 1912, his peak year, Allingham had earned £1,210. His total annual income remained just over £1,000 even through 1916. Figures for the next ten years have not survived but anxiety about money becomes a constant theme in his letters and diaries. The two older children had started at boarding schools, income tax rose and so did the cost of living generally. Perhaps Allingham's expectations had also crept up. He and Em had always liked to eat out when in London; now it was Frascati's, Gatti's, the Cheddar Cheese or the Criterion rather than the ABC teashop. When Allingham was in London on business he usually stayed at the Strand Palace Hotel (5s 6d for a single room with breakfast) – with the children too at holiday times. By 1916 he and his brother Phil had taken over almost the entire shareholding of the *Christian Globe*, which was losing money hopelessly. A photographic redesign was tried but paper rationing supplied the *coup de grâce*. A sale was made but it seems unlikely that either the Allinghams or any of the remaining small investors got their money back.

In the early months of 1914 Allingham had begun supplying reprint fiction to *Sunday Hours*, a superficially evangelical penny paper published by John Leng of Dundee. Religion, however, no longer functioned as the main selling point for a family paper and *Sunday Hours* soon re-titled itself the *Happy Home*. As the war split families apart so the readership of these papers became more exclusively female. The *Happy Home* recommended itself to its readers as an escape from everyday problems. 'In these times it is not good for us to sit studying the war news all day; a little light reading does us good now and then, and in the pages of the *Happy Home*, the RIGHT paper for the family circle, you will find all your needs supplied.' Younger women, working for better wages in the factories than they had earned in domestic service, had a little more money to spend on their own entertainment. John Leng (in association with DC Thomson Ltd) offered them *My Weekly*. It too used Allingham reprints.

Soon Allingham started writing directly for this new audience. His stories no longer shared the action between couples, as his *Butterfly* serials had done, but focused solely on the heroines whose survival was at stake, together with the survival of their children. Readers of the *Happy Home*, it seemed, had an appetite for maternal suffering and child insecurity – as long as it was safely displaced onto gentry families, whose problem might be finding the money to keep the child's pony, not finding the money to pay the rent or put food on the table. Public emotion around motherhood, already high before the outset of war, swiftly rose higher – to a point where death in childbirth could be equated with dying on the battlefield. Public interest in woman as part of the workforce came a little later.

The first story written specifically for *Happy Home* readers opened on 10 October 1914 while Allingham was refocusing *Human Nature* for the *Butterfly*. *Don't Leave Us, Mummy!* was a *Mother Love* derivative evoking emotions around maternal anguish and protectiveness. It highlighted the vulnerability of children in a world of absent fathers and cruel stepmothers and used the same *East Lynne*-inspired trope of the disguised mother. *Mother Love* itself had already appeared in the *Happy Home*'s companion paper, *My Weekly*, as *Spare My Children!* 'The most intensely pathetic story that has ever been written' announced the editor. In late 1914-1915 it ran in the *Christian Globe* and was taken by the *Happy Home* as soon as *Don't Leave Us, Mummy!* finished. *Don't Leave Us, Mummy!* then moved to the *Firefly* as *The Drama of Life*. Later in 1916 Allingham supplied the *Happy*

Home with *The Heart of a Mother* and in 1918 with *A Mother at Bay*, still commodifying the same emotions into near identical formulae with just a twist to the plot and a change of setting to make the stories feel different.

Neither the *Happy Home* nor *My Weekly* was notable for humour, sparkle or originality. They were comfort papers – none the worse for that, if that's what their readers required – but not such fun to write for as the *Butterfly* group. Nor did they pay as well. Meanwhile, and fortunately for Allingham, the AP was developing its own contender for the *My Weekly* market, the younger working-woman. 'It was in 1916 that two determined women journalists, Maudie Hughes and Winifred Johnson, first climbed the stairs of the Amalgamated Press. Between them they were to run a newer-than-1917 feminist paper, *Woman's Weekly*.'

It really is a pity that no one has written a proper history of the Amalgamated Press. From 1888 those mass-market Harmsworth magazines and their hustling, newly professionalised editors garnered the pennies and halfpennies – the many millions of pennies and halfpennies – that made possible the *Daily Mail*, *Daily Mirror*, the Northcliffe *Times*. The structure of twentieth-century periodical publishing was established, for better or worse, from the accumulated profits made by *Answers*, *Comic Cuts* and the rest. Marx had explained it before it even happened but, for those of us who are a little slower, a properly researched, independent account of the early years would be extremely valuable – and might give those pioneering editors their due. Winifred Johnson, for instance, did not come up those AP stairs for the first time in 1916. She had been tramping up different sets of AP stairs since the early days in Tudor Street where she had worked on *Forget-me-Not*, the fourth Harmsworth paper, established in 1891. Nothing ever outsold

Comic Cuts and *Answers* but *Forget-me-Not* was consistently profitable – once it had abandoned some initial pretensions to gentility and found its audience of shop-girls and domestic servants. The First World War, as is well known, widened the range of jobs available to women. It also made women as workers very much more visible and paid many of them slightly better wages. The new-look *Woman's Weekly* was intended to profit from this.

The internal evidence of the magazine suggests that Johnson was transferred to *Woman's Weekly* in the autumn of 1915, not 1916. That was when Maud Hughes, Em Allingham's sister, arrived. Having started her working life as an assistant in a stationer's shop she had subsequently been employed as a clerk at the Post Office and then had worked briefly for the *Daily Sketch* – apparently at Allingham's prompting. He had also suggested that she should be appointed manager of the *Christian Globe* although there were no obvious vacancies. Only Arthur, of all the Allingham brothers, had joined up at this stage of the war though Claude's name is absent from the diaries for a while and Tod, the youngest joined in 1918.

The AP, being so much larger, was showing the gaps more swiftly. 'Before the end came, some twelve hundred men – directors, editors, managers, sub-editors, book-keepers, clerks, printers and office boys – had left their desks for the trenches.' 'Feminine assistants' were urgently required. Allingham wrote a letter on Maud's behalf in June 1915 and in August Maud went for an interview. Ralph Rollington's daughter, cousin Grace Allingham, went with her. It must have been a giggly journey as the two women decided to change skirts in the taxi. There was jubilation at Layer Breton when Maud's telegram arrived: 'Got it!' It was followed the next day by a letter giving particulars of her interview. This crossed in the post with a letter to her from

Allingham giving the price of *Her Own Game*, a serial he had already planned to sell her.

Woman's Weekly soon looked different. Out went the religious and royal articles and in came a series of female detective stories featuring Phinella Martin, a wealthy private investigator who indulged in such stylish eccentricities as decorating her entire apartment in black and white. These were probably the work of several hands, among them Herbert and Em Allingham – and not inconceivably Maud herself. Editors often did pop a story of their own into long-running series – or supplied plot ideas that others turned into narrative. Phinella Martin has features in common with Margery Allingham's female sleuth in the 1930s series 'Darings of the Red Rose' (which Margery claimed to have based on a character of her mother's). She also resembles the lady detectives in the *Comic Cuts* series to which Allingham had contributed a decade earlier. Unfortunately there is nothing in Allingham's archive that fixes an attribution. All that is certain is that Phinella Martin detective stories commenced in *Woman's Weekly* when Maud arrived at the paper, and ended when she left.

The Girl Who Waited at Home, the first serial story published by the new editors, was certainly a product of the Layer Breton fiction factory. It was attributed to 'Jess & E Allanwood' and was followed by others from the same pen. 'Jess and E Allanwood', 'Tess Allanwood' or 'Tess Allenwood' were all pseudonyms for Herbert and Em working in partnership for 'Maud's magazine' – as Allingham habitually called it, ignoring the fact that Winifred Johnson was the senior and very much more experienced editor. The '-wood' may have been something of a family in-joke as Maud had recently married the *Daily Sketch* sportswriter 'Teddy' Wood. This had to remain a diplomatic secret as, even in wartime, there was still some residual expectation that women would resign their jobs on marriage. Maud – like Harold Garrish, Fred Cordwell and Winifred Johnson – stayed with the AP for the rest of her working life. Allingham was possibly making the same little joke in a 1917 *Woman's Weekly* serial. At the end of instalment one of *The Fascinating 'Miss' Forrest* the innocent-looking heroine gives herself away as she drops a wedding ring in her flight. (Does 'Forrest' suggest 'Wood'?)

As both Maud Hughes and Teddy Wood were working for the same company, and, after the war, frequently for the same paper, it would be surprising if their marriage was completely unsuspected. A passage in one of Lord Northcliffe's letters to the AP chief Sir George Sutton indicates that he knew quite well that another valued female employee was married but chose to ignore this fact. She, like Maud, was referred to as 'Miss'. Editorially, *Woman's Weekly* (while Maud was there) supported married women who worked outside the home and was bold enough to suggest that the 'business girl' might get more out of marriage than her 'dull stay-at-home sister'. This went a step further than Allingham's assertion in the *London Journal* more than a decade earlier, that the business girl might make a more attractive bride. *Woman's Weekly* also supported married women who hoped to stay 'in business' after the war was over. It argued not only that the extra income might be an important factor in a period of rising prices but also that going out to work might be more interesting than staying at home with housework and children. Nevertheless, warned the magazine, the married woman at work must be careful not to abuse her position by failing to show solidarity with her fellow-employees when pressing for pay-rises. 'She must make it clear to herself that she is not a wife who is a worker but a worker who is a wife.'

Maud did not have children. Em, who did, had not worked outside the home since her marriage. Her children did not give her much thanks for this – Margery and Joyce both stigmatise their mother as hurtful and un-loving and the only surviving comment from Phil comes in a letter where he recalls that Em was 'more than usually beastly' to their governess. After the governess left, in January 1915, he and Margery were sent away to school. It may have been their absence, worries about money or possibly some sisterly competitiveness that encouraged Em to commence her first full-length serial story soon after Maud joined the AP. They had a close relationship but one which could be stormy. Some of *Woman's Weekly*'s feminist editorials about the boringness of domesticity may have struck a nerve with Em, living her comparatively isolated rural life with her wayward and ungrateful children.

None Other Gods, Em's first serial, was written for the *Christian Globe*. It is a redemption story in which Molly, a cosseted young woman, discovers that her handsome fiancé is a rack-renting landlord. She meets the children around his tenement block: 'Their little noses were scarlet and they all looked almost perished with cold. There was a peculiar drawn look upon all their faces which the girl did not understand. Was it possible they were hungry?' Her father initially sides with Rex, her fiancé, and accuses Molly of being 'like most women [...] You want the good things of life but you don't want to know too much about how they are got.' Molly acknowledges that there has been some truth in this but she is determined to change. When Rex will not reduce his rents, she breaks off the engagement and finds new purpose in life attempting to help poor families. The published story is ascribed to 'Emmie Allingham' but it's clear from Allingham's diaries that he was fully involved in its composition.

Once again, as in the Ealing days, Herbert and Em were working in partnership. It is not possible to say who wrote what – and it probably varied from story to story. (I find it hard to believe that Em had no input into *A Work-Girl's Love Story*, contributed by Allingham to the *Christian Globe* in 1913 and reprinted as *Molly the Milliner* in *My Weekly*. It is set so precisely in the world where she had worked before her marriage.) In general terms the longer the serial, the more was contributed by Allingham. He would also 'correct' the work that Em produced. I believe that her hand in a story can often be seen in the inclusion of precise details of dress, colour and textiles which are not often found elsewhere in Allingham's work. Molly, for instance, wears 'a dress of shell pink ninon with an edging of fur' on the evening she breaks off her engagement. 'Emmie Allingham's' or 'Tess Allenwood's' stories are shorter than Allingham's usual productions and they are closer to romance than to fairy tale. There are no bizarre disguises, Gothic locations, undetectable poisons or other melodramatic improbabilities that Allingham appears to have enjoyed. Neither are there any of his Dickensian eccentrics.

The best of Tess Allenwood's *Woman's Weekly* serials is *Presumptuous Polly or The Girl Who Looked Like Gladys Cooper*. The heroine here is a typist, living in Clapham and earning 30 shillings a week. The first instalment of this story was written by Em when she was still engaged on *None Other Gods* and was then continued through 1916 by Herbert. It's a romantic-comic serial playing on the themes of identity confusion and rags-to-riches wish-fulfilment. With characteristic marketing flair Maud Hughes included an endorsement from the actress, Gladys Cooper, herself:

Polly Parsons is a very delightful girl. Her adventures as my double become more interesting and amusing each instalment and I have greatly enjoyed reading about her. What I like best is that there is no mercenary motive in her acceptance of the double role that is forced upon her by reason of her extraordinary resemblance to me. The adventures are the outcome of a real girlish spirit which is British in every sense of the word. At heart Polly is a good-hearted, lovable girl and I should be delighted to meet her.

Allingham sold reprint rights to Leng's but I have not been able to trace where it was used. Allingham's *Her Own Game* – which he wrote at the same time as *Presumptuous Polly* but which he had offered to Maud as early as August 1915, actually ran first in the Leng-Thomson magazine *My Weekly* under the title *Her Luck in London*. These two, almost concurrent, printings of the same story in rival magazines offer valuable insight as how context can affect the meaning of a story. *Her Own Game* is a story of a young girl who accepts the sort of risky impersonation deal that might previously have been offered to a hero (for example in *His Convict Bride*). Allingham supplied its introductory editorial puff:

A poor girl – so poor that she does not know where her next meal is to come from – is suddenly offered wealth and all that wealth can buy.

In return she is only asked to play a part – to be an actress, not behind the footlights, but on the stage of Real Life.

She cannot resist the temptation to seize the tempting prize which the hand of Fate dangles before her wondering eyes, and so she becomes embarked upon a series of amazing adventures with only her own brave heart and her woman's wit to save her from disaster.

This story is identical in both papers but is adapted to readers' presumed requirements by editorial signposting and by the style of the illustrations. The *Woman's Weekly* illustrations, by artist Charles Horrell, are crisp and lively and the editorial headings emphasise risk-taking, excitement and suspense. Anonymously contributed *My Weekly* pictures play more obviously to the rags-to-riches theme (one of the magazine's favourites). The heroine is provincially dressed and is frequently depicted in a pleading position. The reader is expected to feel 'sympathy' with her predicament. Editorially she is described as 'caught in the web of Fate' whereas the real point of the story, not missed by *Woman's Weekly*, is that this heroine has chosen to take her life into her own hands. 'Her instinct told her that her only chance was in a deliberate, unhesitating audacity.'

'Sympathy' is not a prime quality of the wartime *Woman's Weekly*. During the period of Maud Hughes's involvement it was tough-minded and assertive in its advice to readers. Domesticity was not ignored – there was plenty of household-management advice offered to 'Tommy's wife on 17s 6d a week'. There was also an abundance of factual information about careers, including an in-house information bureau. 'We have helped hundreds of readers find war jobs. Let us help you.'

Unlike Johnson, who had already spent most of her working life with the AP, Hughes had recent relevant experience of earning a living as a woman outside journalism. The advice was practical – what training would be needed, what hours usually worked, rates of pay and even possibilities for post-war continuation. *Woman's Weekly* correctly anticipated that many of its readers would be thrown out of work after the war so advised them either to consider newly developed careers, such as being a 'phone-girl', which had no tradition of male tenure, or to seize opportunities to build up sidelines, such as insurance agent work, which could provide useful fall-back income. Emotional problems related to women's work are also considered. When the girl wage-earner returns home, for instance, she may find that she is no longer integral to her family's daily life. 'Independence is a splendid thing,' comments the editor, 'but we must pay the price for it.'

Maud Hughes is described in the Fleetway House magazine as 'a tartar to work for though the kindest woman on earth.' Her niece, Margery, later ascribed her aunt's success as an editor to her instinctive understanding of her readers, her closeness to them coupled with an ability to analyse this. She also possessed formidable drive and determination. 'Aunt M was a power and an authority who had learned how to be popular by using her head: she was used to making money and spending it and getting her own way.' Although Maud and Em could quarrel fiercely, they remained close. When there was one invasion scare too many at Layer Breton, Em did not hesitate to send her the children. Margery remembered: 'She and my aunt, her sister, had been having a period of distinct coolness and were not on speaking terms. Mother had lots of friends in London but she sent us to Aunt.'

This was most likely to have happened in March 1917. Dr Salter's diary records a warning on the 24th 'that the enemy's fleet was out. I immediately sent a message to all my head men. We were all at attention. Great excitement.' As one of those head men was Special Constable Allingham it seems likely that this was the meeting that precipitated the decision to send the children away.

> The Old Doctor, who was an important person locally at that time and who was allowed to wear a uniform and a brass hat occasionally [...] had called to see the grown-ups and there had been a hasty conference in my father's study. I had gone nosing round, sniffing excitement in the wind, and had gathered from the muttering in the kitchen that the threatened invasion that had been talked about for months, was actually upon us. [...] When I heard that the grown-ups had decided to bundle us children off to London there and then with Cissie I was more relieved than ever in my life before or since.

There were tidings the following day but the local emergency committee remained in a state of 'expectancy'. On 27 March the cipher warning was cancelled 'so all quiet again as regards invasion'.

March 1917, however, marked the beginning of the closure of the Layer Breton fiction factory. The success of *Driven From Home* and the steady flow of sequels had made it possible to work from such a relatively inconvenient location. After paper rationing was introduced the prices of the halfpenny comics rose to a penny and it would not be long before the penny *Woman's Weekly* would be put up to a penny-halfpenny. Soon they would all be twopence and the payment to writers going down accordingly. Herbert and Em stayed only to hand in their notice to the Rev. Luard, their landlord, and close up the house before they followed their children to London. From December 1917 their new home was a flat in a large mansion block in Bayswater. Margery said that they felt 'like pigeons in a sealed dovecote'. For her, retrospectively, this was the beginning of an eighteen-year paradise-lost-and-regained saga that would eventually lead her and her husband back, with almost the inevitability of one of her father's serials, to take possession of Dr Salter's house in Tolleshunt D'Arcy just in time for the Second World War.

'You will order Kingsley, at the point of a revolver, to descend in the German lines'

Chapter Eighteen
1918: The People's Journal

'The wounded soldier entered the shop, and he walked very slowly, leaning heavily upon a stick'

At the beginning of 1917, when conscription was fully operational and even older married men, like the 49-year-old Herbert Allingham, might be called to justify their remaining out of uniform, William McFee had written to wish him 'a happy, prosperous and non-military new year. Personally I am convinced that you can best serve your country by continuing to entertain those half million people a week and I hope that nothing will happen to take you off it.' There are no diaries or letters for 1917 that record how Allingham coped with the move back to London and the disruption of his fiction factory. He produced only two new serials that year – *The Fascinating Miss Forrest* for *Woman's Weekly*, and *Baby Jess* for the *Happy Home*.

Allingham had begun his career as a writer for boys and had then widened his knowledge of readers and their tastes on the *Christian Globe* and *London Journal*, both of them family papers. His best work had been done for the predominantly adolescent male and female readers of the halfpenny comic-and-story papers. Now he needed to adapt his style to a more exclusively female audience and also to changes in the public mood. Fictional relationships in his new stories became more complex, less ideal. The young couples at the centre of the pre-war *Butterfly* group stories had never doubted one another, though everything external conspired against them. From 1915–1916, second choices and more surprising marriages had become usual. The hero of *London* (written for the *Favorite Comic*) has lost his wife to the man who has betrayed him but finds his eventual happiness with the lively young daughter of the judge who sent him to prison.

Once Allingham is writing for a predominately female readership, some of his husbands become older, more jealous, more controlling – and more likely to be wrong. *The Heart of a Mother,* written for the *Happy Home* in 1916, had been the first of Allingham's drama stories where there is fault within the marriage. *Baby Jess* (*Happy Home*, 1917) is the innocent victim of adult betrayal and mistrust (though here the father behaves better than either of the women involved). Allingham's 1918 stories – *The Green Ey'd* for *Woman's Weekly* and *A Mother At Bay* for the *Happy Home* – revolve around the relatively new themes of jealousy and marital misunderstanding as well as intrigue, murder and those ever-elusive inheritances.

One topic Allingham's 1917–1918 readers did not find entertaining was the war. Back in 1915 when he was sending the hero of *Human Nature* off to serve his country, editors might attempt to use the national situation to promote serials that had no genuine connection. Spy scandals were in the news that year. When the *People's Journal*, in Dundee, ran a fifth reprint of Allingham's *A Devil of a Woman* (first published 1893) the editor did his best to make it topical.

> Within the past few weeks, the country has been astounded by extraordinary revelations concerning people who have lived double lives, posing in our midst as loyal citizens, while all the while they were engaged in the deepest villainy, the most ungrateful and the blackest treachery.
>
> Around just such a character there has been written a powerful and arresting story. It concerns a woman whose beauty, charm and grace of manner were combined with a cunning and a cruelty that amply justifies the title The Wickedest Woman Alive.
>
> Read this great story. It will interest you, entertain you and teach you something you do not know about the world in which you live.

Private John Gilfeather, aged thirty-two, of the King's Own Scottish Borderers, was a regular reader of the *People's Journal*, as was his wife, Isabella. He had left his coal merchant business to join up and was now in Northern France. Isabella would have sent the *People's Journal* to her husband in the trenches, as families were encouraged to do in order to maintain close contact. Sadly John Gilfeather never got the chance to read more than the first instalment of *The Wickedest Woman Alive* as he was killed on the first day of the battle of Loos, 25 September 1915. His son Denis remembers the morning that the news came. Mrs Gilfeather was serving breakfast.

> The kid was in the high chair and she was serving it out when there's a hammering at the door. I remember her slight annoyance at the disruption when she went to answer it. And then I saw her opening

the door and taking the letter. She tore it open, she was nervous, her hands started shaking and then she read it and collapsed on the floor.

John Gilfeather was part of the 6th Battalion of the KOSB. The bombardment of the previous days, which should have cut the barbed wire and driven the Germans back from their front trenches, had been unsuccessful and the men of the 6th Battalion were trapped and mown down helplessly. There were problems too with British-used chlorine gas blowing back onto the advancing troops. Some 358 men from John Gilfeather's battalion were killed or missing that day with a further 272 wounded or gassed. The Dundee *People's Journal* publishedpages of photographs as well as the names of the dead – together with desperate pleas for information about 'missing Soldier heroes'. Given the strong local recruitment basis of the battalions, pages such as these must have had an appalling impact on individual communities. Even today they make painful reading and it's hard to imagine many Scottish readers getting emotionally involved in the fantastical exploits of Allingham's Madge Milton and Frank Darcy in those bereaved autumn weeks of 1915.

By 1918 Allingham had been close to a real-life spy story. Although he and his family were now living in London he had continued to rent a holiday house on Mersea Island, eight miles from Layer Breton. In early January 1918 the weather was bad and Allingham found their small semi-detached house, Glyn-y-Mor, 'a bit crowded' as he struggled to keep up his word count during a family New Year holiday. Then everyone's attention was distracted as a wireless transmitter was discovered in the empty attic next door. The police were called, then more police as fifth-column activity was suspected.

The Island's position at the mouth of the River Blackwater would make it a potentially significant location for invaders and Glyn-y-Mor is at the top of a slight elevation to the seaward side of West Mersea – conditions that might have been chosen for clear transmission or reception of hostile messages. The transmitter was beamed on Germany and had been in use.

Allingham was repeatedly interviewed but not, apparently, suspected of any treachery. He was still, at least nominally, an Essex special constable and had remained in close touch with his friend and fellow-Freemason Dr Salter. Salter spoke to the Chief Constable about the matter and, although Joyce Allingham remembered the incident well into her old age, the family soon returned as usual to London (or to boarding school) and Allingham's diary tells nothing more. Dr Salter's diary for 1918 records regular air raids over both Essex and London, mines washed up on Mersea Island's beaches, attacks on nearby Harwich, local invasion scares and casualties and, when the wind was in a certain direction, the grim and distant rumble of the Flanders guns. None of this – neither the wireless affair nor any other manifestations of war – was used as material in Allingham's fiction.

The casualty closest to his own family, Em's brother, Wal Hughes, had been one of approximately 8,000 Canadians and British wounded or killed at the battle of Mont Sorrel, near Ypres, in June 1916. His body was never recovered so he is one of the 54,900 British and Empire soldiers who died between 4 August 1914 and 15 August 1917 who are commemorated only on the Menin Gate memorial. There must have been a long slow period of dying hope, both for his mother and sisters in England and for his widow, Lilian, in Manitoba.

Allingham experienced air raids in London but seems to

have treated them with indifference. On 18 February 1918 he was at the National Sporting Club watching a boxing match with his brother-in-law Teddy Wood. 'Raid came during the big fight. No one took any notice. Came out at 11.30. Walked to Oxford Circus amid the sounding of the All Clear bugles. Tube to Edgware Road. Walked home.' On 7 March two or three bombs fell in Bayswater, 'one very near', and on 21 March he was at the cinema when an air raid warning was flashed on the screen at 8.40. Most of the people went out but Allingham was still there at 9.20 when the screen announced All Clear.

Allingham was changed by the war. He was left, said Margery, with a hatred of Germans, quite different from his tolerant and interested pre-war attitude when he had read occasional German magazines and corresponded briefly with a fellow writer/editor in Konigsberg.

> Long after the last war it used to astound me that such an extraordinarily tolerant and logical man should grow so coldly savage whenever he spoke of them. 'They have the gift of offence,' he used to say, and I think it may be that there is more in that than I realised. My father believed in Tolerance [...] and in his case I think it was probably this which the 1914 Germans had attacked and all but destroyed and he hated them for that.

That was his personal feeling. Professionally Allingham's job was to continue to entertain, to help readers escape their own grief, war-weariness and daily struggle. He sought entertainment himself. His 1918 diary gives the impression of restlessness: an irritable searching for amusement, new ideas, new markets. He and Em ate regularly at Frascati's in Oxford Street – with the children too when they were home. Christmas there, said Margery, was 'falsely gay'. He played chess, followed up commercial openings, met relatives and friends. As well as visits to the theatre and art galleries Allingham regularly spent two or three evenings each week in the cinema, either alone or with Em or Margery. He was not always complimentary about what he saw but was clearly excited by this new medium – as were his readers. He noted one film that used the same 'mother love' theme he was finding so successful and he hoped, briefly, that *Driven from Home* might be adapted for the screen. He negotiated with a film agent over a comic short story, 'Simon's Evening Out', but nothing transpired.

Living like this in London was not economical. There were school fees to be paid, rent on the London flat and the house in Mersea, occasional domestic help and care for Joyce, extra tuition for Phil and all those meals and tickets. Set lunch for one at Frascati's in the 1920s cost 4s 6d; set dinner 7s 6d. Perhaps not quite as much in 1918 but still a significant amount compared with 'Tommy's wife on 17/6d a week' who gleaned domestic tips from *Woman's Weekly*. Or the widowed Isabella Gilfeather in Dundee struggling to maintain herself and four young children on a pension of £1 2s 6d. One survey found that 12 percent of war widows died within a year of their husband's death. Isabella coped for two and a half years before she collapsed in 1918. Denis Gilfeather remembers:

> After Dad was killed Mum received the magnificent sum of £1 2s 6d that was her pension every week for herself and us four kids. It wasn't enough by any means. Life was very hard and Mum went down with erysipelas and became close to death. I felt my whole world was changing. The sunshine was leaving my life.

Allingham's earnings would have been riches for the Gilfeathers. While *The Green-Ey'd* was running during the first quarter of 1918 he was earning about 9 guineas a week with lump sums if he managed to sell any reprint rights: £68 for instance brought the *Happy Home* a revised version of *London* (abridged, and with some mildly political asides removed). But it wasn't sufficient. When *The Green-Ey'd* finished in May, his income slumped. On 12 June Allingham discovered he had only £8 left in the bank and withdrew £4. He tried to approach a new paper, *Woman's World*, but they wouldn't see him. Garrish, still at the AP, was sympathetic but had nothing to offer. Even the family copy-writing commissions had dried up. An exciting new serial was in prospect but couldn't come soon enough. Allingham was desperate.

He called at Cotterill and Cromb who acted as agents for the Dundee firms of John Leng's and DC Thomson. A meeting was set up for the following Monday, then Allingham and Em went out to *Tales of Hoffman* and afterwards to supper at Frascati's with his brother Phil and Phil's wife Ada. A few days later, when Cotterill telephoned suggesting a sale of copyrights, Allingham was in no position to refuse. He talked tactics with Phil and agreed with the agents that they should have a private meeting before the official session with William Harvey.

Harvey, the Leng-Thomson fiction editor, was an unobtrusively powerful figure. His office was in Bank Street, Dundee, where he commissioned or bought stories for the *Dundee Advertiser, Evening Telegraph and Post, Happy Home, People's Journal, People's Friend, My Weekly* and for the 3d series of *White Heather Novels.* He worked closely with the editors of the separate papers and travelled regularly down to the Fleet Street office to convey their requirements to writers or agents.

He had written directly to Allingham, in mid-May, to request 'a good holding story of the "East Lynne" type suitable for our weekly newspaper the *People's Journal*'. This was the first time Allingham had been asked to contribute to the *People's Journal* since September 1915 and the agent was delighted. 'There's a lot of money to be made in that corner if you lay yourself out for it,' he wrote eagerly.

Allingham was doing his best to oblige but he couldn't wait for the new serial to be discussed, commissioned, written, accepted, published and, eventually, paid for. He was obliged to offer Harvey a selection of copyrights – not for outright sale but on long leases. 'He is going to discuss my suggestions with his people. He is obviously satisfied and they want to secure copyrights but very cautious. Meanwhile I want money – Pity – Puts me at a disadvantage in negotiating.' The agents loaned Allingham £100 after this meeting but it took until December for a final agreement to be reached. Harvey purchased a twelve-year lease on thirteen serials. Allingham, however, was forced to concede the 'power to alter or condense' – something he resented. Once he had paid Cotterill and Cromb's commission and repaid the loan, he earned £392 but lost control of several major stories until the end of 1930. He also came to believe that 'his' plots were being passed round other hack writers on the Leng -Thomson payroll.

Meanwhile, with the immediate crisis staved off, he settled to work on Harvey's new commission for the *People's Journal*. This was the flagship publication in the Leng group and claimed the largest circulation of any paper north of the Forth – in excess of 250,000, with most copies being read several times. It was a weekly newspaper produced in Dundee in both national and local editions and had remained the favourite reading of

Mrs Gilfeather. Denis remembers that the arrival of the paper on a Saturday was the highpoint of his mother's week. His daughter, Irene, describes her grandmother and great-aunt talking over the happenings in their weekly serial and speculating eagerly about future developments. Irene's memories of the *People's Journal* are from a much later date than the publication of Allingham's serials but it seems likely that the style of discussion was much the same. She likened this to the way people might now discuss TV soaps.

In 1918 readers of the *People's Journal* were still being excoriated by news of the deaths of their husbands, sons, neighbours, friends. Deaths in the Scottish regiments serving on the Western Front were more than double those in English regiments (26 percent as opposed to 12 percent) since the Scottish troops were so often used as shock troops in the forefront of a major attack. Van Emden and Humphries suggest that the scale of family tragedy 'was probably greatest in Scotland'. Supplying suitable entertainment to 'hold' Scottish readers through any major offensive might seem a daunting task. Nevertheless Allingham covered the back of his agent's letter in calculations and sent Harvey a synopsis – a chore he never enjoyed. Th e editor replied at length.

Dear Mr Allingham,

I am favoured with your letter of 29th inst., embodying the synopsis of a proposed *People's Journal* story. Generally speaking we think this is on the right lines, but we shall be glad if you will give the following points your best consideration.

(1) So far as the synopsis goes the woman does not seem to have a very compelling reason for deserting her children. The reason, however, may be made sufficiently strong by what you write.

(2) With reference to your remark as to having a little more freedom in the *People's Journal*, we do not want to handicap you in any way, but at the same time we desire to state that we place great value on our stories having the ring of plausibility. Consequently we should like you to be as natural as possible in your incidents avoiding anything which might be called super-fantastic or anything of the ultra sensational atmosphere such as was prominent in the early chapters of your story 'The Steel Clutch', and in an earlier reprint story which we bought from you and which you will recall dealt with the work of a Russian Secret Society in London.

(3) As the *Journal* is a domestic newspaper you must be careful to avoid sexual questions or anything suggesting immorality.

(4) The impression left by the synopsis is that the story will be a rather sad one. We should like you to relieve it in some way but we do not wish you to get this effect by bringing in any low comedy character. We would rather prefer that the element of hope should be introduced by the workings of some character – it might be one of the grandmothers, or an aunt of the children whose business it would be to bring things finally right, and whose efforts towards this would always hold the sympathy of the reader.

These are suggestions only and not meant to bind you or cramp the development of the story in any way. Probably you already see a plan for getting this effect. We know we can safely leave the matter in your hands.

In these days of short sizes a first instalment must not exceed 6,000 words, but I know that you can get a good number within these limits. As I mentioned before, we want to start the story at once, and I shall be glad therefore to have the opening instalment at your earliest.

Harvey rejects both 'low comedy' and the super-fantastic. He wants plausibility, 'naturalness' and the appearance of sexual morality – or at least an avoidance of anything suggesting sexual immorality. He is also anxious that the *People's Journal* readers should never lose hope in an eventual happy ending.

There's no evidence that Allingham ever visited Scotland or met any of his readers there. Nevertheless he was a professional who 'got his living from studying the common people', as he said himself. He chose to follow the spirit rather than the letter of Harvey's instructions. *She Sinned for her Children* (editorially Scottish-ed as *For Love of Her Bairns*) dispenses with the husband completely. He and the heroine's brother have both died in action; her husband at the battle of the Marne, her brother in distant Salonika (where McFee had been stationed). The Will that should have provided for the heroine and her children has been left unsigned (a possible metaphor for the poor treatment of war widows and orphans.) Foolishly, indeed criminally, Mary Keith, the heroine, is persuaded to add her brother's signature. For the sake of her children.

This 'sin' immediately exposes her to blackmail and thence to enforced parting from her young son and daughter. Assumed dead, she returns, with the inevitable pair of heavily tinted glasses, to protect the children as their governess. There is a cruel sister-in-law who steps in as guardian and a sinister foreigner with both sexual and financial designs upon the heroine. Mary suffers, loses her looks but gains strength and self-reliance. 'Little trace remained of the gracious rounded beauty of those days. The face was now thin and pinched and lined with care. It was the face of one who has passed through bitter suffering and tragic despair.' Many of Allingham's readers would recognise that look. She is terrified by the forces ranged against her but once her older child, her son, has shown his true grit, she discovers the courage to dupe the scary sister-in-law and hit the predator over the head with a lighted lamp.

Mrs Gilfeather also pulled through with the aid of her son, Denis.

Your mother's in bed in hospital and they're prophesying her death. I remember saying to her, 'Now you canna go, Mum. I love you so much.' That's when she said to me, 'If anything happens to me, you'll look after the bairn and Annie' – that was the two youngest. I said 'Yes I'll do that.' And that's what I tried to do. Mum really didn't want the family broken up, she dreaded that. I done the things in the house, I began to take authority over the younger ones. Then after about six weeks, Mum started to recover. She was a fighter and though she was still weak, she managed to come home again.

Allingham's heroine realises that she has made a terrible mistake. She has ensured that her children are materially secure in their Kentish manor house – but her action has left them emotionally and physically vulnerable. Allingham calls the boy hero 'Raymond', a name not previously used in his fiction but carrying powerful contemporary resonances. Raymond Lodge, youngest son of the physicist Sir Oliver Lodge, had been killed in action in 1915 and was commemorated by his father in a best-selling memoir of 1916. Raymond Asquith, eldest son of the then Prime Minister, Herbert Asquith, was also killed in action in September 1916. This was a loss that seemed to prove that families of all social classes were united in their sacrifice. When Mary Keith returns in her *East Lynne* governess disguise, little Raymond is angry and adamant:

During these last few weeks he had suffered much. He had been insulted and cruelly treated. He had been caned. He, who never in his life before had received a blow.

But the bodily pain he had endured was as nothing compared with the violence done to his sense of justice.

It was this that maddened him and filled him with a secret, passionate desire to kill and destroy.

One consolation and only one he had. They had not conquered him. They had not made him say he was sorry. They had not made him admit they had any right to treat him as they did. He, the son of Lieutenant Douglas Keith had defied them all and he would defy them to the end. Whatever they did, he would never give in.

Mary begins to realise what she has done. 'What does it avail to have won wealth and success for him in the future if he is to endure thus now? If they break his spirit, if they crush and brutalise him, what kind of man will he be when the time comes for him to enjoy the fortune I have sinned to give him?' She offers Raymond the chance to run away but he is stubborn and means to 'stick it'. 'What, give up Lynwood? Give it up to her? No jolly fear. By rights I'm master here, and in a year or two I'll show her.' Mary learns from her son. '"The boy is right," she murmured to herself. "He will be master here one day. Until that time he must suffer and endure. I will stand by his side and help him to fight his battle."'

Denis Gilfeather would have been just a little younger than Allingham's fictional Raymond. His reminiscence of family life after his father's death presents a vivid picture of fear, endurance and the renegotiation of family relationships. He too tried to take responsibility though there was no manor house, no 'Lynwood'. Denis's way of supporting his mother was to take a job in a jute mill.

I was just a wee boy. I was only nine when I started in the mill [...] Anyway they badly needed the labour because all the men were gone. At the mill they gave young boys a new name, often the name of someone who'd been killed in the war, that was how they got round the rules. In the books I was down as David Morris, I found out later that he'd been killed at the front when only seventeen.

Every few months the school inspector would catch up with Denis and he'd be sent back to the classroom.

They'd be talking about verbs and nouns and semi-colons and I didn't know what they were speaking about but I could cope with that. I was a proud boy because when I got my pay and took it back home to my mum, I knew it would make her happy.'

Denis, like Raymond, was 'sticking it'. In 1918, when *For Love of Her Bairns* was the lead serial, the family were living on the Lochee estate, mill-workers' housing nicknamed 'Little Tipperary' because of the numbers of poor Irish immigrants crowded in there. Denis's mother, his aunt and his grandmother all continued to enjoy the *People's Journal*. Denis, however, would not have been able to join in unless someone in the family read the instalments aloud. Though a highly intelligent and determined personality, he learned little at school. It was not until he had officially left school and escaped the jute mills to work as a delivery boy that he successfully taught himself to read, using Edgar Rice Burroughs's *Tarzan* stories and Wild West novelettes before moving to the 'heavier stuff'. Reading, he says, 'was the only chance I had to find my feet'.

Looking back, in his eighties, Denis Gilfeather found it hard to forgive his schoolteachers for the savagery with which they beat him and his fellows, 'often when we had come to school so cold'. Allingham's Raymond tells his mother exactly why he hates and despises his aunt. 'She whips Bessie, and she likes to hear her cry. She likes it!' Allingham never condoned the physical punishment of the young and neither did many of his working-class readers. His fiction of Mary Keith, 'Lynwood' and 'young master' Raymond may seem about as far removed from the life of widowed Mrs Gilfeather in Lochee as Tarzan was a world away from her son Denis. Yet it succeeded in entertaining and involving sufficient numbers of the *People's Journal* readers to satisfy its editors. In Allingham's story suffering and struggle are transposed into the idiom of another class. War and death happen off stage. Strong emotional involvement is possible but so too is escapism. Young Raymond's and his mother's defiance could have focused the emotions of all who were refusing to give up, whatever their social class.

Allingham takes no notice of William Harvey's suggestion that he bring in some grandmother or aunt to make all well. Instead he makes the *deus ex machina* a wealthy and eligible officer, deeply indebted to the dead brother and ready to solve Mary's problems 'as with the touch of a magic wand'. (This wish-fulfilment character is called Harvey!) Of course it's not as easy as all that – by the time Major Dick Harvey declares himself (instalment nine) Mary has been forced into a Faustian pact with the villainous Sandro Dell. Allingham can afford to shock his readers with this disclosure, knowing that they will have recognised Harvey as Mary's potential saviour and will therefore be sufficiently confident in the eventual outcome to enjoy whatever plot twists are in store over the forthcoming weeks.

William Harvey was also satisfied. After only two instalments had been published (though more would have been approved) he contacted Allingham again with a request for a follow-up. 'We shall soon need to get a story to follow *She Sinned for her Children*. We should like this to be by you. I hope you will be able to send me an opening soon.' No synopsis was requested for this second story, *The Woman Pays*, and only the mildest of anxieties expressed for the heroine's future.

> As you know we do not like anything objectionable in the slightest way, and we are especially anxious to avoid anything that would throw Madge into the power of a man or give rise to anything coarse or suggestive. I mention the matter because of your title but at the same time I know your desire is to give us exactly the kind of story we like.

This was possibly the highest praise Harvey felt able to bestow. By the following month (January 1919) he had negotiated an agreement with Allingham's agents for 8,000 words a week of 'approved matter' payable at three guineas per thousand for forty weeks of every year. Allingham would be continuing to entertain.

Nan Seymour, out of work and starving – easy prey for an unscrupulous man

Chapter Nineteen
1921: The Kinema Comic

'I have quite made up my mind. You will write my next play!'a

FC Cordwell had been away from his papers in the last years of the war but he was back in charge of the *Butterfly* and *Merry & Bright* by 1919 and able to announce his first new comic since the *Firefly* in 1913. This new paper would be called *Cheerio!* and Allingham's work would be its prime attraction, just as it had been in Cordwell's new comics before the war.

> First and foremost there is to be a grand serial story by one of the most successful serial writers of the day.
>
> His work has appeared many times in *Merry & Bright* (and our companion paper, *The Butterfly*) from the first number onwards.
>
> To mention but a few of his successes; *The Girl Who Married a Scoundrel, Driven From Home, Ashamed of his Mother, Friendless, The Girl Without a Home*, etc.

Allingham was frequently introduced in this circumlocutory way, as if it were a guessing game to which no answer was ever provided. His successes were named: he never was. Readers were apparently expected to remember and be excited by the titles of his serials but not to recall their incidents sufficiently clearly to notice when the story was reissued with a new title and new names were given to the lead characters. Four of the five stories highlighted here would be brought out again, lightly disguised, within a few years of this announcement, together with most of the rest of Allingham's pre-1917 serials. It's possible that Cordwell's market research may have told him that the readership was now more narrowly defined by age than it had been previously. If the comics were read only by the new generation of teenagers and not by the decimated population of young adults then wholesale repetition might pass un-observed.

Reprinting was also an economy measure. *Merry & Bright* and the *Butterfly*'s cover prices had trebled during the war but all the signs indicate that they were produced to a very tight budget during the 1920s. Paper costs remained high and management may have been demanding an improved rate of profitability from individual editorial groups. The Amalgamated Press was now a large concern grandiosely accommodated. Its chairman and managing director, Sir George Sutton, earned £30,000 a year. When it was reconstructed in 1922, its capital amounted to £3,800,000 and by 1924 it was issuing 102 periodical publications. Allingham's rate of pay had not risen since 1912, yet over the next few years he would come under increasing pressure to cut his prices or lose the work.

Immediately after the war, however, the editors had some money to spend. New papers were authorised; new stories commissioned. *Judgement*, Allingham's newly written serial for the first numbers of *Cheerio!,* uses an idea of return and change that he also used in another new story of 1919, *The Mystery of Brandon Chase*. The returning hero of *Judgement/His Father's Son* is unrecognisable to his family and has not grown up exactly as expected; the returning daughter in *The Mystery of Brandon Chase* discovers that her father, who has remained at home, is oddly changed. Neither the hero nor the heroine of these formulaic drama-stories is returning from a war, yet the theme of family re-adjustment is unobtrusively appropriate.

Neither Cordwell nor Allingham had been in touch recently with younger readers and the initial success of *Cheerio!* may have been only moderate. A fresh approach was not far away. *Cheerio!*'s next serial from the Allingham fiction factory was *The Fellow Who Loved Violet Hopson,* credited to 'E Allingham' but written jointly by Herbert and Em. The story takes film fascination as its starting point. Billy Poole, a young village lad, is so overwhelmed by his first visit to the cinema, and especially by screen heroine Violet Hopson, that he abandons Mary, his actual sweetheart, in quest of the celluloid image. He forfeits his home and his money as well as his good sense.

The Fellow Who Loved Violet Hopson has some features in common with *Presumptuous Polly: The Girl Who Looked Like Gladys Cooper,* which 'Tess Allen-Wood' had written for *Woman's Weekly.* By the time it was published in *Cheerio!* Maud Hughes was running a new magazine for the Amalgamated Press. This was the *Picture Show* – her great achievement and a major success over the next forty years.

The *Picture Show* carried lengthy excerpts from the opening instalment of *Cheerio!*'s serial together with a letter from Violet Hopson. Like Gladys Cooper, Hopson claimed to have read the story 'with great interest [...] I think it a very charming tale'. Although Hopson is calling it a story, rather than allowing the pretence that the adventures are 'real', the joint authors leave themselves plenty of scope to play with their readers' possible confusions between art and life. 'She's [Hopson's] only a picture,' Mary tells the infatuated Billy before leaving home to become an actress herself and a friend of the 'real' Violet Hopson. 'She is so sweet and always so nice,' claims fictional Mary – a sentiment which would surely have been taken for truth by *Cheerio!* readers who were also Hopson fans.

In the *Picture Show* Hopson is placed at the centre of network of commercial endorsements. Hughes ran a series of 'Violet Hopson's Beauty Tips' in close proximity to advertisements for products such as 'Harlene Hair Drill' (copy for which was often provided by Allingham and which may have been brokered by his brothers' agency). An art plate of Hopson was the *Picture Show*'s special December offer whilst readers of *Woman's Weekly* were offered a 'companion plate' of her leading man, Stewart Rome. Forty years earlier a similar offer in an Allingham family paper might have featured a portrait photograph of the Rev. Charles Haddon Spurgeon or Rev. T de Witt Talmadge.

Cinema audiences had increased dramatically during the war years. Men and women as well as boys and girls began attending regularly and, as the cleanliness and comfort of the picture palaces improved, so did their appeal to the respectable classes and to families. The Allinghams went at least once or twice every week – sometimes more often – as well as to theatres and other London entertainments. By 1921 Margery was living full time in the Bayswater flat with her parents. Phil was at the Forest School, Snaresbrook, and Joyce, aged eight, was boarding at New Hall convent school near Chelmsford in Essex. Margery had enrolled at the Regent Street Polytechnic to study elocution and drama as well as reading English literature with a private tutor, rather as Allingham himself may have done at the same age. Similarly, her partisan following of Ernest Milton, a Shakespearean actor, in his various roles throughout the year recalls Allingham's own youthful enthusiasm for Henry Irving in different guises.

There was so much more entertainment available to teenage Margery and her family than there had been forty years earlier to her father. Some had a home-grown quality as she and her fellow-students frequently gave recitations or organised amateur theatrical performances as part of their college life but this was atypical. For most people – especially those youngsters who might be buying and swapping copies of *Merry & Bright*, the *Butterfly* or *Cheerio!* – entertainment was highly organised, slickly commercial and centred on the cinema.

By 1919, writes cinema historian Eric Rohde, 'Hollywood was everywhere recognised as the dream capital of the world.' 'Dream' is the important word. The same pattern of capitalistic accumulation and centralisation that had taken the print industry from a craft through a manufacturing stage to an all-inclusive factory system had happened much more swiftly in the film world. A small number of powerful studios had the actors, the scriptwriters, the technical personnel and the machinery of production bound together by draconian contracts, feeding their products seamlessly into the networks of distribution. Another of *Das Kapital*'s powerful insights into the working of capital concerned the 'fetishising of the commodity' – maximising its appeal to people's imaginations as well as to their material needs, thus increasing profitability for minimal extra input. The culture of celebrity is an outstanding example. The box-office value of an actor's participation in a play or film can be hugely magnified simply by emphasising the actor's fame – a fame that exists mainly because it has been brought into existence by conscious promotion and marketing.

This is not a phenomenon confined to the cinema, of course. The impact of CH Spurgeon's sermons or Moody and Sankey's evangelical tours was all the greater because the portrait photographs, the personal anecdotes, the statistics of their success had been so energetically disseminated by papers such as the *Christian Globe*. People like Molly Hughes's mother in Islington were attracted to a meeting simply because she'd heard so much about the evangelists. She had no interest in their message but still spent money on a hymn book as she left. Now the Hollywood stars were getting the same treatment. It was not just their film exploits that fed viewers' dreams but carefully disseminated information about all aspects of their lives and personalities that made them supersize.

In England Maud Hughes was at the forefront of these developments. One of her innovations at *Woman's Weekly* had been the regular cinema column she wrote from 1916 under the pseudonym 'Fay Filmer'. She provided information about new releases and about the reception of films – by the troops in France, for instance. Many of her anecdotes centred on the doings and sayings of the stars. Hughes herself was a film fan as well as a clever and determined woman. She built up a network of contacts in film publicity and marketing which she put to immediate use in 1919 when she persuaded the AP management to allow her to found the *Picture Show*, Britain's first magazine for cinema fans. 'Devised on ingenious lines and printed by the most modern methods, it was an instant and enormous success,' said the Fleetway house magazine. In the wake of the *Picture Show* she founded and edited *Boys' Cinema*, *Girls' Cinema*, regular Christmas annuals and other more ephemeral periodicals, such as *Joy*, a weekly paper for flappers.

The directors of the Amalgamated Press had been shrewd in agreeing to fund Hughes's new venture. Even before the First World War commentators such as Florence Bell in Middlesbrough and Arnold Freeman in Birmingham had noticed the impact of the moving pictures on working-class districts. Bell's study was first published in 1907 and reissued in 1911. In four years the number of music-halls showing moving pictures on the cinematograph had leapt from two to ten. She noticed women emerging with babies in their arms 'looking pleased and brightened up'. Arnold Freeman recorded forty-seven 'picturedromes' in Birmingham in 1912, with a seating capacity of 32,836, then added a footnote to say that a further fifteen applications for 'cinematograph exhibitions' had been received and were under consideration in 1913.

> It seems to me unquestionable that it is the greatest formative influence at the present time in the life of the working boy. I gave up asking the lad if he went to the cinema as the response was invariably in the affirmative. Usually the boy will go about twice a week. It costs him at a cheap show not more than a penny or twopence a time and it occupies practically his whole evening.

Freeman also noted that many of his boys spent an additional twopence going to the music hall on Saturday evenings as well as buying their various halfpenny comics throughout the week. Editor Fred Cordwell had been quick to incorporate some of these enthusiasms into his papers. *Fun & Fiction* ran a 'Footlight Favourites' series from 1911 and *Merry & Bright* had used images of music-hall comedians such as TE Dunville and Little Tich in its front-page comic strips almost from its inception. It was not long before the music-hall stars were superseded by cinema comics such as Louise Fazenda. There was not too much difference between cartoon slapstick on the front page and black-and-white slapstick on film. Apart from the printed acknowledgement to a film studio (such as Mack-Sennett Productions for Fazenda) the comedians in this context had about as much reality as the *Butterfly's* 'Portland Bill' or *Chips'* 'Casey Court Kids'.

In 1920 the escapologist Harry Houdini made a well-publicised visit to England. *Merry & Bright* responded to its readers' interest by giving them *Houdini's Schooldays* as their weekly serial. As the editor explained, 'A man like Houdini could not fail to have had a wonderful early life and these stories tell of his adventures while still at school.' In *Merry & Bright*'s version, however, the boy Houdini was not Erich Weiss, the rabbi's son from Budapest, growing up impoverished in America; he was a cricket playing, boater-wearing fine young fellow at Rathgar College. He was in fact Will Holt, Allingham's Duffer, with the Dufferish-ness reduced a fraction and the agility played up. Only a few new sentences and occasional descriptors were needed to make this happen and, apart from a change of proper nouns, *Houdini's Schooldays* was simply the fourth printing of *A Regular Duffer*, the story that Allingham had first written in 1904 for Aldine's *True Blue*. This seems to have been Allingham's own initiative. A diary entry for 10 June 1920 states that he 'went to New Cross and saw Houdini. Fixed up with him about school days. Wrote him and Cordwell.'

Like Maud Hughes, Fred Cordwell responded to the enthusiasm for the cinema with a long-running print success. In January 1920, while *The Fellow Who Loved Violet Hopson* was running in *Cheerio!*, he founded *Film Fun*, a comic paper which lasted until 1962 and attracted generations of children from across the social classes. *Film Fun* took the overall format and the most popular fictional elements of the *Merry & Bright*group and glossed them, far more thoroughly than before, with the personalities and vocabulary of the silent cinema. It was advertised as 'An Absolutely NEW and ORIGINAL comic paper [...] All the REAL Film Favourites in Flickers of Funniosity, *Film Fun* strikes an entirely new note in both humorous and cinema papers. NOTHING ELSE LIKE IT ON THE MARKET.'

Almost uniquely among Cordwell's post-*Butterfly* creations, *Film Fun*'s opening numbers did not carry a serial by Allingham. That situation was soon rectified and from 1921 to 1927 Cordwell busily reprinted Allingham's earlier stories one after another – with the names of film stars attached. His *The Steel Clutch* (*Butterfly*, 1916) became *The League of the Yellow Hand* 'by' Japanese film star, Sessue Hayakawa; *The Girl Who Married a Scoundrel* (*Merry & Bright*, 1912) became *The Price of his Silence* 'by' the same author. *Don't Leave Us, Mummy!*, a 'mother love' tale written for the *Happy Home* in 1914 was reprinted in *Film Fun* in 1922 as *A Woman Against the World*, once again 'by' Hayakawa. 'Jorkins & Co', a short story series developed from 'The Duffer, Detective' (*True Blue*, 1906), was ascribed in *Film Fun* to Houdini, the Handcuff King. In the *Picture Show* Allingham wrote two serials 'as' the film star, Norma Talmadge.

Just four months after the launch of *Film Fun*, Cordwell re-branded *Cheerio!* as *Film Fun*'s value-for-money companion paper, the *Kinema Comic*. The lead serial was Allingham's *Peg of the Pictures*, a self-referential comedy in which he gives a witty twist to a young boy's quest to win his inheritance and introduces a modern-day princess – a shop girl who has escaped the slavery of her uncle's department store and gone on to become a film star. Allingham's private joke is that the film, *The Comic Convict*, which the hero, Charlie Chester, produces in an attempt to fulfil the terms of his comedian uncle's Will, is so sad it has to be released under the new title *Driven from Home*. More reprints followed. In the *Kinema Comic* authorship of the third reissue of *Max the Magnificent* (*New Boys' Paper*, 1907) was ascribed to 'Winkle' (Harold Lloyd) and the second reissue of Allingham's *Ashamed of his Mother* (*Butterfly*, 1911) to 'Fatty' Arbuckle. A sketch of Arbuckle, pen in hand, formed part of the story's header.

> Like most big men he [Arbuckle] has big ideas on all sorts of subjects. He can write better than most professional authors, and he has published several books. Others from his pen will appear shortly.
>
> I have just read a story by him which to my mind is one of the finest stories ever written. [...]
>
> I am so impressed by the story that I have arranged for its publication in the *Kinema Comic*. The opening chapters will appear next week, and if, when you have read them, you send me a postcard letting me know just what you think of Fatty Arbuckle as an author, I shall be much obliged, and so will Fatty.

In 1920, when these claims were made, Arbuckle was under a million-dollar contract to Paramount films and being pushed to the limits of productivity, working on as many as three films at once. There is no evidence that he (or Sessue Hayakawa or Norma Talmadge or Harold Lloyd) ever met Allingham or knew about the stories that were being re-produced under their names, though presumably some deal must have been made between the AP and the stars' agents or studios. Allingham supplied the editorial paragraphs drawing attention to Arbuckle's presumed serious side, 'a big man with big ideas'. Cordwell meanwhile was running him as a series cartoon character in 'The Funniosities of Fatty Arbuckle' on the *Kinema Comic's* front page. What were the readers supposed to think?

One portrait of a 1920s *Kinema Comic* reader exists but it is an editorial feature and gives nothing away about the subject's level of belief in the celebrities who were offering themselves for his entertainment. Albert Watson was a fourteen-year-old from a family of ten brothers and sisters living off London's Old Kent Road. He had won a 'five-shillings-a-day' competition that had been part of the marketing campaign for the re-branded *Kinema Comic*. The editor had gone to visit Albert at home. Much is made of the cheerful street life surrounding the Watson family ('small boys play cricket in the old-fashioned way using lamp-posts for wickets, girls are constantly skipping and the air is full of shrill cries and happy laughter') yet the winner himself seems depressed. He has recently turned fifteen and can no longer stay at school.

> Now he has made a start in life and has completed his first month as a leather worker in a nearby tannery.
>
> I asked him whether he liked work.
>
> 'I'd rather be at school,' said he.

Poor Albert. Tanneries – along with their associated glue works where the animal bones were boiled down – were among the most unpleasant of south London's small industries – as the Fabian women had noticed. As a junior employee Albert was probably given the task of scraping the last gobbets of decaying flesh from the hides before they entered the curing process. The smell would have continued to cling around him long after the end of every working day. When the editor offers to pay Albert's winnings as a single lump sum instead of a daily postal order he accepts, explaining that this would enable him to buy a new suit of clothes and other things.

> 'Besides,' Mrs Watson, Albert's mother, interposed, 'the lad is rather run down and a holiday will do him all the good in the world. If he has the lump sum he can have a nice week in Brighton which will set him up splendidly.'

Albert assured the editor that he intended buy the *Kinema Comic* 'for the rest of my life'. One can only hope that it continued to divert him.

The first biography of Harry Houdini was written in 1928 from the recollections and documents of his wife, Beatrice. Allingham had contributed a series of 'Houdini' stories for the *Kinema Comic* in which he had invented a cheerful cockney named Arth Wright as a resourceful boy assistant for the escapologist and had introduced him to one of his series detectives, Pelham Webb. The biography went out of its way to deny any connection:

> In England a tuppenny weekly, the *Kinema Comic*, which provided literary nourishment for persons of moderate intellect, was beginning a serial entitled 'The Amazing Exploits of Houdini – Written by Houdini Himself' which was to run for several years. None of the Exploits was authentic, none was written up by Houdini; but the term 'amazing' was fully justified.

Only the first thirty stories in this long-running series were Allingham's. Early in 1923 FC Cordwell instructed him to drop 'Houdini' and cut the current serial he was writing for the *Kinema Comic* from 4,000 words per instalment to 3,000. 'Houdini' was continued by other anonymous writers and most of Allingham's subsequent *Kinema Comic* serials were reprints rather than new work. 'My price too high,' wrote Allingham in his diary. It was an ominous sign of trouble ahead.

'You won't tell anybody you saw me here?'

Chapter Twenty
1923: 'His most industrious apprentice'

Few parents, I suspect, would choose to be recorded by their volatile, sensitive, frequently bored sixteen-year-old. Allingham's daughter Margery gave him mixed reviews. Her diaries are patchy and personal. They are, as far as any diary can be, private documents, frequently incomplete and often mundane. Because of this they often seem to succeed in conveying the texture of ordinary family days. Her diary for 1921 is pocket-sized. 'Errands. Practised elo [elocution]. Wrote play till dinner. Continued till tea and after til 6 when to elo class. Returned and continued with play til 10 o'clock when Daddy came in. Mother read serial she is writing for Daddy. To bed.'

This was the year after she had left school and was living at home with Herbert and Em. The family home was a flat in Hurlingham House, a mansion block in Bayswater, not far from 'Little Venice', a location later used by Margery in one of her most successful detective novels, *Death of a Ghost*. Today the immediate area seems scarred by main roads and railways, ugly, unimaginative and disconnected building projects and the gaps still left from the Second World War. Its 1920s atmosphere has gone. There must, presumably, have been one yet it has left little discernible trace in either Margery's or her father's diaries. The Hurlingham House flat is somewhere to be, to go out from and return to. Not somewhere to savour.

Allingham had rented himself studio space in Chancery Lane so as be able to work away from the distractions of family. His return home each day – when no one was going out to a show or to eat at Frascatis – was often noted by his daughter – sometimes negatively: 'Daddy late and ratty'; 'Daddy very tired and nervy'; 'Daddy unreasonable and fidgety'. There are rows when Daddy is 'very beastly', moments of penury: 'everyone very hard up. Daddy only gave me 2/6 of my 5 s this week' and appreciated moments of affluence: 'Daddy gave me £2 for chintz'; 'Daddy is an old dear.'

Mother, more frequently present during the day, is a much less interesting figure in her daughter's eyes. She falls ill for a few days and has to be nursed – a duty from which Margery escapes with alacrity as soon as Daddy comes home. She 'waxes incoherent' on some religious point when they are out to lunch and nags when they are at home. 'Mother worried at Daddy and so made me cry.' 'No maid. Another row.' 'Mother worried at Daddy and so nagging me. I think I shall go mad may the Lord help me.'

So far, so teenage. From the perspective of the fiction factory, however, 1921 was the crucial year during which Allingham began to feel excited by his older daughter's potential. After this year he came to believe that she had 'a spark of genius in her'. 'What a splendid woman she is becoming,' agreed McFee, who kept Margery's photo in his cabin. 'I don't wonder that you are interested and preoccupied by her future.' Margery herself described this period as her 'apprenticeship', claiming in later life that she left the Perse School in Cambridge and 'came to London to learn to write under my father' as if it were some almost formal arrangement. Certainly she looked to him as her most regular companion and mentor. 'To pictures with Daddy' – 'Walked with Daddy' – 'Talked to Daddy' – similar entries run through her diary like a refrain to each day.

Writing for Daddy was more problematic. Even before she had left school Margery was already hard at work on the projects that appealed to her – plays, short stories, historical recitations – none of them comfortably within Allingham's area of expertise. He could not direct her work as securely as he did Em's or his younger brother Claude's – or the fellow professionals with whom he had worked as editor. In adulthood Margery paid him one of her characteristically twisted tributes. 'My father was one of those born editors who was able to inspire almost anyone to write anything but whose decisions are in any case final,' she said. Perhaps not the ideal approach when you're dealing with an emotional, inarticulately determined sixteen-year-old. Her diary for March 1921 evokes his editorial style: 'Re-wrote "When the Bell Rang". Read to Daddy. He wants last scene re-written'; 'Re-wrote last scene'; 'Copied out "When the Bell Rang". Daddy says not so good as other'; 'I wrote that verse for Daddy. Some words over it. He shouts and I cry again.'

Allingham's approach to the craft of writing was willed and cerebral, though shot through with a displaced hunger for colour, excitement, excess. Em described him as 'an intellectual, interested mainly in ideas which found an outlet in his plots'. This doesn't quite tell the whole story. Allingham was not cold – and possibly not quite as rational as other people thought.

Years previously, when he had been editing the *London Journal,* he had used the persona of Mab to appraise as well as advertise his own writing.

> 'Silverdale', the first story in the Christmas number is, I think, a particularly good one. It is a little improbable, perhaps, *like all this writer's work,* but it is profoundly interesting and if the central incident is improbable, the characters are real-life and human [my italics].

Allingham, as editor, allowed himself his improbabilities. As a writer he longed for imaginative freedom and was less comfortable with editors, such as William Harvey, who placed great value on stories 'having the ring of plausibility'. Margery, as a teenager, was not in the least attracted by plausibility. Shakespeare was her guru and her inspiration came from the big personalities of history and pre-history. When her father attempted to persuade her into realistic or contemporary writing, as he did disastrously in 1923 with her novel *Green Corn*, apparently in the belief that this was more 'serious' work, her sparkle deserted her – just as his did when editorially forced to abandon his improbabilities. He even made her write a synopsis for *Green Corn*, a chore he personally loathed.

For all his experience, thoughtfulness and professional reflection, Allingham may never quite have plumbed the central mystery of his own art. When all stories used similar formulaic elements, when all were written to order, what was it that made some noticeably better or more successful than others? Questions of fit are essential – produced for the right periodical at the right time – but so is congeniality. Allingham's best stories were written for editors who enjoyed, encouraged, paid generously and left him alone. These stories retain vitality and their own type of truth. Ship's engineer McFee once likened Allingham and his fellow serial writers to the turbines in the SS *Carthago* but even top-quality engines run better or worse in different climates and with better or worse human attendance. Margery Allingham grasped the importance of the pleasure principle in fiction production far more securely than her father – though not until after she had left home. Looking back, much later, she said that previously 'I had always assumed that utter solitude, not to say boredom, was the only condition in which fiction could be produced.' A depressing reflection on the environment in which her father passed his long working life.

Margery also made a crucial distinction between what she called left and right hand writing: 'Right hand writing is the story one tells spontaneously at the party. Left hand writing is the one one is made to tell by somebody else.' One might assume that all of Allingham's work was 'left hand' and there would be truth in that but not unmitigated truth. Writing *A Devil of a Woman* for himself at the *London Journal*, 'Gaston Gaters' and *Plucky Polly Perkins* for HJ Garrish in the early days at the AP, *Driven From Home, The Girl Outcast, His Convict Bride* and *Mother Love* for the *Butterfly* and Cordwell's new comics in the years immediately before the war, Allingham might well have experienced a sense of excitement, of being valued for his expertise, of having a degree of choice in his work.

In the 1920s he was locked into a contract with Leng's that required two newly written serial stories from him for forty weeks of every year. Welcome security in uncertain times but not work to quicken the pulses or foster much illusion of spontaneity. He was beginning to struggle to maintain his productivity. I found a handwritten chart where he attempted to log at which times of day he found it easiest to work. He also consulted some sort of specialist and was delighted to discover that his word count rose as a result. For a while...

One evening, during their summer holiday on Mersea Island in August 1921, Allingham, Margery, 'young' Phil and a family friend, George Hearn, decided to amuse themselves 'playing the glass'. This involves a type of automatic writing where an upturned tumbler, touched by the fingertips of all participants, moves from letter to letter, apparently of its own volition or under the influence of a spirit. The Allinghams had played this game before. This time their level of success took Allingham completely by surprise.

> The glass began to move as soon as we touched it and we found ourselves apparently in communication with a person called Joseph Pullen. Pullen is a common name on the island, familiar to at least three of us. We therefore attributed this early success to auto-suggestion. We asked Pullen how long it was since he lived on the island. He replied two hundred years. After one or two unimportant questions and replies, Hearn asked Pullen if he knew anything about smugglers. This proved a happy suggestion. Pullen was an old smuggler and after this he spoke freely.
>
> Then someone (Margery) suggested asking about the old Ship Inn. On a previous visit to Mersea we had heard a story about the Ship. The building is now demolished but it was once a notorious smuggling centre. A murder is said to have been committed there and the place was reputed to be haunted. There are still old residents on the Island who will tell you that they have seen the ghost. This much we knew when we asked the question that led to such surprising results.

'Joseph Pullen' gave them the names of the people who had been involved in the murder at the Ship Inn and a variety of details about their characters and their lives. 'It is difficult to describe our sensations at that first sitting,' wrote Allingham. 'We all had a feeling amounting to absolute conviction that we were receiving an account of actual incidents which had occurred and of actual people who had lived on Mersea Island over two hundred years ago.' Better still – when the four of them tried again the following evening, other characters were apparently waiting to spell out their part in the story letter by laborious letter.

> We questioned these about the affair at the Ship and they all gave their evidence just as though they had been witnesses in a police court case. As the story unfolded itself new facts came to light and new actors in the little drama were mentioned. At subsequent sittings we called up all those who seemed to have a bearing on the story and questioned them in turn. Nearly all of them answered freely and during the eight sittings [...] we had communication from twelve different spirits each one of which had a distinct and strongly marked personality.

All four of the participants in these evening sessions were or would become writers. Allingham and Hearn were already earning their livings by their pens, Margery was serving her 'apprenticeship' and fifteen-year-old Phil (who, Allingham said, had entered the proceedings 'inclined to scoff') later worked as a journalist and a copy-writer as well as producing a small amount of fiction and a best-selling autobiography. In August 1921 Phil was as convinced as his father that they were in touch with historical people. He went to the local record office to check details and, when he returned to his boarding school, spoke up for the truth of spiritualism in the debating society. Surely this was a team effort? All of them asked questions that helped to push the story on and, if either the make-up of the group or its location were changed, the 'spirit' messages petered out. Ultimate responsibility, however, was ascribed to Margery. When they returned to London after the holiday she began using the story as the plot to her first novel.

Immediately the working relationship between herself and her father became easier. Allingham was aware, perhaps overly aware, of the gulf between the serial stories he (and Hearn) produced, and stories constructed in novel form and destined to be produced as a book. 'You cannot call yourself an author,' he told his youngest child, Joyce, 'until you have been published in hard covers.' He believed that what his friend McFee did, and what Margery was now doing, was something by its nature different from his own writing and superior. Margery worked at her novel unaided, then in the later stages she discussed her work with her father on their walks and read it to him in the evenings. No adverse comments or emotional upsets are recorded and by April 1922 the completed novel had been sent to McFee's literary agent, AP Watt. Meanwhile, more pragmatically, Aunt Maud began to use Margery to write up silent films for her *Girls' Cinema* magazine.

Still Allingham had not quite grasped how his daughter's creativity worked. Margery later described herself as 'primarily an intuitive writer whose intellect trots along behind, tidying up and saying "oh my".' At this moment her father undervalued her personal inventiveness (or their dynamics as a group) and assumed she must be a medium. This worried as well as excited him. He hoped there would be a rational explanation. He made contact with the Psychical Research Society who explained a theory of 'retrocognition' defined as 'a knowledge of the past supernormally acquired'. According to Joyce he wondered for a while whether Margery's mediumship was a practical gift that could be harnessed to help him push his own work on. Margery's diary mentions several abortive sessions with the glass in the company of her father but nothing similar to the séances on Mersea Island.

Her own interests remained focused on the Polytechnic and the theatre. As her father became more fascinated by her potential – 'I feel she may "go off" in any direction' – she began to spend to significantly more time with her fellow students. In November 1923 Allingham firmly took her away to a rented cottage at Lyminge in Kent where she was to get on with her second novel, the ill-conceived *Green Corn,* in which those fellow students were to be turned into literary copy. Three weeks of walks and talks, reading and comfortable companionship produced some thousands of words from Margery but nothing of imaginative quality. She tried working in her father's studio but found it cramped and dirty. Allingham agreed to move into a space more suitable for shared work – on the condition Margery pay for any redecoration. Once the children had left school he was strict about money. Em found them a room near the flat but still the success which Allingham so confidently anticipated for Margery eluded her. The first Mersea Island novel, *Blackerchief Dick*, was published in 1924 to an uncomfortably mixed reception; the second, *Green Corn*, remained a heap of typescript.

'My poor father was bitterly disappointed at the mess I made of it all. He was the kindest man alive but in one of his stories I would have been beautiful as well as industrious, witty, resourceful and above all lucky.' Margery was right. Even at that moment the serial Allingham was writing for the *Picture Show* was *Luck in London*, subtitled 'the story of a boy, some girls and a song which swept the world'. Allingham writes wish-fulfilment fiction; hence his heroines possess beauty, wit and resourcefulness, and their endings are invariably happy. The realism comes from the part played by luck. Telling people who are trapped by an unfair social system that if they looked more beautiful, made more jokes or worked a little harder they would inevitably succeed is a lie. Without luck people do not often escape their surroundings. This is the fairy-tale element of Allingham's art – and its truthfulness to his readers' experience of life. Richard Hoggart explains:

> To working-class people luck figures as importantly and naturally as steady endeavour or brains or beauty: it is as much an attribute that you have to accept. They are prepared to admire these other qualities, but give as much importance to the sheer chance of having luck with you. It may partly be explained in terms used before by referring to the fact that in a life so materially limited one is led to hope for the sudden chance of fortune from heaven. But it is also rooted in a supernaturalism which has survived centuries, and is still enjoyed, not as a makeshift for the rewards that have not yet come, but because it makes life more interesting.

Aged nineteen, Margery may have felt hurt, misled by her father, resentful at having been exposed too young to what she later described as 'the dead sea fruit of authorship'. She retreated to the fiction-factory activity of writing anonymously for Aunt Maud. Allingham struggled with his frustration at her underachievement. 'Margery has not done any serious work this year,' he wrote towards the end of 1925. The rows had begun again, in 1923, mainly over money, though this was probably a cover for rows over work.

Phil had also left school and was living at home failing to find his way professionally. The ability for all adult members to earn their own living was deemed as essential in the Allingham family as in the families of his readers. No solid regular parental salary could keep post-school children in idleness – or allow a budding author time to make mistakes privately. 'They seem to see me as some kind of cuckoo in the nest,' wrote Margery. As early as Christmas 1921 she had begun to feel the burden of expectations from her friends and family: 'I wondering what will happen if I don't do something someday.' Now she knew.

Allingham's dealings with his daughter over this period show him as optimistic, as loving and as fallible as most other parents of teenagers. That's on the personal level. Vocationally, the aspects of their relationship that focused on writing – Margery's self-styled 'apprenticeship' – may be viewed either as showing some naivety in Allingham's approach to fiction writing or as highlighting the difference in their genres. Florence Bell in *At the Works* said that she thought it was a pity that the same word 'read' was used to cover the separate processes of reading for education and reading for escape. Perhaps it is the same with the word 'write': what Allingham was doing as his daily work was not the same activity as what he was trying to help Margery towards and he was therefore not well qualified to assist. He once reassured McFee that 'the joy of craftsmanship comes to the maker of doll's houses as well as the builders of cathedrals.' The joy may be comparable but the skills are not and neither are the audiences.

Allingham knew that his work only succeeded because he was attuned to his readers: he doesn't seem to have realised that the same might apply to Margery. Hodder and Stoughton published *Blackerchief Dick* as a 7/6d hardback: the

Amalgamated Press had already rejected it. An editor at *Red* magazine complained that the novel had 'a curious air of unreality. Situations seem to be lacking in grip and there are too few of them for a magazine serial.' When *Green Corn* was rejected by Hodder's Allingham was aghast. 'It only needs a real man of letters to read it,' he insisted, idealistically forgetting that the literary market place is still a market place.

'Things not joyous at home,' wrote Margery, in August 1924. 'Think I shall leave.' And, aged twenty, she did – only as far as a bedsit in the garden of Hurlingham House. This, and her work from Aunt Maud, made her both financially and practically independent. When Herbert and Em moved out of London again in 1926, she remained behind. She still loved her father and was grateful for his support and the help he'd tried to give her. Allingham's style is evident throughout her work. In 1934 when she wrote her 'Little Venice' novel, the geographical souvenir of this period in their lives, she dedicated it to him 'from his most industrious apprentice'.

'"I am Miss Sunny Ray, of the firm of Michael Power," said Sunny boldly'

Chapter Twenty-One
1924-1928: The Girl He Thought He'd Married

THE economic optimism of the early 1920s had soon waned for Allingham, his employers, and for many of his readers. There would be more than a million workers unemployed on average through most of the decade and, for those fortunate enough to be earning, income tax rose to an unprecedented 5 shillings in the pound in an attempt to service war debts. By New Year 1924 Allingham was once again overdrawn and had to resort to borrowing £25 from Cotterill and Cromb, to put this straight. By the end of 1925 he was £250 in debt.

Slowly his quantity of work was dropping away. In 1923 he had written two original serials, a large number of short stories and supplied ten reprints to the AP comics. In 1924 four new short serials, no stories and eight, shorter, reprints. In 1925 three new serials and six reprints. In 1926, the year of the General Strike, was an especially bad year. In January Cordwell lost two of his papers, the *Butterfly* and *Merry & Bright*, which were redirected to serve younger readers. Leng's the *Mascot*, which, as the *Happy Home*, had been publishing Allingham's work consistently for twelve years, closed down during the strike and never re-opened. A promising new opportunity with Anne St John Cooper, a women's magazine editor at the AP, also came to nothing when her paper failed.

In December 1926 Allingham and Em decided to economise by moving out of London. They had already spent much of the year living near their Essex relatives: cousin Grace at Pope's Hall and Allingham's older brother Will at Sible Hedingham. Finally they signed a three-year lease on another decrepit old vicarage, this time at Letheringham in Suffolk (village population 164 and falling.) Allingham had paid the deposit on a car and Margery learned to drive, though her parents did not. The Old Vicarage was not too far from a railway line, the rent (£65 pa) was less than the combination of flat plus studio. Without the temptations of restaurant meals and theatres – and with the two older children left to support themselves – the daily cost of living would also be reduced.

So, unfortunately, would Allingham's contentment. He had enjoyed the comings and goings of the grown-up children and their friends. He was happy in the company of Maud and Teddy Wood, his brothers Phil, Tod and Claude and other relatives of his own generation. Staying at Pope's Hall over the summer, there had been constant communication with his friend and fellow writer, Richard Starr and his wife, as well as frequent visits from the children and other relatives. Many of the older generation were gone – James and Louisa had both died in 1920 and wild Uncle John a couple of years later, smoking a last cigar. Emily Jane (Granny) spent much of her time at Pope's Hall, or in London with Maud, busily writing spidery letters to more distant relations keeping them all up to date on each other's news. McFee came to stay in the autumn of 1926 – and later used Pope's Hall as a setting for a novel entitled *Family Trouble*, a novel in which at least three of the characters earn their livings writing or illustrating serial stories.

Winter in agriculturally depressed East Suffolk was less fun. Allingham donned a tweed suit, acquired a dog, bought his cigarettes at the village post office and went with Em to the cinema in the nearby small town of Woodbridge. Family visitors still arrived but it wasn't the same as dropping in and out of each other's homes and offices in London. Em became involved with the local church and visited Dr Salter in Essex with increasing frequency. Allingham found little to do but 'work, read and potter around the garden'. The sense of relief in his diary when he travels back up to London, goes to a show and sits up till midnight 'talking shop' with Maud is patent. Then he has to return to Letheringham where there is a phone but no electricity, the only light during the long winter evenings being provided by Aladdin lamps. 'Fire smoking, dinner poor, don't feel happy.'

Somehow the economies hadn't been as effective as he'd hoped. By January 1927 Allingham was so far in debt to his agents that he had to propose a £5 10s weekly repayment plan, as well as the recently agreed 10 percent commission on *all* his output (except work for the *Picture Show* which was 5 percent). As he negotiated all his business himself, other than with 'The North' (Allingham family slang for John Leng or DC Thomson) these extra commissions, which the agents had done nothing to earn, were more like bank charges (or money-lender's fees). He sought help from Harold Garrish, who was now a director of the AP Garrish used his influence and RN Chance, then editor of the *Boys' Friend,* reluctantly offered Allingham a commission for a school story, *The BATs*. [*The Backward and Troublesomes*]. This and a final serial for *Film Fun* helped

Allingham to earn £920 (before tax) in 1927 – a large sum compared with his readers' likely wages but one that was earned with increasing anxiety and humiliation.

Internal restructuring (and possibly editorial in-fighting) had provided Allingham with his entrée to the Amalgamated Press in 1907. Now it may have felt as if corporate events beyond his control were forcing him out again. Lord Northcliffe had died in 1922 and eventually the decision had been reached within the Harmsworth business empire that the AP must be sold to pay his death duties. Reluctantly Sir George Sutton negotiated its sale to the Berry brothers, a younger, energetically entrepreneurial family from South Wales. This was completed early in 1927. Inevitably it created uncertainties before the event: 'Sutton going to *Mail*. Lynforth also leaving. Clark or Tod Anderson may be the new chief.'

In fact the transfer of ownership appears to have caused minimal disruption. This, in itself, illustrates how far the company had changed from its nineteenth-century conception as the property of a pair of brothers to its twentieth-century status as a corporation. Allingham's editors kept their jobs and most of their papers but the change of proprietorship may have encouraged a new hardness in negotiation – and thus an awareness in an individual 'outside' worker, like Allingham, of the essential insecurity of his employment.

On the day in 1927 that Allingham had called at the AP office and heard speculation as to the identity of the new chief, Cordwell had offered him a serial for *Film Fun* – though only at three thousand words per instalment, not the usual four. This serial, *Mother's Boy* (1927–1928), was Allingham's last original story for Cordwell's papers. He struggled to write it and when *Mother's Boy* ended, early in 1928, Cordwell told

Allingham that he was 'not in need of another story at present'. Garrish had already warned him that his regular rate of two guineas per thousand, which he had been paid since 1912, was unlikely to be afforded in the future. The new 'Big Five' comics from DC Thomson of Dundee had grabbed the attention of the teenage public as firmly as the *Gem*, the *Magnet*, the *Butterfly* and *Merry & Bright* had done almost twenty years earlier. The circulation of the *Kinema Comic* was falling and Cordwell decided to redesign his better-selling *Film Fun* so as to include more direct links with the cinema. 'Films in *Film Fun*,' Allingham noted in his diary. ' No room for me.'

Allingham couldn't afford to give up. He tried again, two days later. 'Called on Cordwell again. He had seen Garrish. No work. I tried to see Garrish. Saw Chance. Offered to work at lower rate. He promised to tell Garrish. Saw C&C. Cheery but not hopeful.' When next he saw Cordwell the editor told him that he was no longer allowed to pay more than 25s per thousand words and, even at that rate, he had no work to give out. Allingham offered old school stories at £1 per thousand words. He may have sold one or two to the *Boys' Friend* Library. Garrish tried again to help by putting Allingham in touch with the editor of *Merry*, a children's magazine, who took some stories based on Allingham's 1907 'Sport Monkimore' style. An updated rewriting of the *Motor Man* adventures (*Chips*, 1908) was published in the *Gem* as *The Robot Man*. These crumbs of work demonstrate the limited extent within which a cordial relationship between supplier and buyer could still assist.

By 1928 Allingham had been working for the AP for more than twenty years but he had built up no personal security other than goodwill and his remaining copyrights. These were valuable only when he could find buyers. More than once he noted in his diary 'Garrish refused to see me.' Sometimes even Cotterill and Cromb were too busy to see him or could not help financially. 'Letter from C&C. No cash. Balance at bank £1.' He wrote hairdressing copy for his brother Phil and borrowed money where he could. He looked out some old stories of Em's and helped her sell them as cheap books and delightedly accepted an offer of £25 for *The Rod of the Oppressor* from DC Thomson who had already bought it in 1912; tried to cut down expenses.

Margery's career meanwhile was beginning to take shape. Even in December 1925 when Allingham was writing anxiously that 'Margery has done no serious work this year' he was sufficiently trusting (or astute) to guess that his daughter was 'thinking and subconsciously making plans'. As well as her 'left hand' work for Aunt Maud, Margery produced a few markedly original, though un-commercial short stories and a play during 1926. Then, in October, she and her father talked over the plot of a detective story and in March 1927 he had a first reading. A month later it had been accepted to run as a serial in the *Daily Express*. In the interim period Margery and Pip Youngman Carter announced their engagement and Allingham wrote affectionately to his own first girlfriend, Lilian Carter, née Robinson, the mother of his prospective son-in-law and former editor of *Amateur Scraps*.

Lilian Carter remains a shadowy figure. She was by now a respectable, middle-class widow from Watford. Her response to the engagement and to Allingham's fond reminiscence was an expression of anxiety about her son's selfishness and the likelihood that this would impact on his ability to be a good husband. Shrewd enough, as it turned out, but lacking Herbert's emotional generosity. Margery, he wrote, 'is all the world to me'.

Fortunately Allingham liked his prospective son-in-law.

Pip had first come to see him in his 'draughty attic' in Chancery Lane and been in and out of their household for several years. Allingham had continued to welcome him even when Pip and Margery's relationship was difficult. He wrote again to reassure Lilian that all would be well but there was little subsequent coming together of the families. Perhaps it would have been different had there ever been grandchildren but there never were.

A relative of Lilian's officiated at the wedding. Allingham gave Margery away and Phil was best man. The reception afterwards was at Maud's flat. 'God bless,' wrote Allingham, uncharacteristically. Then, in the car going back to their hotel that evening, he was forced to ask his youngest brother, Tod, for a loan of £27 to cover Joyce's school fees at the Perse. It would have been awkward if Tod had refused as Em and Phil had already put Joyce on the train back to Cambridge.

On the scanty evidence available one might guess that Em Allingham and Lilian Carter would never have become soulmates. Although it appears deceptively easy to build a picture of Em from her daughters' perspectives – possessor of a hurtful tongue, a religious crank, flashy, 'not really safe with people' – seeing her through her husband's eyes after twenty-five years of marriage is harder. Allingham's surviving diaries and letters are not personal documents and it is extremely rare for him to make any derogatory comment about those closest to him. He once stigmatises a letter from his son Phil as 'silly' and on another occasion comments that he is 'a difficult chap to help'. And this through a period of Phil's young adulthood which many parents would have found extremely unsatisfactory and frustrating. Joyce, poor Joyce, is scarcely mentioned. Allingham pays her school fees, corresponds with her teachers (no letters survive) and notes her occasional presence at home. As Joyce once claimed that she considered her main childhood accomplishment was the ability to slip in and out of rooms unnoticed, perhaps this recognition is something in itself. She admired her father for his work ethic and loved him for his kindness. And he did once find a story of hers 'surprisingly good'.

Allingham's companionship with Em is a given: they walk together, go to shows, house-hunt. He corrects her writing and, on the rare occasions that he is ill, she helps him with his. They also function separately – he goes to play chess; she attends a flower show. Her daughters resented her visits to Dr Salter at Tolleshunt D'Arcy and felt jealous on their father's behalf. Clearly there was deep emotional involvement on Em's side but it was scarcely a conventional extra-marital affair. Salter was now in his mid-eighties and Em felt no awkwardness about what Margery described as her 'obsession with him'. Her husband, Em wrote later, 'was part of herself. He did not come into the picture at all.' Perhaps Allingham understood her well enough to understand this. It must have helped that they were also cousins and he could remember her as a child. He knew, for instance, that 'she very often says more than she means' and he probably sympathised with her own admission that she did not have 'a contented mind'. When he once comes close to criticising – on his birthday, 18 December 1925 – 'Em too much occupied by church work,' he almost immediately qualifies this. 'On the other hand… Em is having a full life and is happier than formerly.'

Marriage was a main theme in Allingham's writing for the Leng-Thomson magazines during the 1920s but its presentation had shifted once again. A group of stories which he produced from 1924 proved particularly successful. I call them the 'Tricked into Marriage' group, from Allingham's working title for the first serial of this type, *The Girl He Thought He'd*

Married (*Mascot*, 1924). In all these stories good women marry under false pretences. The heroes are blinded or amnesiac and become quite disorientated in the midst of a plethora of true and false wives, heroines and impersonators, good-time girls and devoted nurses. The women are persuaded to 'trick' the heroes into marriage by economic need, self-sacrifice and compassion. As a group, these 'Tricked into Marriage' stories can be viewed as dramatising a perception of change in gender relations, a new 'structure of feeling' to use Raymond Williams's term. Between 1924 and 1931 twelve of the stories written by Allingham include a catastrophe for the hero. When the men are weakened they become more perceptive. The women, meanwhile, have greater scope for action – whether for good or ill.

This fictional disabling of men and the demonstration of women's different reactions to disability makes sense in the post-war situation – particularly when the story shows two women competing for one man. Public anxieties were centred around the increased ratio of women to men in the population, the numbers of surviving men who were physically or emotionally maimed, and the complex realignments of male-female relationships resulting from women's new legal and political status. Once again Allingham's art is as responsive as journalism to the contemporary mood. Women had been given the vote but their jobs had been taken back by men. All the heroines in the 'Tricked into Marriage' group are fatherless (motherless too, but that appears less significant) and it is in part their economic desperation that persuades them to substitute for the anti-heroine, the good-time girl, who rejects the hero because of his disability.

He doesn't write in his old jolly masterful way. His letters are timid, almost apologetic and yet he wants to see me. And I can't! I won't! Suppose I gave way and married him out of pity. It would be hideous! I've got my own life to think of. I can't bear illness of any kind. I'm healthy and I must have healthy people about me. It sounds heartless but I can't help it. That's my nature. Besides I must have money and when I marry it must be a man who, if he isn't rich, must be able to make a good income.

This story cuts immediately to the amnesiac hero, poignantly weakened, yet romantically, naively, passionate and constant. 'God help me win her and be worthy of her!' Dramatic tension is thus set up – how can this situation be resolved without inflicting further pain on a character who is already suffering? In 1918, when Harvey had given Allingham his detailed instructions to ensure that *She Sinned for Her Children* was suitable for readers of the *People's Journal*, he had insisted that the heroine must have 'a good reason' for deserting her children. In the 1920s heroines are allowed far more latitude and are dealing with more complex situations. In *Her First Born Son* (the *Happy Home*, 1920) a young war-widow gives up her child for adoption but does not tell her new husband. She has a new baby but discovers that the first child is being ill-treated and that he, not his brother, is the true heir to a fortune. Then her husband loses his memory. What should she do?

Bigamy and illegitimacy were recognised post-war problems. These stories approach them indirectly. *Her Darling* (*My Weekly*, 1928) has two sisters: Alice, respectably married but childless, Lucy, secretly married, assumed widowed, pregnant. So Lucy gives Alice the child. Then Alice dies, her husband remarries, the new wife has a child of her own and the first little girl is sent off to the baby farmers in Walworth. How will her original mother rescue her? It's a new twist to an old plot. Children had been swapped in their cradles for as long as folk and fairy tales had been told but usually by some malignant agency. Now good characters in respectable family papers are agents of their own difficulties and yet retain the readers' sympathy.

Three more Leng stories, *The Custody of the Child* (1928), *The Stepmother* (1929) and *Her Stolen Bairn* (1929), all use divorce as the factor separating mothers from their children. Not only had the law made divorce more easily available to couples from a slightly wider social range, but the publicity spotlight on Hollywood ensured that the news of celebrity marriages was swiftly followed by tales of celebrity divorce. If there had been any intention to present film stars as reassuring exponents of family values, it had already backfired. The front-page photograph in the *Picture Show*, 11 February 1928, for instance, depicted Mr & Mrs Reginald Terry awaiting their final decree with their young daughter, Barbara. 'Why can't they be happy?' asked the caption. The featured article was written by the husband that Maud Hughes could not publicly acknowledge. 'Unfortunately for Hollywood the powers that be have always made a feature of personal publicity,' wrote Edward Wood. 'They were right that the public liked to know about its favourites and they reaped the reward of that publicity.'

Gwendoline Freeman, a collector for the Provident Bank, who made many friends in the slums of Birmingham during the 1930s, saw the role of the press in telling tales of film stars' eventful personal lives as positively beneficial: 'When anyone in the Lane begins to read the papers or go to the cinema regularly it is always a sign of progress. It shows a certain amount of interest in the world: interest in something beyond one's family circle, to go and look at American pictures or read about the latest murder.' Freeman viewed the cult of personality as a means by which this wider world could be assimilated within the Birmingham back-to-backs. It offered a 'human angle' and enhanced a good 'mag' (a women's gossip session). Here she describes a mother and her two daughters making magging into an occasion.

> We would have a special tea – tinned salmon and tinned peaches. I listened mostly but the others gossiped until tears ran down their cheeks with laughter [...] They had a wide range of subjects but always saw things from the human angle. The affairs of the Duke of Windsor were a gift and we had endless anecdotes culled from the Sunday papers [...] They told me at length the plots of the films they saw but Hollywood provided more than that. The film stars' private lives were a rich mine.

This intensely pleasurable social bonding seems not unlike the eagerness with which Mrs Gilfeather and her sister in the tenements of Lochee are said to have discussed the incidents of their weekly *People's Journal* serial. Reports such as Freeman's offer a more humane perspective on the culture of celebrity than that expressed by some highbrow critics. 'The cult of the movie star, fostered by the money of the film industry, preserves not the unique aura of the person but the "spell of the personality", the phoney spell of the commodity,' sniffed Walter Benjamin in 'The Work of Art in an Age of Mechanical Reproduction.' 'A commodity,' commented Marx, more wisely, 'appears at first sight a very trivial thing and easily understood. Its analysis shows that it is in reality a very queer thing, abounding in metaphysical subtleties and theological niceties.'

Looking back to Lady Bell's study of the working women

of Middlesbrough in 1907 should persuade us all to raise two cheers for commodity culture as it had developed over Herbert Allingham and Maud Hughes's working lives. She described 'Mrs Z' as

> a typical and extreme case of want of interest in her surroundings and indeed in her existence. She was born in the next street to the mews she now lives in and this was almost all she had seen of the town. From year's end to year's end she hardly ever went out of the house, excepting to shop as near her home as convenient. It did not occur to her to go out for air and exercise: she had never been down to the river or across the ferry to see where her husband worked.
>
> Many of the women get into a frame of mind where they simply accept, in a sort of inertia, what life brings to them, as though they had given up the idea, if they had ever had it, of the possibility of making anything better of it.

Women like Mrs Z 'do not read at all, and do not therefore use that means of diverting their thoughts and supplementing and enlarging their limited experience. The result is that they have minds curiously devoid, so to speak of points of comparison. This again tends to their remaining inarticulate.' It was for these women that Lady Bell wanted entertainment 'which would give them change of ideas and bring some relief to the monotony of their lives'. Just what Geraldine Freeman had noticed happening twenty-five years later in the Birmingham back-to-backs.

Meanwhile, down in the Suffolk countryside, money matters were not getting easier. 'Your resilience has always been a marvel to me,' wrote McFee consolingly. By the end of 1928 Allingham's income had dropped to £653 5s 2d. He had taken on more work for the North but his end of year summary was depressed:

1928. Lost my work at the AP. Started work for P Dunn of Dundee. Marge wrote and sold Black Dudley. PWA took his future in his own hands and went on the road. Many money worries. A little tired. Aged 61.

'Harvey Price stood motionless as Marion lifted the poisoned peach to her lips'

Chapter Twenty-Two
1931: The Family Journal

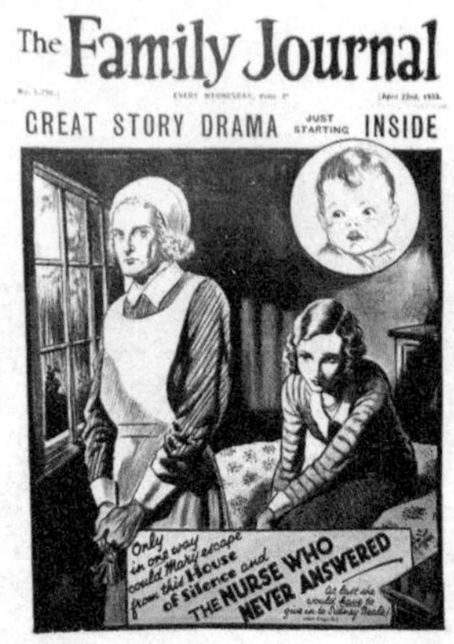

'Get as much as you can for it (one serial use) – there is a run on me just now. My Indian summer I suppose!' Allingham's instructions to his agents in December 1931 show a cheerful confidence compared with the occasionally desperate tone of his diary entries in the later 1920s. His earnings were rising again. From the depressed levels of 1928 and 1929 (£658 and £698 respectively) his total income for 1931, 1932 and 1933 was £1,305, £1,546 and £1,537. Only in 1934, Allingham's last complete production year, did it begin to drop away. New stories were once again being commissioned and old stories finding new incarnations in a different set of magazines.

The most important factor shaping Allingham's success in the early 1930s was his editor. Anne St John Cooper, editor in charge of a clutch of successful story-papers for the Amalgamated Press, was the second wife of Henry

St John Cooper, one of the writers whom, twenty years ago, Hamilton Edwards had held up to Allingham as an exemplary producer of boys' school stories. They were both long-standing AP. authors and their output had overlapped in other areas. In 1909, for instance, when Allingham was writing *Plucky Polly Perkins* for the *Butterfly*, St John Cooper was producing stories about 'Pollie Green', who demonstrated similar qualities of wit, assertiveness and willingness to stand up to authority.

They were close contemporaries but there's nothing to suggest that they met socially – the passing of the old ramshackle Fleet Street bohemianism amongst common writers was one of the changes Ralph Rollington deplored in his account of old boys' papers. Once Allingham had left London to set himself up in his fiction factory (or as an outworker in the corporate enterprises of others) he was effectively isolated by the demands of deadlines and productivity. He had occasionally attended Freemasons' meetings in Essex but otherwise chose to spend his leisure time with his family or his chess club. By the later 1920s, however, St John Cooper's son, Robert, was one of the group of friends which included Margery, Pip and Tibby Clarke. 'Coop' became a cartoonist, responsible, for instance, for the Tate and Lyle advertising character 'Mr Cube'. He was still sufficiently close to AP contacts to help gain Margery a lucrative commission to write the first of her three serials for *Answers* in 1931.

Few members of this next generation followed their fathers down the mine (or into the Amalgamated Press) for long. Instead they used their inherited understanding to achieve success in new areas of the burgeoning communications industry. The informal level of expertise developed by childhoods in the fiction factory was demonstrated on the occasions when Maud Hughes's husband, Teddy Wood, or Maud herself, were too incapacitated by whisky to file their copy. Not only Margery but her younger brother, Phil, could step in and file for them. By the early 1930s Margery's career as a 'middlebrow' detective novelist was well underway and Phil was making a series of broadcasts for the BBC.

Henry St John Cooper had died in 1926 and Allingham sent a letter of condolence to his widow (Robert's stepmother). Allingham had been searching for new markets at that time and it had come as a great relief when Mrs Cooper (as Miss McGlachan) had approached him for reprint material to use in one of her story papers, the *Home Mirror.* Unfortunately the *Home Mirror* did not survive and in 1927 its readers were redirected to the *Home Companion.* No subsequent invitation to contribute appears to have been extended until 1930 when Anne Cooper (using her married name, now she was widowed) editor of the *Home Companion,* requested a second use of *Out of the Past,* one of the aborted *Home Mirror* stories. At the same time she bought second serial rights to an Allingham 'Mother Love' story for her main paper, the *Family Journal*, and followed it immediately with another.

This was the beginning of a working relationship as close and almost as productive as that established with FC Cordwell on the comic-and-story papers in the years before the war. From 1930 until autumn 1937, more than a year after Allingham's death, there was not a week without an Allingham serial in the *Family Journal*, sometimes two or three running concurrently, as well as reprinted stories in the *Home Companion* and in Cooper's other story-papers *Poppy's Paper,* the *Oracle* and the *Miracle.*

Cooper possessed the prime editorial quality of putting herself in the place of her common readers. Just as Maud

Hughes's personal enthusiasm for films and film stars underpinned the success of the *Picture Show*, so Cooper presented herself as reading her magazines' fiction for her own pleasure. She was ready to be delighted:

> I thought the instalment received this week for the *FJ* serial now running was wonderful. I'd never in my wildest flights of imagination thought that the burgled house was going to be Phil Rodney's.
>
> You are astonishing in your surprises!

Such generously expressed enthusiasms probably facilitated Allingham's acceptance of her occasional criticisms and suggestions.

> I love all the characters in your new first instalment, but most of all I love TOBY TILES. What a creature!!
>
> The one criticism I have to make is the curtain. I am making this my autumn boom story in the *Family Journal* and the curtain is not strong enough to carry a leaflet. As I do not know what is in your mind in the way of developments I am rather at a loss to know how it can be strengthened up.
>
> Will you give me some idea of what is to happen in the second instalment as then I might be able to add a piece on to number 1?

Presumably one reason that Anne Cooper felt confident in letting Allingham work out his stories in his own way is that he already had a lifetime's understanding of the medium in which they would be published. Cooper's two main papers, the *Family Journal* and the *Home Companion*, could serve to exemplify the way in which aspects of nineteenth-century evangelicalism had been commodified into entertainment, secularised into the family paper and finally narrowed into the domestic women's magazine. In the late 1870s James Allingham had tried unsuccessfully to use the success of the *Christian Globe* to establish a *Family Paper* and a *Ladies' Journal.* The Harmsworths had achieved this in the 1890s. Their semi-evangelical *Sunday Companion* (1894) had been notably successful (mentioned frequently by the iron-workers of Middlesbrough, among many) and had soon spawned a 'weekday edition', the *Home Companion* (1897). This was the paper into which Cooper recruited Allingham in 1930.

The *Sunday Companion,* edited by Hartley Aspden, had encouraged Bible study and support of the Barefoot Mission; the *Home Companion* was ostensibly committed to the 'sanctification' of the home but was actually dominated by romantic fiction, household hints, a children's page, a members' club and incessant self-interested aphorisms concerning the duty of parents to encourage right reading. 'You can't gather figs from thistles and you can't make good men from boys who read bad books.' Most of the exhortation was directed towards mothers. Nevertheless there were clear domestic roles for fathers too and membership of the 'Red Rose of Courage' readers' club shows a 50-50 male/female balance. Members, including the editor, pledged themselves to 'Say No to Gambling, Profane Language, Intemperance, Lying, Dishonesty, Impurity, Evil Speaking and Bad Literature.' (Northcliffe, not personally keen on temperance, had to find ways to distance himself from his editor's more enthusiastic crusades.)

The *Family Journal* (founded 1909) was a comfort paper targeting the same mixed, domestic audience and glossing its entertainment with secular piety. It was hugely successful – in 1925, for instance, its annual sale was 341,000,000 copies – more than 6 million a week. Henry St John Cooper had been a key contributor from the first issue. His dramatic story *Master of the Mill* opens with a violent scene in which the hero is disinherited and his cousin plots against him. In the middle of this opening page is an inset box proclaiming:

> **A United Happy Family Life is the Basis of a Prosperous Country.**
> **Those who love the name of Father, Mother and Home are asked to join our Family Club.**
> **The Key that unlocks the entrance to a successful career is True Family Life.**

Such exhortations remained a feature of the *Family Journal* and were regularly inserted in the midst of Allingham's 1930s dramas of divorce, bigamy, illegitimacy and betrayal. There was a 'Family Club' whose president was 'Mother'. This functioned partly as a pen-friends' agency putting the lonely (and often the disabled) club 'sisters' and 'daughters' in touch with one another and was also used to advertise lodgings. The 1930s *Family Journal* still possessed some regular male readers, old and young. Among the dress patterns, recipes and household hints, there were handyman's features, often beginning 'Down at our Working Man's Club the other day...' A long-running cartoon, 'The Gay Goblins', aimed to appeal across the generations.

The *Family Journal*'s success in retaining the vestiges of a mixed-gender readership was unusual by 1930. As periodicals continued to proliferate, the category of family magazine had fragmented. Families had changed too. Family sizes had dropped, disposable family income (for many) had risen and by the 1930s a slightly higher proportion of even working-class housing offered some more private and differentiated spaces as well as better lighting (in urban areas). Family reading aloud had declined as the literacy gap had closed and as the wireless offered more sophisticated opportunities for families to listen together. A move out of inner cities to the new suburbs often changed the way a family unit functioned and, for many women, the 'sanctification' of the home took ever more material forms as the housewife became a solitary labourer within its servant-less, sometimes child-free space. The loneliness of *Family Journal*'s married 'club daughters' who hope to hear from 'sister members' is as patent as the financial neediness of the single club members who advertise for others to rent small furnished bedrooms or share their homes as a paying guest ('very small premium asked').

Anne Cooper understood her readers and was protective towards them, especially the readers of the *Home Companion*, who were now almost all female:

> I am exceedingly sorry, but the instalment of *Cora Royle* received today is much too strong for the *Home Companion*. I am returning from page nine to you and hope that you will be able to develop it without so much shooting and without making Baron Sarke so dreadful in appearance. I hope you will not mind doing this but as it stands it is not really *Home Companion* stuff.

This seems to have been the only occasion that she found it necessary to make such a comment to Allingham. Usually she relied on his understanding of the paper's special needs. 'Meantime, have you any story that you think would be suitable for the *Home Companion*? If so would you send it onto me to look at?'

Many of these stories had originally been written for the young, but were now being read by the mature middle-aged – to judge from the number of front-page advertisements for dress patterns 'flattering to the older figure'. Some of Allingham's 1930s readers could have been from the same generation who had first thrilled to *Driven from Home* in 1909. Their approbation was crucial in consolidating his final period of success. However friendly Anne Cooper might be, or however much she might personally relish his work, she was not an autonomous or disinterested reader. Nor was she a powerful leader in the Victorian editorial mould. She was an employee of the Amalgamated Press and, as such, accountable to its directors. She and her papers needed to show results.

Allingham's 'Indian Summer' of prosperity blossomed from the renewed success of the *Family Journal*. On 28 October 1931 he noted what Anne Cooper told him. 'While other papers went down during the crisis the *FJ* went up. The people downstairs asked her why this was. She replied Mr A's story.'

The story was *The Child She Dared Not Claim* (aka *Her Hidden Past*): the crisis was the fall of the Labour Government on 24 August coupled with the decision of the Prime Minister, Ramsay MacDonald, to form a new 'National' Government with the Conservatives and Liberals. There had been an acute financial emergency with worries about basic food supplies. This had triggered an attempt to pass draconian legislation reducing payments to teachers, civil servants and members of the armed forces as well as to the unemployed. Then, in September, came the psychological blow when Britain was forced to abandon the Gold Standard. The navy mutinied at the government's cost-cutting measures; teachers and civil servants lobbied successfully for some reconsideration, but there was no such reprieve for the millions of people dependent on unemployment benefit. The Conservatives had demanded a General Election and won it on 27 October, the day before Allingham's diary note.

1931 has been described as a political 'watershed' and its events as having 'an impact in countless working-class homes'. Was it a need for comfort that persuaded more people to buy the *Family Journal* over this period or did the sheer grippingness of 'Mr A's story' serve to take their minds off their problems? Editorially, comfort and exhortation were being dispensed in large helpings – together with economy household recipes, such as the making of sheep's head broth. 'Mother' in 'Our Family Club' assured her members that everyone was sharing the need to make sacrifices:

> There are few indeed among us who will not feel some difference for a time. The plans we've made may be subject to alteration and we shall all have to make some little retrenchment. But the present state of affairs is one of national importance. Pride in our country will urge us to do our bit towards keeping our beloved country in the front rank among the nations.

She promised readers that the hard times would not last.

> Make no mistake about that. Our troubles and trials – whatever they may be – are purely transitory. They will assuredly pass, as those we have known before have passed. Look back over your life and recall the difficulties you have known. At the time they were present in your life, you saw no way out – the whole future seemed clouded over, with no ray of light to relieve the blackness. Yet those trials passed away, and once again you saw the light [...] If trial be

your lot today, remember you have come successfully through trial before. Similarly you have had your happy days, and will have many more at the direction of a wise and merciful Providence. The right thing to do then is to face up manfully to your present difficulties, and await with confidence the turning of the tide.

Week after week, in Allingham's stories, the heroes and heroines are trapped into impossible situations and week after week they escape, only to face some new disaster. Like fairy tales these stories are characterised by their 'heroic optimism'. Although the prison warders do not crash through cottage doors in the 1930s stories quite as frequently as they did before the war, they, and the baby-farmers and the keepers of the sinister private asylums, have certainly not gone out of business. Additional threats to family stability in these post-war stories come from misunderstandings and failures of trust between hero and heroine, usually precipitated by the malice of others. They are dire (as in *The Child She Dared Not Claim*) but under the providential direction of the author, happy days always return. The readers can thus face their fears, enjoy the periods of adventure and suffer the 'heart-pull' of sympathetic emotion, knowing that all will come right in the end.

One might wonder whether it was a validation or a condemnation of Allingham's art that readers turned to it in this period of crisis. Was he part of a capitalist conspiracy to keep the common people quiet whilst the elite manipulated the situation to their own advantage? 'All fiction from the mushroom libraries downwards is censored in the interests of the ruling classes,' stated Orwell, firmly. Allingham was not directly censored but he was an experienced interpreter of the expectations of others and the dynamics of the field within which he worked. 'I know your desire is to give us exactly the kind of story we like,' William Harvey had written, encouragingly, and Allingham knew, as well as any other supplier, that if his product failed to please it would not be published and he would not be paid – a strong incentive to self-censorship.

The problem in 1931 was that 'Mother', the spokesperson of the Amalgamated Press, was not telling the whole truth. 'Little use to resent such trials,' she writes, 'They fall to rich and poor alike, for trial and adversity are no respecters of persons.' As the 1930s wore on, it became increasingly obvious that the burden was not being shared equally: whole areas of the country – the distressed areas, 'graveyards' of the industries whose workers had given Britain such ebullient prosperity in the nineteenth century – were suffering disproportionately.

One lie that Allingham's fiction never told was that rich people, as a group, were no happier than poor people. The rich, in his stories, are nakedly powerful. They can hire detectives, impress policemen, lawyers, doctors and nurses; rush across the country in powerful cars and pay whatever fees the baby-farmers and the private asylum keepers require. His fiction strips out whatever legal and financial safety nets there actually were in the early twentieth century, to present the central injustices starkly. The rich are warm and comfortable while the poor are anxious and hungry: the rich are believed, the poor are not. When Harry Dare, son of the titled owner of the advertising agency in *The Child She Dare Not Claim*, tells his parents that he has fallen in love with Milly, a shorthand typist, she is dismissed at once. When she marries a Manchester industrialist, who is murdered and his will forged by his scheming cousin (who then pays an eminent doctor to commit Milly to an asylum) no one makes much of a fuss.

Little thought was given to Milly. She was just a work girl who by her pretty face had inveigled Brand into marriage... No one greatly blamed the dead man for his duplicity. It was felt that he had always loved his cousin. *That was proved by his Will.* Milly by her wiles had caught him in a weak moment but *being what she was* had been unable to hold him [my italics].

The readers know that Milly is competent, intelligent and loving; good at her work and a keen reader of what her unsympathetic father calls 'trashy novels'. Yes, she has an illegitimate child. Few will blame her: she was so young, so trusting, her 'guardian angel looked away' at one crucial moment. It was Fate. Then the forces of snobbery and hard, unforgiving respectability combine against her – in Ealing (where Milly's father is a grocer) as well as in Tudor Street (where Harry Dare's father has earned his knighthood by covering up for a politician). The power of money is spelled out again by the wicked cousin, Julia, speaking to a sub-villain, Ramon Carr.

'You foolish little man,' said Julia with a light laugh. 'Don't you see that if you utter a libel against me you will at once be arrested and sent to prison for a long term? You will not even be allowed to tell your story in public. I am rich and powerful; you are poor and with a bad record. I think I am right in saying you are known to the police. You are not very intelligent but surely even you can see that you have no earthly chance against me?'

'Then you mean to fight?' snarled the man, assuming a crouching attitude which somehow made his grotesque little figure look indescribably absurd.

'Fight? Oh no, it won't come to a fight,' replied Julia with another irritating laugh. 'If you annoy me again you will be sent to prison and I shall save thirty pounds a month. Now stand still and listen and I will tell you exactly what is going to happen. You will leave here at once and return to London where you will live quietly on your allowance which will now be reduced to twenty pounds a month. This reduction is a punishment for your insolence today. If you repeat your threats or annoy me in any way in the future your allowance will be stopped completely. That is all. Now ring the bell and a servant will show you out.'

Carr leaves. The narrator, however, points out that Julia's arrogance may be a weakness. 'It did not occur to her at that moment that her victory has been a little too easy. She forgot that in warfare it is never safe to despise one's enemy, however weak and contemptible they may be.' Read in the context of the 1931 crisis it's quite possible to see different social and political attitudes being dramatised here. As he leaves, Carr sees the child who will inherit the fortune. '"Yes! That's the boy," he muttered to himself. "That's the prize we are all fighting for!"' Allingham offers no political solution: what he does is what he has been doing since at least 1909, he offers a framework for emotion, a structure on which readers can hang their personal hopes and fears without the discomfort of actuality.

Milly is one of Allingham's more feeble heroines – as much a victim as a protagonist. She can't bear the thought of her repressive father and disapproving sister discovering her pregnancy so she runs away from home. Later she cannot face telling her respectable husband about her first love affair. This leads her to deny her own child, thus delivering both the child and herself into the power of wicked cousin Julia. Yet the narrative is unfailingly sympathetic towards her: the forces of inflexible respectability are presented as truly daunting. Milly is too young, too weak to tackle them alone. As a result she suffers abandonment, marriage and miscarriage, blackmail, incarceration and unremitting persecution. Early in the story she has no 'mother-instinct' but finally, in the last instalment, when the choice appears to be a new marriage to a man whom she does not love, or continued imprisonment in an asylum, one look into her child's eyes gives her the strength to resist:

> She was no longer in the sitting room of the dingy Paddington flat but in the open air on a lonely island in one of the upper reaches of the Thames. The sun was shining in a blue sky and she was gazing into eyes as brown and as serious as these. But they were not the eyes of her baby boy; they were the eyes of his father, Harry Dare.

Eyes are conventionally eloquent. This vision compels her to reject the marriage-and-safety offer, making one of those fictional decisions that seem irrational but by the emotional logic of the story turn out to be right. Before the instalment is out her enemies have been routed, her true love has returned and, finally, they can live happily ever after as a family.

Robbed of Her Child!

Chapter Twenty-Three
1932: Driven from Home, again

HAD Em Allingham, meanwhile, been living in her own fantasy? Her friendship with Dr Salter had been important to her ever since Layer Breton. Salter took a continuing interest in all the family. He had praised Margery's achievement when she was the young author of *Blackerchief Dick* and he attempted to influence Phil Allingham to continue trying for Oxford University even when Phil and his father knew that he had been categorically rejected. Every year members of the Allingham family were among the guests at Salter's annual garden party at Tolleshunt D'Arcy and he, occasionally, visited them in London. The friendship with Em, however, was special – for her at least. Towards the end of his life she was visiting every few weeks.

Em may have helped Dr Salter with his reminiscences – he

claimed to have documented every day in his life from the age of eight, every child brought into the world and every purchase ever made. A note in Allingham's 1920 diary says that Em had been 'writing Salter's stuff'. A few days later he 'corrected' it for her. We'll never know the extent of the Allinghams' involvement as the many volumes of Salter's memoirs were stored in Chelmsford during the Second World War and destroyed in a direct hit. In the abridged version of Salter's *Diary and Reminiscences*, published in 1933, Em and her family are never mentioned. The doctor had died in 1932 and producing a memorial volume so soon after his death meant that very many people might have expected to see their names included. The editor opted firmly for discretion. 'The entries and detail appertaining to his profession of a country doctor were innumerable but, unfortunately, not of a nature to allow publication.'

Nothing survives to tell what Em or Herbert thought of the abridgement. What had already mattered, catastrophically, was Em's partial exclusion from Salter's will. The doctor had left her a financial legacy (£500) but did not name her among his executors – and, worst, did not leave her D'Arcy House, as she had believed he would. Why Em should have expected this remains a mystery. D'Arcy House had been the doctor's home since 1864. In his *Reminiscences* he (or the editor) presents it as pervaded by the spirit of his much-mourned wife. It was at the centre of Tolleshunt D'Arcy village and housed his GP's surgery. Minor operations, such as tonsillectomies, were routinely carried out on the premises. As Salter had no immediate family he left the house to his partner, Dr James, who continued the practice. Even if Em and the doctor had been enjoying a passionate affair for years it would still have seemed out of character for him to leave her such a locally important bequest.

It seems unlikely that they were lovers. Allingham's diaries contain no hint that he disliked this friendship although Margery later recorded her own resentment at being dragged round the D'Arcy House gardens in her mother's wake. Granny, writing to Maud, mentioned an occasion in 1931 when 'poor Emmie came home upset from the Doctor's' but Allingham's frequent diary notes – 'Em to Salter's', 'Em back from Salter's' – carry no emotional charge whatsoever. They are identical to 'Em to Pope's', 'Em to the cinema', 'Em to Maud's'. His wife had her own life and interests as he had his. Perhaps he felt excluded but he doesn't say so.

Allingham's diary records that Dr Salter died on 17 April, 1932 at 2.30pm. At 3.35pm his head gardener, Herbert Bullard, rang the Allinghams to break the news. On the following day Em went down to D'Arcy and a few days later, on Thursday, they attended the funeral. Real trouble began on the Saturday when a letter arrived from Dr Salter's solicitor. The whole family went over to Chappel, the village where Margery and Pip had been living since August of the previous year and which had long been the home of Herbert and Em's favourite cousin, Grace. This was the traditional refuge in times of upset but Allingham's diary gives no clue as to whether the letter and the visit were connected or coincidental. He remained at Chappel the following day while Em returned to their home, the Dairy House, Shelley. She then visited Tolleshunt D'Arcy on her own, and came later to collect Herbert.

'Home left to Dr James.' There was no mistake. Allingham and Em went immediately to London and sought professional advice. Em requested a copy of the will. She became 'nervy'. Salter's solicitor refused to provide a copy. Em became 'abnormal and fanciful'. Herbert took her back to Margery's house in Chappel where her condition worsened. Different doctors were consulted and the family considered a nursing home. Instead they took the advice of a specialist recommended by Margery's friend Ronnie Reid.

Turnbull came. Strongly against a nursing home. 'Only chance of recovery immediate action under proper medical treatment.' Advised St Andrew's. Arranged during day. Car took her away at 9pm. She was willing and eager to go. Will write all I remember elsewhere if I can.

St Andrew's was a private mental hospital. If Allingham did write an extended account of his feelings and actions around this time it has not survived. There had never, in his fiction, been a justified committal to such an institution. It was invariably a hostile act. Even the most benign – as in the most recent example, *The Child She Dared Not Claim* – are unwittingly cruel. Wicked cousin Julia gains immense social credit by paying 'a thousand a year' for Milly to be incarcerated in a mental home with 'smooth velvety lawns, bits of woodland and masses of spring flowers'.

For nearly five months Milly had lived in this beautiful joyless paradise but to her it seemed like five years.

At first she had been frantic, protesting angrily, telling her story to everyone but that was long ago. Now she had sunk into the apathy of despair.

She had been treated with the utmost kindness by the attendants, by the doctors by everyone with whom she came into contact. It was this very kindness that had first driven her frantic and then crushed her spirit. Everyone was so gentle and sympathetic and no one believed a word she said.

The day after his wife had been taken away, Allingham briefly collapsed. 'Made a fool of myself. Empty emotion. Boys took me to Colchester and saw *Congress Dances.* Girl amazingly like Em as a child.' Theirs had been a long relationship.

Phil Allingham had arrived in Chappel at midnight, some hours after his mother had left. He rallied round his father, taking him home to Shelley to sort out practicalities and then, a couple of days later, up to Northampton to visit Em in hospital. Allingham then settled with Margery and Pip at Viaduct Farm and got back to work. He had just finished a new serial for *My Weekly* for which, confusingly, he had used an old title, *Driven from Home* (published as *The Woman Cast Out*); now he was re-writing an old serial, *Justice*, under a new title, *The Woman Who Loved Him Best.*

His weekly word count had dipped in the depressing years of the 1926–1927 and it had been a shock to him when he discovered that one reason he was no longer being offered commissions for new serials was that he was considered too slow. From that time on he became more punctilious about recording his weekly word counts in an effort to keep himself up to scratch. A mix of re-writing old stories and composing only one or at most two new serials helped him achieve a fairly steady 8,000-10,000 words a week for most of his 1930s 'Indian Summer'.

Margery also mentioned her father's slowness – later in life she worried that she was becoming like him when she found she wasn't able to work as swiftly as before. Sometimes Allingham described himself as 'lazy'; more often he worried that he was blocked, that he 'couldn't' get on. The crisis with Em had shaken him but he knew that, however sympathetic his editors might be on a personal level, there was no compromising with the need for copy once a serial was running. Fortunately, re-working *Justice* appears to have been a straightforward task and there was no new work required until July (though it was August before he delivered). Living with his hard-working daughter and her husband must have been a little like the old days in Layer Breton when visitors from London would come to stay with him and Em, bringing their deadlines with them.

There were many letters to be written – to Em, to editors and to other members of the family. There also seems to have been some unspecified complication with Colonel and Mrs Tabor, his and Em's landlords at the Dairy House, Shelley. They had moved to Shelley in July 1929 when the lease on the Old Vicarage, Letheringham, had expired and its owners decided to sell. Allingham had wondered briefly whether he could afford to buy the Old Vicarage but knew he could not. The rent at the Dairy House was his cheapest yet, only £40 per year. It was near the small market town of Hadleigh, was accessible to other family members and had provided regular writing-holiday accommodation for Margery and Pip while he and Em had moved to London to stay in their flat. Neighbourly relationships appear to have become difficult. Em and Mrs Tabor were embroiled in some way over the Girls' Friendly Society, Em's regular charity, and Allingham needed to pass messages between the two women while Em was away.

His relationship with his wife also had to be handled with great care. He, after all, was the one who had taken the responsibility of committing her. She was angry with him and said so – but it passed. When Em came out of hospital Allingham took her first to lunch with Maud in London and then to stay with Cousin Grace. 'All's well,' he wrote in his diary with relief. It was three more weeks before they returned to the Dairy House and by then they had decided to move on. For the first time in their lives the Allinghams were going to buy a house. The abandonment of the Gold Standard during the crisis of 1931 had brought interest rates down, while many people with money to invest now felt safer in building societies than in the stock market, which had crashed so spectacularly in 1929. The 1930s saw a boom in home-ownership, in the south of England anyway. Em's forthcoming legacy from Salter enabled her to supply the cheque for the deposit and Allingham's 'Indian Summer' of success in Anne Cooper's papers meant that he could be confident in his ability to pay the rest. Once Em was safely settled at Pope's Hall, Allingham hurried back to London and talked to his agent, and his editor. 'Cooper wants all the old stuff I can find her', he noted in his diary.

He also talked to Maud. She and Teddy had bought a house in suburban Thorpe Bay, just outside Southend-on-Sea in Essex. After a lifetime of either metropolitan or rural living this represented something different – perhaps not completely unlike the 'third England' that JB Priestley identified in his 1934 *English Journey.* Most of the houses were post-war, there was a direct rail link to London as well as the metropolitan pleasures of nearby Southend – a theatre, amateur dramatics, a chess club and a good restaurant, Gavron's. A fortnight later Herbert and Em left Pope's Hall to stay at the Queen's Hotel, Westcliff-on-Sea. Within a few days Em had found them a house in Thorpe Bay Avenue, Allingham had discussed their plans with the Abbey Building Society and they returned to the Dairy House only to give their landlords notice and pack up for the move. By September they were installed in their final destination.

The whole episode – an unexpected and unjust will, a couple split apart, the heroine's committal to a mental institution, then reunion in a new home, looking forward to the future – could have been an abridgement, or a parody, of one of Allingham's own stories. Except that Herbert and Em were no longer a young couple with children growing up sturdy on the green lawns of one of his fictional dream homes: she was in her early fifties and he was almost sixty-five. Retirement wasn't an option but they were downsizing. FA Wickhart, former editor of *Spare Moments*, sent good advice.

I can quite understand the wrench it must be and the pathos of having to go through old letters and destroy them. But be careful not to burn those that may be wanted later. Two or three large boxes might hold the lot and be put on the 'wain' with your other goods. No doubt a cupboard at Thorpe Bay might store them until you get time to wade through them. It was the keeping of old letters that won me the Bradley action. There may be some among your old papers that may preserve your rights in some direction so go through them carefully before you commit them to the flames. Possibly this will come too late to save many but MSs I should certainly preserve. RIP to those that have gone.

A charming letter had arrived a few days earlier from Anne Cooper: 'I want to tell you how much I have enjoyed the story that is at present running in the *Family Journal* and I am going to be very, very sorry when it finishes.' Things were evidently going well in her professional life. As well as the *Family Journal* and the *Home Companion*, she was editing a paper for younger women, *Poppy's Paper* (for which Allingham had already re-written one of his DC Thomson stories using the pseudonym 'Victoria Strong'). She was now busy establishing yet another new story paper, the *Oracle*, and, just as Fred Cordwell used to do, she wanted it to open with a serial from Allingham. At Christmas she was taking a few weeks rest in her favourite location, Broadstairs, but she still wanted to hear from her current favourite author. 'Mrs Cooper asks me to add that the instalments you write will be sent on to her – to brighten her up and act as a tonic. So, to use her own words, "make them good!"'

'Mary pressed on desperately'

Chapter Twenty-Four
1934: Married to a Monster

At the beginning of 1934 Allingham was working simultaneously for Cooper and William Harvey. For Harvey he was in the later stages of a new serial, *Married to a Monster*, while for Cooper he was re-writing *The Woman Pays*, first produced for Harvey's *People's Journal* back in 1918–1919. This serial had been conceived when many men were not yet home and some families were wondering how to meet again, whether they would manage to re-establish their relationships after such traumatic change. Allingham had been working as usual through emotional displacement. The separation of hero and heroine had not been caused by war but by a naïve addiction to gambling, specifically horseracing. Jack Wallace was blithe and boyish when he was parted from his loving wife: he returns aged, emotionally scarred, facially unrecognisable, with a devoted but sinister Japanese manservant in attendance. Husband and wife are finally reunited but the brutal plots against them and the story's gothic elements (such as a mysterious oriental drug capable of freezing living beings into an inanimate suspension) make for a somewhat dour reading experience.

This was not what was required in 1934. Allingham's rewrite, *The Wife of a Hunted Man*, still values endurance and devotion but chooses to emphasise happiness coming unexpectedly from misfortune; change being potentially constructive and re-vivifying. The *Family Journal* was all about positive attitudes. The homiletic jingles which were printed within each instalment of Allingham's serial constantly urged readers to look on the bright side, count their blessings, relish new possibilities and 'Carry on! Keep doing your Bit!'

Never say fail
Keep pushing – 'tis wiser than sitting aside
And dreaming and sighing and waiting the tide.
In Life's earnest battle they only prevail
Who daily march onward and never say fail.

Despite the evangelical antecedents of her papers, Anne Cooper's editorial standards of morality were more accommodating than William Harvey's. She had no problem passing stories of Allingham's that included sex before marriage, adulterous sex and bigamous sex, as long as the protagonists were more sinned against than sinning and it was tastefully managed. As she said in a letter on the question of the husband's premarital affair in *The Child She Dared Not Claim*: 'This is not a big point and in your own inimitable way you will gloss nicely over anything of this sort.' In 1934 AP Herbert's *Holy*

Deadlock put reform of the divorce laws on the public agenda. Allingham's *Family Journal* version of *The Woman Pays* does not use divorce (which remained difficult and expensive for the poor) but does allow the heroine's new love to triumph over her first husband. Madge and Jack are not re-united. She has children by two different fathers – who grow up to love and care for one another. The hero too has a new relationship, with a very young girl from a different social class.

Anne Cooper's lighter touch was manifest as she wrote to Allingham telling him of a change she had made to one of his curtains. 'I like your third instalment. I have altered the last three lines and made Nan say, when Jack asks her what she is going to do now that she has discovered who he is, "Nuthin'. Let's go off together and be sweethearts".' It's hard to imagine Harvey allowing such a line, let alone editorially dabbing it in. Nan represents Allingham's final version of the supremely competent, tough, inventive slum-girl. She is the daughter of a Gypsy who has been left to fend for herself in a dingy east London coffee shop. She has saved her pennies and survived, adopting Tricksey (a comically inept old crook) as her 'father' and now Jack as 'Archie', her brother – though she makes it perfectly clear that she wants him as a sweetheart. But Jack is married:

> 'I can't have you as my sweetheart, Nan, I've got one already!'
>
> The girl nodded as if it was of no importance. 'I reckoned you would have,' she said. 'Is she nice?'
>
> 'Very nice!'
>
> 'And pretty?'
>
> 'Very pretty!' [...]
>
> 'And now the cops have given up looking for you, I reckon you are going back to her?' suggested the girl petulantly.

Jack shook his head.

'No, I am never going back to her. I shall never see her again.'

Young Nan's face cleared immediately

'Then that's alright,' she said cheerfully. 'Having a sweetheart you never see is like having a shilling in someone else's pocket. It don't count!'

Nan's humour and pragmatism offer a welcome contrast to the anguished heroine. Madge, however, finally surprises the reader when she accepts that her love for her second husband (Lord Swaley) is a more adult and serious passion than her girlish marriage to Jack. Nan and Jack are also allowed to grow up – and the change in personalities, in this second version, is linked specifically to the experience of war.

The War had intervened and that world-tragedy had drawn a thick line across the page of history.

People who survived did not take up the old life again where they had dropped it in 1914; they began a new life with new ideas and new aims. Everything had changed. Even human nature did not seem the same.

In the final episode of *The Wife of a Wanted Man* Madge and Lord Swaley are both dead, Madge's children (one from each father) are financially and emotionally secure and Jack and Nan are living in New York under somewhat bizarre disguises as 'Count Varano' and his secretary 'Miss Brown'. At long last Jack takes the initiative.

'Nan,' he said, in a quite changed tone, 'I wish I could understand you. You always give me the idea that you rather despise me.'

A smile flickered over the girl's face but she did not reply.

'When we first met … you called me a softy, do you remember?'

The girl nodded but still did not speak.

'Well, ever since then you've treated me in the same way – as though I was not quite right in the head. I won't say you haven't helped me. You have in a hundred ways. You've been a brick! But you've never treated me seriously – not as though – well as though you cared for me, I mean. Why is that?'

Nan rose from her chair and stood back with her hands on her hips, an attitude reminiscent of the childish Nan of years ago.

'Archie,' she said, looking him squarely in the eyes. 'When I was a kid I said you was a softy. And I said something else. I said: "Let's go off together and be sweethearts." That's what I said – and you turned me down. Well I ain't going to say it again. If you want me you've got to ask me proper, like the gentlefolks do.'

She was trembling and all the cultivated refinement of recent years had fallen away from her.

The next moment Jack's arms were round her and he was looking into her tear-dimmed eyes.

'Nan – my dear, dear little Nan,' he said softly. 'Will you be my wife?'

'That's what I've been wanting all along,' she said, sniffing. 'You are a softy, Archie. But, oh my dear I do love you so very much and – and I will take care of you!'

And so it was that Jack Kingsley, under another name, found happiness himself and gave it to the one who, in his hour of need, had proved so true and loyal a friend.

THE END

It's interestingly different from the 1919 tableau ending when Jack and Madge and their daughter Jenny are seen reunited in their picturesque Heather Grange from where the story had begun. Lord Swayne, the 'true and loyal friend' of this original version, is left an adoring bachelor while Madge gazes fondly at her and Jack's new baby sleeping in the cradle by her side. The 1919 ending offered reassurance that fractured families can rebuild their lives together: the 1934 marital swap-about affirms the positive aspects of change.

Allingham's other January 1934 serial, *Married to a Monster* (published in *My Weekly* 1933-1934 as *The Hate of a Woman*) turned out to be the last serial that he wrote for the North. For the only time on record there had been sharp creative disagreement. In the middle of January 1934 Harvey returned an instalment with a request for alteration.

> You appear to have transformed Charles Crewe and he has become a very respectable character. I have no doubt that you have a perfectly good reason for this but it is a bit puzzling and I am wondering whether the reader should not be let into the secret of why he is reformed. [...] I am returning the instalment to you so you can look at it in the light of these remarks.

'I will of course do what you like with this story,' Allingham replied,

> but I cannot help feeling that you are taking a lot of the interest out of it. Surely one murderer in a story of this kind is enough? I cannot see that CC has had a changeover in character. I have known many writers only out for a good time (one or two in my own family) but not one of them would have committed murder or failed to be shocked by it.
>
> This is how I meant to go on [...] But, as I say, I will think out an entirely new continuation for you if you want it.

Harvey remained unconvinced:

> There is no doubt that in the earlier episodes he was depicted as an absolute rascal, just the last man that the reader would imagine would boggle at a murder or indeed at any crime. He had been a waster. He had disappeared from the family home. He had reappeared unexpectedly. He had made it clear that he was out for a good time come what may and generally he was really the bad man of the piece. It seems to us that he has made a wonderful somersault and we have no doubt that our readers will be disappointed with this changing of character.

As far as Harvey was concerned a bad character should be completely bad. The time taken for him to receive and disregard Allingham's explanation presented a threat to his production schedule. 'I know you will do your best to meet our view, and as some days have been lost over this correspondence, I sincerely trust that you will be able to let me have the revised instalment by Monday.'

The presses were imposing their timetable on both editor and author. Harvey's letter was dated Thursday 25th and arrived on 26th. He also sent a telegram. Allingham complied – as Harvey had known he would. On Saturday 27th he altered the instalment and posted it to Dundee. On Monday 29th he received a telegram from Harvey confirming that the instalment was 'now OK' and by Thursday he was at work again on the next instalment.

Poor Charles Crewe, the character who had caused the trouble, soon found himself dispatched to yet another of those convenient institutions 'run for private profit' where he was put on a diet, deprived of 'all the little luxuries to which he was accustomed' and subjected to a very rigid discipline. He had, as Allingham had tried to explain to Harvey, been a cheery black sheep, not averse to a little light blackmail but loved devotedly by the old housekeeper and completely outclassed by the wickedness of his own daughter. He was also fatally apt to get drunk at the wrong moment. It's hard not to wonder which members of Allingham's 'own family' he had in mind when he wrote Charles Crewe's defence: Teddy Wood, who failed to arrive that weekend as expected, having been left behind 'ill'? Cousin Grace's father 'wild Uncle John'? His own son, Phil, regularly disappearing from the family home and re-appearing unannounced?

Allingham completed the assignment as requested – seventeen instalments which ran in *My Weekly* until May – then he uncharacteristically neglected to provide any more opening instalments and allowed several weeks to pass before reporting for instructions when 'our Mr Davidson' was visiting London. When he finally attended an appointment he was given the plot for a new serial but did nothing about it. Feelings were hurt. The agent, JH Cotterill, did his best to jolly the writer along.

> Davidson was in London last week and was asking after you. He feels your desertion of Dundee very much; doesn't think that they deserve it. I told them we would do our best to bring the straying sheep back to the fold. No it is not going to be a case of leading a lamb to the slaughter. Now get busy on that story you started for Harvey like the good chap that you are and let us have you writing regularly again for Leng's.

Cotterill appears unaware that Allingham might have had any reason for this unexpected recalcitrance. He feels no need to represent Allingham's point of view to the publishers – or even enquire whether he has one. Allingham should simply 'be a good chap' and write. 'Leading a lamb to the slaughter' seems an entirely apt description.

Even if Allingham had wished to respond to such a mutton-headed letter it was no longer possible. A few days previously he had granted Anne Cooper the first option on all his reprints and accepted an advance of £250 'to help my married daughter buy a house.' Dr Salter's legatee, Dr James, had been killed in a car accident and his executors were selling D'Arcy House. Margery and Pip wanted to buy. 'Have odd feeling that these things are ordained somehow,' wrote Margery. Allingham had also offered not to write for anyone else for three years – as long as Anne Cooper continued to want his stuff. This offer appears to have been made voluntarily. He knew he 'owed' Dundee one more story but was doing his best to manoeuvre himself out of their orbit. He had been supplying 'the North' continuously since 1914 and writing for them on a contractual basis since 1919. He and his family would not have survived without this steady flow of work. Nevertheless resentment had been building up. Margery's *Death of a Ghost* was published in 1934. Privately Allingham used the occasion to poke some angry fun at his Scottish editors.

Dundee

<u>One Scottish B-d</u>

Jaime, th'Allingham bairn's another book oot. Seven an' sax. It's dedicated to her father. We could buy it oot right for five pun ten.

<u>Other S B</u>

It looks awfu' dry Donal. She hasna got her faither's geeft.

<u>One Scottish B-d</u>

The owd man's awfu' lazy. Twa months with the last instalment.

Other S B

Aye the bairn's mair speed on her.

One Scottish B-d

Wad we offer fifteen shilluns fur a first number? Likely she get the owd man's idees and the Johnnie MacDonald, Ronnie Duncan, Jessie Stuart and owd uncle Tammas McTavish culd have a spier at them for their new stories. Wuldn't that be economical?

Other S B

Fifteen shilluns! Ye spendthrift! It's awfu' expenseeve. Still the owd man has gran' ideas...

(They write and offer ten bob.)

'Bastard' (if that's the word) is very strong language for Allingham. He had grown grumpy at the constant haggling over money (first evident in 1907 in correspondence with Harvey's predecessor, WF Anderson) and resented the restrictions imposed on his style – no low-life comic characters, for instance. Allingham also had definite views about the sanctity of plots. A plot was a tangible thing, with a commercial value. If he had used a friend's idea or asked a fellow writer to complete a story from his outline he expected to pay appropriately.

Later that year he 'gave' a plot to Margery, which she said she might use (but possibly never did). He also wrote to Harvey offering, somewhat awkwardly, to return the plot that Davidson had given him. 'I would not bother you with the thing at all only the plot is yours which precludes me from offering it elsewhere.' Privately Allingham appears to have believed that the editors at Dundee were regularly guilty of just such underhandedness – passing one writer's ideas to others without payment or permission. It's a difficult accusation to substantiate when relationships between author and editors were so close and when one editor, such as William Harvey, was supervising the work of a large number of authors across so many publications. More difficult still when the entire method of operation is based on common understandings of narrative formulae.

Falling out with Harvey and selling reprints to Cooper left Allingham free, for the first time in years, to take a summer holiday. Phil Allingham's autobiographical *Cheapjack* – an account of his fairground adventures as a 'grafter, knocker-worker and mounted pitcher' – had been published in May 1934. 'Surprisingly good and unlike anything else,' wrote Allingham in his diary. 'May easily make a hit. Pip is taking it to Heinemann tomorrow. My prayers go with it.' His diary for May and June lists generous reviews and exciting sales. Phil was invited to do a series of broadcasts and Margery, who had worked hard to make *Cheapjack* publishable, felt just a little jealous. Her father clumpingly made this worse by taking her aside and reminding her to 'let Phil have the credit for his book.' Margery 'was so angry that I almost wept'.

At the end of July Allingham and his son set off from Thorpe Bay to Cardiff, via Fleet Street. Addie, a young girl who Phil used as his model in hair-waving demonstrations, travelled with them and was put in the charge of various landladies in the lodging-houses where they stayed. For ten days they criss-crossed South Wales including Dowlais, Aberdare, Tonypandy and Pontypridd as well as the seaside resort of Tenby and Pembroke Dock. Allingham met Phil's Gypsy friends, the Lorenzos, in their caravan and was introduced to them as the father of 'Orlando' (Phil's Gypsy name). Most evenings they ate fish and chips and went to 'bevvy' with Phil's fellow grafters: 'the Strangler', 'Randall the Great' and a man named Gordon who travelled with his girl-friend Mattie and two sisters referred to only as '18' and '22'.

Allingham's diary suggests that he noticed some emotional complications involving Phil and one or more of these young women. 'Silent 18 contrives a long private interview with Phil.' Margery had edited Phil's sexual experiences out of *Cheapjack* and Allingham describes himself as rather slow on the uptake, 'At first I don't get the full strength.' He betrays no shock when Phil explains 'the whole bloody how d'y do' – whatever it may have been. This was a dads'n'lads holiday. Allingham and Phil share bedrooms and talk into the small hours. Then they sleep late in the mornings and spend the day shuttling between market centres until it is time to bevvy again.

Em and Joyce meanwhile had gone to the Passion Play at Oberammergau. Joyce, in adulthood, remembered little of their holiday. Her father's trip with Phil had been, in her view, one of the highpoints of his life. His diary reveals pride but little surprise at Phil's success as a mounted pitcher, setting up his stall, drawing and holding a crowd then 'coming to his bat' with practised skill to sell his sets of hair-wavers. He watches his son reconnoitring the markets, selecting and haggling for his site, then pitching for two or three hours at a time. He notes Phil's daily takings and understands how hard the work can be with an unresponsive or impoverished crowd.

On August Bank Holiday they are at Chester racecourse where Allingham finds the fairground fascinating but exhausting. He goes out and finds a café, which he describes as 'a bit arty but not too crowded'. Meanwhile Phil has worked from 2pm to 8.30pm and earned £11 4s. They take Addie, the girl model, back to their digs, garage the car and go out to celebrate with chops, steak, lager and cigars in 'the best hotel in the place'. Addie is then discovered to have 'grown up' so Phil decides that she should return to her mother for a while. He and his father set off (via Manchester, Oldham, Huddersfield and Leeds) for the north east of England – Stockton, Darlington and South Shields. So many places where Allingham's stories have been read but which he has never seen.

There's a great welcome and a meat tea at Phil's regular lodgings in Stockton and more happy reunions with old friends in Darlington. In South Shields, however, Phil's previous models Susie and Jenny Johnson are disappointingly unavailable and another sister is substituted. A day at Blackpool and the holiday is coming towards an end. A night at Peterborough and a few pounds earned at the market in Swaffham. Then they are on the road for Viaduct Farm, Chappel, where they arrive at ten minutes to midnight. The household is waiting for them: 'Pip, Marge, Cooee, Robin, Grog. Great reception. Marge gives dramatic account of Pope's Hall tragi-comedy.'

Once again Allingham is in the thick of his family's affairs. There has been a scandal concerning cousin Grace. 'Marge gives us the news – dramatically!' In his rough holiday notebook, but not in his formal diary, he scribbles that 'it doesn't seem to matter'. The following summer, 1935, he stowed away with Phil again.

'Her father was the last person she wished to see'

Chapter Twenty-Five
1934–1936: Deserted

'Oppressed with the thought of futility, futility, futility.' Allingham's brother 'big' Phil died in October 1934 – 'old' Phil as he had more recently become in Allingham's diary. The doctor wrote to offer sympathy: 'The marvel is he lived so long under the very serious conditions from which he suffered. I rather think he felt the end was near since we had difficulty in getting him to take his food and to look forward to getting better [...] You have been a most devoted brother to him for many years.'

As a boy Allingham had spent much of his time with his older brother, Will, and as adults they had regular dealings with each other over Will's property problems in Essex. He kept in touch with his next brother, Arthur, an artist, and helped where he could. Arthur's wife, Florence, undertook Allingham's typing. Claude, a failed actor, he saw frequently and supported with small writing projects. 'Tod', the youngest, he worked with at the agency and admired for his business acumen. 'Al' (Albert) seems to have faded from the family scene but 'Wal' (or 'Tub'), an invalid, was still in regular touch. 'Big Phil' had been different. He was twelve years younger than Allingham, born just two months before Em, and like her had the touch of flamboyance that Allingham loved. He was the first to go to work in the advertising agency with their father; he made and lost money, took risks in his relationships, experienced divorce. Allingham sought out Phil. They talked, worked and went out together. Phil was the brother to whom Allingham turned in times of trouble. He was the first of them to die and it was a moment of deep sadness.

Allingham's grief could not be allowed to stop him working. He wrote 1,500 words on the day after he'd heard the news and 1,500 on the following day when Margery, Pip, Phil and Joyce came to visit. Jane Carter, the heroine of his current serial, *Deserted,* had already sought refuge among the kindly working people of Kennington. Jane has an illegitimate child and she is angry. Angry with the weak upper-class boy who has deserted her; angry with the world where such things happen. Unlike Milly (heroine of *The Child She Dared Not Claim*) Jane's 'mother instinct' has not been damaged by her abandonment. On the contrary she is ready to 'rob the world left and right' to give a better life to her child. 'He shall want for nothing. And in the days to come if he ever meets his father they shall meet in equal terms. He will be as well educated, as well dressed and he will hold his head as high.' Fortunately (for the plot) the stranger in whom Jane confides is himself a member of a criminal gang. When she returns to her lodgings that night she has money in her pocket and a mission in prospect.

But when a responsible single mother embarks on a life of crime, she needs to arrange childcare. Jane appeals to her landlady. 'Mrs Martin, Jane's landlady, was a typical member of her class. Her figure was shrunken, her face lined with care and overwork but her eyes were brave. After a lifetime of struggle and suffering she had retained her power to sympathise with others.' She and her disabled daughter, Sarah, sound just the sort of people who might enjoy the *Family Journal* if they had a couple of pennies to spare. Jane tells Mrs Martin that she has 'a situation' and explains that this will mean she has to go out at night. She is worried that the baby may wake up while she is away.

'Promise me that one of you will always be in the room till I come back and then I'll give you half a crown for your trouble.'

'Half a crown! It must be a pretty good situation you've got, my dear.'

'Yes, I think it is.'

'Or maybe you've found a friend? But there that ain't no business of mine …'

Does Mrs Martin wonder if Jane is selling herself? If she does, she's not shocked, knowing that Jane's earnings will benefit the child.

'It's lucky for him that your luck turned when it did, my dear. I've seen many a fine 'ealthy babby ruined by underfeeding. If you can't get enough to eat when you're young, you can't never make up for it afterwards.'

'My boy will always have enough of everything,' declared Jane, her arms tightening around the tiny form she was hugging to her heart.

'Ah!' said Mrs Martin with a sigh, 'It's a comfort if one can believe that.'

The instalment Allingham wrote in the days after his brother's death complicates the character of the master-criminal, the unscrupulous financier, Valentine Finch. Is he a murderer or not? A double-crosser yes, but what are his motives? Perhaps he is a more interesting, more human character, with weaknesses. His associates discuss him.

'Val is too reckless. Why does he go in for crazy adventures of this sort? Why can't he stick to the money-making game? He understands that but I doubt he understands women. They'll be his ruin sooner or later, you mark my words.'

This was what Allingham thought, sometimes, about his son, Phil, and about Phil his brother too.

Deserted ends in 1935 with the death of Finch and the contrite return of the child's weakling father. His snobbish mother is sorry too and all is set for the happy ending. But Jane cannot quite forget.

All the events of the last year, which had grown so vague and shadowy, returned to her one by one, and she saw them all quite clearly. And yet they did not seem real but more like pictures on a screen.

The people she had met went by in a kind of procession, each one playing his part and then vanishing. Only one figure constantly returned and seemed always somewhere near. He was dead she now knew – killed by his own hand – yet he seemed more alive than any of the others.

His bold handsome face, his mocking and yet good-humoured eyes, *his reckless laugh* all came back to her in the still watches of the night.

And then, quite suddenly, the conviction came to her that there is nothing in this world so enduring as the influence of a strong and masterful personality [my italics].

'...and Phil's shrill laugh of enjoyment rises above the din,' as Allingham had written in 1886, listening to his younger brothers at play. *Deserted* ends on the evening before Jane Carter's wedding 'and for a brief second she was not thinking of the man who on the morrow would become her husband.' It's quite unlike Allingham's usual idyllic family tableau. Jane will marry the father of her child but will also keep the cottage by the sea that Valentine Finch had given her. Moreover, she will keep it exactly as it has been left to her, with her new husband's understanding and agreement.

These last months of 1934 saw Margery and Pip buying Dr Salter's former home in Tolleshunt D'Arcy with a generous gift from Lilian Carter and £250 advance to Allingham from the Amalgamated Press. It should, overall, have been a satisfactory year for the family but even on Christmas Day Allingham recognised that Margery was 'sub-consciously worried by her responsibilities'. He was troubled too.

The year ends anxiously. Work not going well. Bank account very low. Inc tax due.

The Year: Phil's *Cheapjack* and Broadcast.

Marge – *Death of a Ghost*, story in *News Chronicle*, D'Arcy House bought.

Em & Joyce, German trip.

My trip with Phil.

Joyce secures job & flat in London.

Old Phil died.

Deserted (published as *The Silence of Jane Carter)* was the last of Allingham's new stories to be an unequivocal success. In the way of AP editors, the good results of her core magazines encouraged Anne Cooper to start new papers. The *Oracle* (1933) and the *Miracle* (1935) were both women's story-papers rather than family magazines. They were thus subtly different from the *Home Companion* and the *Family Journal*, which had their roots still in the distant evangelical entertainments of Allingham's childhood. They were competing in the section of the market occupied by DC Thomson's *Red Star Weekly*, a paper that had serialised Allingham's murder story *The Silent Lady of Deadman's Lane* in 1929.

There was no vestige of piety and little domesticity in these new papers. Murder and violence by men against women were their dominant themes. Instead of reassuring their readers, they seemed intent on arousing the shudder factor. AJ Jenkinson, who conducted a survey of adolescent reading in 1940, called such papers 'erotic bloods' and pointed out that, although they were marketed to adult women, they were especially popular among senior school girls – the girls who would not be staying on in education but would be out and at work by age fifteen.

> The Senior School girl can look forward to earning money at 14+. Throughout her short Senior School life she is rapidly nearing a job. She is much closer to the task of earning a living than is her contemporary in a Secondary School, closer to what are termed the 'hard realities of life'.

The AP had been losing readers to Thomson's in their women's magazines as well as in the comics. Anne Cooper's *Miracle* was part of their fight-back. It announced itself as being 'full of really grand stories that will make you want to pull your chair up to the fire and have a good read'. Its first lead story was *Daughter of the Scaffold* by Walter Tyrer, who had been writing similar capital punishment tales for several years for *Red Star Weekly*. Cooper selected and cut several of Allingham's earlier convict stories for her new papers, as well as reprinting *The Silent Lady of Deadman's Lane* and immediately asking him for an additional re-write. Allingham could and did write murder stories for both Thomson's and the AP but they were not his forte. His first story for the *Miracle* had been hastily pulled, presumably in response to poor sales figures, and although he was later asked to re-write it for the *Family Journal* he was too astute not to notice that his editor's strategy had changed. 'Tyrer the great favourite now with Mrs C but she is anxious to hold me.'

Allingham was always quick to worry if he didn't hear from an editor or they didn't seem 'friendly'. Despite his lifetime of steady work and achievement, a phone call from an editor that was unsatisfactory in some way could unsettle him for days. Now, in 1935, aged sixty-seven, he was finding it unusually hard to summon enthusiasm for new work and his perception of Anne Cooper's changed priorities made even re-writing old stories difficult. 'Had a shot at *Girl*. Afraid this story is not in line with Mrs C's present policy.'

His second summer holiday with Phil had taken them from their starting point of D'Arcy House to London. Then to St Alban's – Bedford – Southampton – Alton – Newport – Cardiff – Treorchy – Porthcawl – Llanelly – Nottingham – Thirsk – Stockton – Darlington – Blackpool – Middlesbrough – Whitley Bay – Blyth – Newcastle – Redcar Bay – Whitby – Scarborough – Newcastle – and finally home to Joyce's London flat. In three weeks they had travelled 2,133 miles, with any amount of criss-crossing between different destinations on the same day, irregular and late hours. With hindsight this was probably not an ideal holiday for someone of Allingham's age and usually sedentary life. Yet Margery remembered one of her father's catchphrases as being 'it's all very interesting' – and clearly it was. He was thrilled by Phil's new commission (six talks for the BBC on 'The England I Know') and his 1935 diary regularly records which markets Phil was working and how much he took.

As far as he himself was concerned, it should have been business as usual once the holiday was over. He saw Mrs Cooper and her assistant Mr Lewis the day after his return to London, and then went home to Thorpe Bay with Em and an idea for the next serial. Somehow it wouldn't go. Quite uncharacteristically Allingham found himself having to re-write and revise again and again. 'Can't write, can't think, don't know what to do.' He calculated that he'd had to write 15,000 words to achieve a single passable instalment. Nothing like this had happened before and his brief diary notes make increasingly painful reading: 'Up to Town two or three times. Mrs C cooling off. Can't get going. Rather worried.' The assistant editor took him out to lunch and talked about Phil. Allingham was cheered but not reassured. His anxiety was such that he forced himself to try once again to begin writing for Mr Davidson at Dundee. But, even with Em's help, he could sustain nothing beyond an instalment or two. He tried dictating to her, which felt constructive but only produced a 'jumble'.

The final crisis came on 6 November. 'Frantic phone call from Mrs C. Number no good. Went to Town with Em by car. Saw Mrs C. Told her I could not go on with story. Asked her to lend me £200. Came home and went back to bed.' His beautiful flowing handwriting, perfectly clear for the printer or typist and producing a regular hundred words per page for so many years, degenerated overnight into poorly formed pencil jottings and ceased on 13 November. Margery was anguished. The last words her father wrote in his last diary were 'R e a d m a r g e r y s s t o r y'. The pencilled letters trailed down the page.

Margery's own diary for the first weeks of 1936 tells a sad tale:

1 January: Getting the furniture settled and fixing Emmie's room. The Old Boy seems a little better. Feeling the stress of Em. A dreadful opening to the New Year.

2 January: Pip to London. Terrible sense of oppression. Feel Em and the Old Doc have caught me. Emmie vague about the Old Boy. Feel I must see him. Cocky home. Sayers backed out of book. (*Six Against the Yard*) Saw to Daddy's papers (Northampton insurance. Howell etc).

3 January: Saw Daddy – worse – so weak and speechless. Letter from Hearn. Em more than trying – feel disaster has come over me. One of the two supports of my world going and it looks as though I must live with Em. Boys very very good . Em says extraordinary things that she is destined to live here.

4 January: Mother unbearable. Father worse. Phil, Joyce and Francesca down. Luard rang up. Played rummy.

5 January: A terrible, terrible day. The old boy much worse. Did not see him. Phil and Joyce went together – anxious not to intrude or, more honestly, to share. Em horrible over the book – dreadful scene, just like her. Kids thoroughly frightened of her. Seems to have come down and taken possession of our house. Kids off to town. Pip amazingly good. Frightened myself. Em talking of old Doc.

6 January: long sad day. Em saw him and he's very weak. His pulse fluttering and weak. Phil brought Claude and Tod to see him and on here to tea. They wouldn't stay. Em very nervy of course but

dare not get too sorry for her. Awful situation. Em came back wearing Salter's ring which she had taken off Dad's hand.

7 January: Not a good day at all. Emmie fancied Pip did not speak to her when she met him in the passage and came to make a scene with me just as I was setting out to see Dad. Broke down and made a fool of myself. Saw Dad. Very very weak poor old boy. Feel very helpless and lonely but Cocky wonderfully good. Went on to Pope's. Grace and Steve anxious to help if she has any cash. They're broke. Saw Granny – a dear old thing. Had long reasonable talk with Em in the afternoon. Made her see that she could not live with us but offered her the room always and emphasised that her furniture was only stored here. She seemed to get the idea perfectly and was a different woman – a visitor again. Quite happy and not resentful. Very very tired and miserable. Did an idiotic thing and ordered £5 worth of stuff from Harrods (glass, wine and linen). Cheered me up. Bed early and read a [...] short story. Comfortingly good.

8 January: Corrected *Devil and her Son* and sent it to Chenery. Em in with Daddy nearly all day. Trying evening.

9 January: Grog and Pip to town. Em in a bad mood. She went in to see Daddy. Says he is very drowsy. Cooee hunting. Emmie talking of her own extraordinary virtue and my sinfulness all the rest of the time. Pacified her a bit. Feeling dizzy and utterly wretched. Corrected 20,000 words *Devil and her Son* and sent it off to Chenery.

10 January: Daddy died this morning in his sleep. Undertaker – matron – registrar. Grace, Steve, Miss Bates. Letters. Phoned Joyce and others.

11 January: Mother on mourning ...

12 January: Tired out and miserable. Had the horrors.

13 January: Finished dress. The idiocy of it all. Em religious and spiteful and tragic.

14 January: Daddy's funeral – very quiet and pleasant upon the

hill with Blackwell and a nice priest in charge. Not horrible or terrifying. Only a personal grief. I felt *he* was alright. Horribly miserable.

None of the papers for which Allingham had written mentioned his death. As he had never really existed for the readers, he could not really die. His stories continued to appear in the *Family Journal* until autumn 1937 – the AP had its £200 loan to recoup. Then, after more than thirty years when there had always been an Allingham serial running somewhere, there was nothing. Millions of readers had pulled out their pennies to catch the latest instalment of his work, had discussed it with their workmates or neighbours and looked forward to discovering what would happen next. He died as unobtrusively as most of them would, mourned only by his family and friends.

George Hearn wrote a letter to Margery, which she described as 'heartbroken', and William McFee never really got over his loss.

Since the old man died, Marge, I have missed his letters so much. For many years he and I corresponded and it left a terrible gap in my life. I still have his last one which ended all scrawly and illegible because he had lost control of his muscles. So you must take his place.

In the days immediately after Allingham's funeral Margery described her mother as 'radiant and very important. Feel horrible – I do miss the old man – but it's much better she should take it like this. Oh dear, I don't know what I think, life is very complex.' Margery remembered that her father had looked at her before he died and laughed when she promised 'idiotically' that she would 'look after' her mother. The house in Thorpe Bay Avenue appears to have been closed up, but mother and daughter failed to live together comfortably even for a few days. Margery patently loathed and felt threatened by her mother at this time of her life and Em said of Margery that 'her personality is too strong, she exhausts me.'

Em went as a paying guest to cousin Grace at Pope's Hall and spent some restless months there, and with other relations, until she settled as a live-in housekeeper to an Essex vicar whose wife was a long-stay patient in a mental institution. Em Allingham's life-story is an obscure and a troubled one. Margery said later that 'my mother is not really safe with people' yet she had, it seems, been safe with Allingham. Safe enough to experience an intense emotional attachment to Dr Salter, secure in the knowledge that her husband would not object. In 1932 she had described Salter as 'a Master of Men'. 'Her husband' she added, 'did not come into the picture at all... the Doctor was a materialist, a man of action – the husband intellectual, interested mostly with ideas that found an outlet in his plots.' Her husband was, she added 'a part of herself.' When this 'part of herself' had gone, she did no more writing and appears to have taken no further interest in the work he had left behind. His possessions were dealt with at D'Arcy House.

24 January: 144 boxes arrived for Daddy's stuff. Cocky cross. Sorted out Daddy's stuff. Awfulness.

25 January: More sorting.

26 January: Still sorting out Daddy's stuff. Got it done and boxed up at last.

Margery kept her father's papers safe through the Second World War, through her own troubles and domestic rearrangements until, on her death they passed to Joyce. Fifty years after Margery had boxed them up, Joyce pulled them out again and we looked at them together. Their lodging with me has been temporary. Now they should find their place in the history of mass-market literature.

As a father, Allingham was beloved: as a worker, his job had died with him. Between the publication of *Barrington's Fag* in 1886 and the eventual cessation of stories in the *Family Journal* in 1937, Allingham had contributed almost three hundred serial stories (originals and reprints) for his readers' entertainment. From 1907 to 1937, there had always been an Allingham serial running somewhere. His pay was good, his job security shaky and his public recognition non-existent.

There are occasions when his editorially determined anonymity seems even more than usually perverse. Margery's word 'exasperating' might come to mind. Introducing *The Girl Who Loved Him Best,* in June 1932, Anne Cooper (or her sub-editor) wrote: 'Those who remember that wonderful love story, *The Man Who Stole Her Heart*, will be delighted to know that this new serial, starting today, is by the same author. And my new readers will take care never to miss another story by this great writer.' But how were readers expected to do this in the absence of the great writer's name? In fact Allingham was contributing so much to the *Family Journal* at that period that it would have been impossible to identify him. His *Where Are My Little Ones?* had ended that same day. It had been presented as 'by The Author of *The Child She Dared Not Claim* etc etc.' Linkages work on the principle of recommendation; different sets of linkages suggest that there are a variety of writers at work – which wasn't true. At that moment all three of the *Family Journal*'s serials were by Allingham.

'Stick to it, old boy and you will make a Name!' Ralph Rollington had written cheerfully to his nephew in 1886. In fact the longer Allingham had stuck to it the more invisible he grew. The more stories he wrote, the more reprints he spawned – and reprints were rarely attributed. When Allingham began writing for the *People's Journal* in 1918 he had specifically asked William Harvey whether he could be named. The request was complied with for the first two, higher-profile, serials, and then identification was quietly dropped. Comic papers have a tradition of anonymity. Partly because they are collaborative productions but perhaps also because recognising an author's personality might introduce an intrusion between story and reader.

Accepting anonymity was not the same as abdicating personal responsibility for his stories. While Allingham was alive he was usually anxious to retain control of his material. His fiction however was published as journalism. Every instalment had to be 'passed' by an editor before it went to the printers and sometimes it was sent back for alteration. Allingham always did as he was asked, however reluctantly. He knew, additionally, that his stories might be cut and re-shaped in the editor's office. This varied from Anne Cooper adding a sentence or two 'to strengthen a curtain' to the wholesale re-writes by which the AP recouped the money advanced to him at the end of his life, first for D'Arcy House and then to support him in his last illness. The 1919 arrangement made by Cotterill and Cromb with 'the North' had explicitly allowed editorial re-writing without consultation. The quality of stories such *as Clara Brent – the Woman who Had Hate in her Heart* (an AP office version of *The Girl Outcast*) and *The Fateful Hour* (a Leng's cheap book version of *The Rod of the Oppressor)* is demonstrably rougher than Allingham's originals. *Clara Brent* is structurally weakened at a crucial moment and *The Fateful Hour* shows a coarsening of the main working-class characters that is quite untrue to Allingham's idealisation of 'the common people'.

Such comparisons help demonstrate the extent to which Allingham was a craftsman, not a hack. His writing is a form of word art where the words are not memorable. He writes with cadence and simplicity but his style eschews individuality either of diction or of metaphor. In Allingham's narratives words are used instrumentally. They set up a situation, sketch in a character type, fix the lighting, stimulate an emotional response. They make pictures and it is these stereotyped images (often aided by the magazine illustrations) that remain in the memory when the words have slipped unobtrusively away.

Allingham's editors were the only professional reviewers of his work and they were necessarily partisan. When composing their brief announcements of forthcoming serials the editors first needed to attract readers and then, once the serial was running, to retain them, whilst drawing in others. Their choice of features to praise was a guide to the interpretation of the story rather than the recording of a judgement. Naturally they did their best to predispose readers to enjoy what they were being offered. Their introductions offered a initial evaluation, which was supplemented, as the stories progressed, by their choice of sub-headings, running titles and closing rhetorical questions. They were also selective about which stories were given advance billing. Readers probably picked up on this and assessed the stories' perceived value accordingly. In 1929, for instance, the editor of *My Weekly* announced *The Wicked Guardian*, 'A story that will set all women talking':

The story of Harriet Yorke and the Carter children is such as has never been told before, written in the simple moving language of a master-storyteller, it gives you vivid pages of stirring emotions and depicts strong incidents that will grip you and live in your memory for ever.

The editor was being economical with the truth when he claimed that the story of *The Wicked Guardian* had 'never been told before'. It was yet another re-write of *Mother Love* (1912), another take on the story of the cruel stepmother versus the never-truly absent mother. These are archetypal themes. In 1929 however, unlike 1912, the emotional emphasis of Allingham's narrative falls more powerfully on the pathos of the children than on the anguish of the mother. Its most enduring image, for me, is of an exhausted little girl dancing late into the night in a squalid circus ring, watched greedily by the circus master who is planning how best to market her – rather as the editor was marketing his 'master-storyteller'.

Pip Youngman Carter, Allingham's son-in-law, described him as 'one of the last of a race of giants who made fortunes for others in the formative years of the pulp press'. Allingham's working life had been spent in the culture industry. It had existed before he was born, then had burgeoned in the hands of his contemporaries such as Alfred and Harold Harmsworth and the hard men who ran the Hollywood studios. In the decade after Allingham died the precise term 'culture industry' would be coined by Marxist critics Theodore Adorno and Max Horkheimer in a 1944 essay, 'The Culture Industry: Enlightenment as Mass Deception'. As their title suggests they were not impressed with what they saw.

> The sociological theory that the loss of the support of objectively established religion, the dissolution of the last remnants of pre-capitalism, together with technological and social differentiation or specialisation, have led to cultural chaos is disproved every day; for culture now impresses the same stamp on everything. Films, radio and magazines make up a system which is uniform as a whole and in every part.

The authors charge the culture industry with centralising the consumer, identifying their needs through market research and then designing art-products to almost-satisfy them, whilst simultaneously titillating their appetite for more of the same. 'The culture industry perpetually cheats its consumers of what it perpetually promises' – almost like a semi-addictive patent medicine. Precisely the aspect of Allingham's work that might be cited in its defence: that it was shaped according to a perception of people's emotional need; that it offered them alleviation and escape through the fictional expression of their hopes and fears, is condemned. 'Pleasure promotes the resignation which it ought to help to forget.'

No pleasure for the proles then? George Orwell's critique of 'Boys' Weeklies' was written a few years before 'The Culture Industry' – at the beginning rather than the end of the Second World War. He, too, presented writing for the mass-market as cultural brainwashing in the interests of the ruling classes. Frank Richards was moved to respond.

> Every day of happiness, illusory or otherwise – and most happiness is illusory – is much to the good. It will help to give the boy confidence and hope. Frank Richards tells him that there are some splendid fellows in a world that is after all, a decent sort of place.

He likes to think himself like one of those fellows, and is happy in his day-dreams. Mr Orwell would have him told that he is a shabby little blighter, his father an ill-used serf, his world a dirty muddled rotten sort of show. I don't think it would be fair play to take his twopence for telling him that!

Ada Chesterton, a middle-class journalist who deliberately made herself homeless in the mid-1920s, explained how material privation altered her aesthetic perceptions. She went to the cinema and watched 'a story of a conventional type in which a poor girl becomes a leader of society', just the sort of wish-fulfilment story *My Weekly* would regularly have offered its readers and which Mrs Chesterton would usually have dismissed as clichéd (or to use her actual words 'garish' and 'impossible'). In her new circumstances she was amazed by the intensity of her visual response, her empathy with the heroine.

> I dwelt with rapture on her dinner with the hero in an expensive restaurant. I noted with extraordinary precision everything she ate [...] I would not have forfeited any one of the thousand mechanical sensations she enjoyed [...] When you are hungry and cold, without a home and without hope, the 'Pictures' warm your imagination, heat your blood and somehow vitalise your body.

Allingham's readers were not experiencing homelessness but they were not financially secure and their lives generally were neither varied nor exciting. During 1929 there were very occasional contributions from *My Weekly* readers, introducing themselves and their work. One woman described work in a pickle factory, another woman was a gardener, there was a male reader who worked in a hat factory. *My Weekly*'s offer of 'vivid pages of stirring emotions' sounds appealing. The magazine's circulation was in excess of 200,000 throughout the 1920s. In the absence of explicit testimony from readers themselves, we must assume that they continued to buy the magazine, and the editor continued to commission Allingham to write serials for it because many of them had been moved, stirred and gripped by *The Wicked Guardian*. How bad was this?

Adorno and Horkheimer perceive the cultural consumer as passive and homogeneous:

> Marked differentiations such as those of A and B films, or of stories in magazines in different price ranges, depend not so much on subject matter as on classifying, organising, and labelling consumers. Something is provided for all so that none may escape; the distinctions are emphasised and extended. The public is catered for with a hierarchical range of mass-produced products of varying quality, thus advancing the rule of complete quantification. Everybody must behave (as if spontaneously) in accordance with his previously determined and indexed level, and choose the category of mass product turned out for his type.

We know that this is true and that, in our own generation, the techniques for profiling consumers and second-guessing their buying choices have become unimaginably more sophisticated.

But we also know how often these assumptions are wrong. On the few occasions when actual readers of Allingham's stories have been identified – the three boys in Birmingham, the Gilfeather family in Dundee – they have been discovered to be distinct individuals making their choices and developing their own identities and relationships within the imperfect circumstances of their lives. The two hundred ironworkers' families interviewed by Florence Bell within the culturally limited environment of Middlesbrough had made a multiplicity of individual decisions: whether to read, what to read, who read and how they read. Every social survey of a defined area, such as a street or a group of families on similar incomes (Maud Pember Reeves *Round About a Pound a Week*, or Gwendoline Freeman's *The Houses Behind*), reveals the diversity of ways in which people actually live their lives. Allingham's skill lay in creating a narrative space where large numbers of working-class readers could feel comfortable whilst retaining their right to individual discussion and response.

Over the fifty years of Herbert Allingham's working life the particular set of circumstances that can be caught in a snapshot of 1867, the year of his birth – the struggle towards democracy, state-enforced literacy, sophisticated capitalism, technological advance and just a little more money flitting through the pockets of the working population – effected a cultural revolution, which was revolving again by the time that he died. Silent films were being replaced by talkies and wireless sets were becoming part of the furniture in many homes. The year of his death, 1936, was the official launch of the BBC television service. In January 1937 the world's longest running soap opera began wireless broadcast in America.

The dominance of print as the medium for drama-in-instalments was coming to its end. Today, most of the periodicals for which Allingham wrote have ceased publication. *My Weekly* (1910), *Woman's Weekly* (1911) and the *People's Friend* (1869) survive but printed serial fiction is no longer an exciting, mainstream genre. Reading itself has to jostle for space in amongst the available variety of mass-market entertainment.

At the end of most literary biographies – or biographies of creative artists generally – comes the comforting reassurance that their works live on independently. For the common writer this is not so. Herbert Allingham would have remained anonymous forever were it not for the devotion of his daughters and their conviction that his intelligent, conscientious life's work had been worthwhile.

Papers are often the key to a plot dénouement in Allingham's serials – a lost letter, the true copy of a will, perhaps. As the lawyer/editor FA Wickhart advised him in life: 'It was the keeping of old letters that won me the [...] action. There may be some among your papers that may preserve your rights.'

And so, I hope, it has proved.

JUSTICE!

'Lucy finds a paper in her father's handwriting'

Notes & Sources

Abbreviations
MA: Margery Allingham; HJA: Herbert Allingham; ASL: Special Collections, Albert Sloman Library, University of Essex; *OH*: *The Oaken Heart*; PYC: Pip Youngman-Carter; WM: William McFee, *DoY*: Dance of the Years; *CG:* The *Christian Globe; CGW:* The *Christian Glowworm;* RR: Ralph Rollington; HJG: Harold Garrish; *Butterfly*: The *Butterfly*; FCC: Fred Cordwell; WH: William Harvey; *AMA*: *The Adventures of Margery Allingham,* C&C: Cotterell & Cromb; AC: Anne Cooper. More detailed information including letters to editors, bibliography and PhD thesis *Family Fictions* can be found at www.fiftyyearsinthefictionfactory.com

Introduction

p 1 'This chap Anon': 'Greensleeves', Michael Flanders & Donald Swann.

p 2 'most industrious apprentice': MA dedication to *Death of a Ghost* (London: Heinemann, 1934).

p3 'I get my living': HJA letter to Lord Northcliffe, April 1915, ASL.
Hue and Cry (1947) written by TEB Clarke, starred Alastair Sim.
John Mullan, *Anonymity: a Secret History of English Literature* (London: Faber, 2007). Mullan focuses, for instance, on the anonymity which cloaks a writer whose voice is too individual to be socially acceptable or a writer who endangers themselves by expressing seditious or risqué opinions.

p 5 'Like hair-dressing and hotel keeping': MA *Flowers for the Judge* (London: Heinemann, 1936) p218.
'lined with an impressive glazed bookcase': MA draft material, quoted AMA p34.

p 6 'I never wished': *OH* (London: Michael Joseph, 1941) p222.

p 7 'with donnish precision': PYC, the preface to *Mr Campion's Clowns* (London: Chatto, 1967).

p 9 Julia Jones, *Family Fictions: the Working Life of Herbert Allingham 1867-1936* (University of Surrey, 2006).

p 10 Jonathan Rose, *The Intellectual Life of the British Working Classes,* (Newhaven & London: Yale University Press, 2001).

p 11 EH Burrage, *The Ruin of Fleet Street* (London: EW Allen, 1882) www.geocities.com

Chapter One

Books I found particularly helpful in this chapter were Geoffrey Best's *Mid-Victorian Britain 1851–1875*, Paul Foot's *The Vote* and Francis Wheen's *Das Kapital: a Biography.*

p 13 'The only thing we can do', Robert Lowe 15.7.1867 (Hansard).
'if it is not efficient', Asa Briggs, *Victorian People* (Harmondsworth: Penguin, 1954) p265.

p 15 Charles Booth, *Descriptive Map of London Poverty* (booth.lse.ac.uk).

p 18 Eric Hobsbawm, *The Age of Capital 1848–1875*, (London: Weidenfeld & Nicholson, 1975).
Karl Marx, *Das Kapital*: the edition used was David McClelland, *Capital: a New Abridgement* (Oxford: OUP, 1999).

Chapter Two

Margery Allingham's *Dance of the Years* and *The Oaken Heart* are central to this chapter. Another useful book is Richard Martin, *Ink in her Blood.*

p 20 MA *Dance of the Years* (London: Michael Joseph, 1943).
'was born in 1800': *OH* p191.
'You know how we all feel': Letter Philip Allingham to MA, ASL.

p 21 'as one of our family': *OH* p80.

p 22 'all day': *OH* p267.
'It was in Penton Place': *DoY* p106.

p 23 'The large ivy-covered house': *DoY* p157.

p 24 Michael Collins, *The Likes of Us: a Biography of the White Working Class* (Cambridge: Granta, 2004).

p 25 Mary Boast, *The Story of Walworth* (Southwark Libraries Dept., 1976)
'The market-night': George Gissing, *Thyrza* (1887).

pp 27-31 'Saxdell Road' and all subsequent quotes in this chapter: HJA *The Lights of Home* (first published 1910-1911 in *The Jester*).

Chapter Three

p 32 HJA diary 1886.

p 33 'Pastors of churches': *CGW* July-August 1874.
'More reading matter': *CGW* May 1875.

p 34 'Question: If you were a teacher': *CGW* July-August 1874.

p 35 'This number of *The Glowworm*': *CGW* July-August 1874.

p 36 National Archives reference number: NA BT31/14535/9609.

p 37 'Mr Calvert': Arnold Bennett, *The Card* (London: Methuen, 1911) p44.
'Their street corner betting': Richard Hoggart, *The Uses of Literacy: Aspects of Working-Class Life with Special Reference to Publications and Entertainments* (Harmondsworth: Penguin, 1958) p73.

p 38 'Why pay rent?': *The Starr-Bowkett Journal and Building Society* News 2.1.1882.
'Perils': Arnold Bennett, *Clayhanger* (first published 1910. Edition used Harmondsworth: Penguin, 1975) p242.

p 39 'He worked out the cost': *DoY* p149.
'One day, as he watched': *DoY* p151.

p 40 Hartley Aspden, *Fifty Years a Journalist* (Clitheroe n.d.). Aspden became editor of the Amalgamated Press magazines *The Sunday Companion* and *The Home Companion.*
'You ask me for my photograph': *CG* 1875 p1.

p 41 'Stay-maker, horse-keeper': NA BT31/14535/9609.

p 42 'sociology of investment': MJ Daunton, *House and Home in the Victorian City: Working-Class Housing 1850-1914* (London: Edward Arnold, 1983).
'Involvement with a Christian group': John Kent, *Hold the Fort* (London: Epworth Press, 1978).
'It is pleasant': *CG* 10.5.1900.

p 43 'It's wonderful': *DoY* p155.

Chapter Four

p 47 'Let me sit down': *CG* July-August 1874.
'In London alone' and following quotes: Albert Fenning, *Every Mother's Book*. Wellcome Collection.

p 51 'Surely to mislead': *Advertised Remedies Exposure Campaign* (Southend, 1929). Wellcome Collection.
British Medical Association, *Secret Remedies* (London: BMA, 1909 & 1912). British Library.
HG Wells, *Tono-Bungay* (London: Macmillan, 1909).
'The price is sixpence': James Grant, *The Newspaper Press Volume II* (London: Routledge, 1872) p143.

p 52 'An important fact': Henry Sell, *The Philosophy of Advertising* (1883). Item SL09 in the History of Advertising Trust Sell Collection.
'so-called religious': ES Turner, *The Shocking History of Advertising* (London: Michael Joseph, 1952) p175.
'A respectable married person': CG 24.11.1876.
James Greenwood, *The Seven Curses of London* (London: Stanley Rivers, 1869).

p 54 'How to make children lovely': CG 2.1.1890.

p 56 'He has sprung': W Stead Junior, *The Art of Advertising* (London, 1899).

p 57 I have not been able to trace business records for the Bradleys. The firm of AC Bradley, Ltd. and CW Bradley & Co. is the same entity.

Chapter Five

p 58 'Non-collegiate students': WW Grave, *Fitzwilliam College Cambridge 1869-1969* (Cambridge: Fitzwilliam Society, 1983).

p 60 'I really must': HJA diary 1886.
Exam lists consulted in Cambridge University Library.
'A disorderly collection': CNL Brooke, *A History of the University of Cambridge*, vol. 4 (Cambridge: Cambridge University Press, 1993).

p 61 'For me admission': Sir Maurice Amos, quoted CNL Brooke, above.

p 65 'Unfulfilled romance': PYC *All I Did Was This* (London: Sexton Press, 1962) p34.
'You and I': HJA to Lilian Carter, April 1927, ASL.

p 66 All quotes from *Amateur Scraps*, HJA collection.

Chapter Six

As well as HJA 1886 diary and Ralph Rollington's memoir, an invaluable source both for this and the following chapter is Frank Jay, *Peeps in the Past*, www.geocities.com. Jay almost certainly knew both HJA and his uncle John (Ralph Rollington). ES Turner, *Boys Will Be Boys* gleaned some of his information from HJA's son-in-law Pip Youngman Carter.

p 69 'to my seven paternal uncles': MA dedication to *Police at the Funeral* (London: Heinemann, 1931).

p 70 'My grandmother': MA *The Relay* (unpublished manuscript).

p 71 'I well remember': RR, *A Brief History of Boys' Journals* (Leicester: H Simpson, 1913) www.geocities.com. He and his bohemian friends represent what collectors would call the 'fierce' boys tale as opposed to the *Boys' Own Paper* 'goody-goody' style.

p 72 Robert Kirkpatrick, *Encyclopaedia of Boys' School Stories* (Aldershot: Ashgate, 2000).

p 73 'I remember a good many years back': RR, *Brief History*, above.

p 74 Copies of John Allingham's papers are extremely rare. There is a run of the *New Boys' Paper* in the British Library Ono collection and some numbers of the *Boys' World* among the Opie papers in the Bodleian Library.

'Arthur brought the first number' and all quotes: HJA diary 1886.

p 82 'My wife tells me': letter 43 (8.04.1905)

Chapter Seven

Andrew King's research and writing on the *London Journal* has been particularly valuable in this chapter. Both his PhD thesis *Periodical Places* and his book *The London Journal 1845-1883.*

p 84 'Can't you see': HJA 'The Duffer Detective', *True Blue* 1905.

p 86 'Eventually Stiff worked up': Henry Vizetelly, *Glances Back Over Seventy Years* (London: Kegan Paul, 1893)

p 87 'There is a mighty potentate': *Macmillan's Magazine* 1866 quoted King.

'So cleverly did JF Smith': Vizetelly, above.

'*Cassell's Magazine*': Molly Hughes, *A London Family 1870–1900* (Oxford: OUP, 1991) p130.

p 88 'Give the poor man sensation': Pierce Egan II, quoted King.

p 89 'Then, early in 1887' and 'Mr CW Bradley': Frank Jay, *Peeps in the Past.*

p 90 'You think you have a gift': WT Stead, *Answers* 1893.

p 91 'Stick to it': letter 1, John Allingham to HJA (1886).

p 92 'The terrible old building': WM letter to MA (5.6.1948) ASL.

p 93 'A devil of a woman' and all quotes: HJA *London Journal* 1893.

Chapter Eight

p 96 'I remember you': letter 244, FA Wickhart to HJA (3.10.1932).

p 97 'too Mephistophelean': letter 58, *Puck* editor to HJA (30.11.1905).

'Somewhat too sensational': letter 118 WF Anderson to HJA (3.6.1907).

p 98 'less busy than usual': Mab's Gossip, *London Journal* 16.9.1893.

p 99 'The Editor had with him': Mab's Gossip, *London Journal* 27.4.1895.

p 101 'As I anticipated': Mab's Gossip, *London Journal* 1.4.1893.

p 102 'They're servants mostly': William McFee, *Casuals of the Sea* (London: Secker, 1916) p151.

p 103 'Besides I suppose': Mab's Gossip, *London Journal* 4.11.1893.

p 104 'The other day I took Margery': *Mab's Gossip*, *New London Journal* 1906.

p 105 'Love Lady Shield': *London Journal* 1.11.1890.

p 107 'A mysterious Grecian': *London Journal* 18.2.1896.

p 108 The secret of a good complexion': *New London Journal* 13.12.1906.
'My correspondent is the wife': *New London Journal* 13.12.1906.

Chapter Nine

p 111 'In the Christmas Number': *New London Journal* 27.12.1906.

p 112 'You thought me worthy': HJA 'The Conversion of Gerald Dane', *CG* Christmas Hamper 1890.

p 113 'You shall have the finest Christmas': HJA 'The Redemption of Richard Deane' *CG* Christmas Hamper 1895.

p 114 'a gloomy-looking house': HJA 'Our Madge', *Tit-Bits* 21.12.1895.

p 115 Joel Weiner, *Papers for the Millions: the New Journalism in Britain 1850s-1914* (Westport: Greenwood Press, 1988). Kate Jackson, *George Newnes and the New Journalism in Britain 1880-1910: Circulation and Profit* (Aldershot: Ashgate, 2001).

p 116 'The New Journalism': Matthew Arnold, *The Nineteenth Century* May 1887.
'Schemo Magnifico': *The House of Northcliffe: the Harmsworths of Fleet Street* Paul Ferris (London: Weidenfeld & Nicolson, 1971).

p 118 'We were all smart men' and subsequent quotes: HJA 'The Achievements of Michael Power', *Pearson's Weekly* Jan-Feb 1901.

p 124 'One day a group of men' and subsequent quotes: HJA ' The Garden of Glory', *CG* Christmas Hamper 1901.

Chapter Ten

p 128 'Williams with stories': HJA diary 1886.

p 129 'I like your friends': HJA ' The Garden of Glory', *CG* Christmas Hamper 1901.

p 130 'Isabella Beeton': Kathryn Hughes, *The Short Life and Long Times of Mrs Beeton* (London: Fourth Estate, 2005) p67-68.

p 131 'There was an almighty row': *DoY* p207. Em was married from an address in Gunnersbury, the parish in which she had been born.

p 132 'hated to be bored': *OH* p355.

p 133 'All my dull days': HJA to WM 19.8.1920.

p 134 'Well, I expected': WM to HJA 18.6.1918.

p 135 'Men were beasts': WM to HJA 14.11.32.

p 136 'The more I study children': Mab's Gossip *New London Journal* 1906.
'If you had kept your story': letter 5 Frank Girlman to HJA (16.3.1904).
'In going through your serial': letter 6 Charles Sisley to HJA (2.6.1904).

p 137 'I have now given the subject of your serial': letter 14, Editor *Pearson's Weekly* to HJA 29.11.1904.

p 138 'Why doesn't your firm pay more promptly?': letter 28, HJA to editor of *Puck* (January 1905).

p 140 'Between ourselves': *True Blue* December 1904.
'The principal reason': letter 34, editor *Boys' Leader* to HJA (14.2.1905).

p 141 'I doubt': letter 35 HJA to editor *Boys' Leader.*
'after that I notice': letter 44, A.C. Murray to HJA (17.4.1905).

p 142 'Dear Murray': letter 38 HJA to editor *True Blue* (n.d.).

Chapter Eleven

WOG Lofts and DJ Adley, *The Men Behind Boys' Fiction* and Alan Clark *Dictionary of Comic Artists, Writers and Editors* are useful reference guides.

p 144 'I am returning': letter 83 Edward Hawke to HJA (10.6.1906).

p 145 The editors of *Yes or No* were Isabel Thorne and Agnes Carruthers.
'I called about a little matter': WM *Casuals of the Sea* (London: Martin Secker, 1916).

p 147 'She was one of those remarkable women': MA preface to *Mysterious Mr Campion* (London: Chatto, 1963).

p 148 'A very excellent': letter 107, Charles Perry Brown to HJA (21.2.1907.)

p 150 'I regret that I am unable': letter 138 Hamilton Edwards to HJA (23.4.1908).
'Dear Sir, I am obliged': letter 139 HJA to Hamilton Edwards (n.d.).

p 151 'spacious Victorian days': *The Autobiography of Frank Richards* (London: Charles Skilton, 1952) p19. Frank Richards was the favourite pen name of Charles Hamilton, prolific author of school stories and creator of Billy Bunter.
'I should go straight in': letter 51, Frank Atkins to HJA (16.10.1905).

p 152 'One day he was asked': *The Autobiography of Frank Richards* p25.

p 153 Hamilton Edwards to Lord Northcliffe, BL ADD MS 62182A.

p 154 'Instalment of Comrades True': letter 128, HG to HJA (1.7.1907).
'Saw Garrish': HJA diary 1909.

Chapter Twelve

p 156 'When Sport Monkimore': HJA *Jester* 22.8.1908.
p 157 'Don't think I am dissatisfied': HJA *Jester* 26.09.1908.
p 158 'I want you to close up': letter 132, HJG to HJA (16.9.1907).
'He then adopted a conversational method': Frank Richards, above.
p 159 'I am very glad': letter 126, HJG (26.6.1907).
'And I am a clerk': HG *Thirty Bob a Week* (*Jester* 25.8.1906). Rowton Houses were working men's hostels.
p 160 'having a flair': George Dilnot, *The Romance of the Amalgamated Press* (London: The Amalgamated Press, 1925) p18.
'He opened his heart': HJA diary 6.1.1909.
'Imagine a man': HJA *Girl of my Heart* (*Puck* 1908–1909).
p 161 'Tuesday: ('Nuff said.): Easter double number, *Comic Cuts* 1907.
p 162 'Flossie will enchant you': *Butterfly* 1908.
p 165 'We are right out': letter 147, HJG to HJA (20.8.1908)
'He had not meant': HJA *Lights of London Town* (*Butterfly* 1908).
'You will be glad to hear': *Butterfly* 2.1.1909.
p 164 'Can I get you anything, sir?': HJA *Plucky Polly Perkins* (*Butterfly* 26.12.1908).
p 166 'If you want to beat Tom Mullins': HJA *Plucky Polly Perkins* (*Butterfly* 10.4.1909).
'You never walk far' and all quotes: George Orwell 'Boys' Weeklies' *Collected Essays, Journalism and letters* vol 1: *An Age Like This 1920–1940* (Harmondsworth: Penguin, 1970) p505.
p 168 'She had the tired look': HJA *Miss Maggie McFee* (*Puck* 1909).
p 169 'The proof of popularity': letter 126, HG to HJA (26.6.1907).

Chapter Thirteen

p 171 'It was a pitch-black night': HJA *Driven from Home* (*Butterfly* 1909-1911).
p 172 'This was the first': letter 307, HJA to Anne St John Cooper (Nov 1934).
'I think that': letter 154, FCC to HJA (29.9.1909).
'Thanks for *Driven from Home*': letter 160, FCC to HJA (5.1.1910).
p 173 'one of the men' Dilnot *Romance of the Amalgamated Press*, above.
'*The Butterfly* has been': for sales figures see BM ADD 62182 B.
p 174 'In her thoughts of books': Gissing, above.
'Who created, wrote, drew and edited': Alan Clark, *Dictionary of Comic Artists, Writers and Editors* (London: British Library, 1998).
p 175 'Saw Dad, John, Phil, Ernest': HJA diary (6.1.1909).

p 177 'a tour-de-force': Frank Richards, above, p45.
'*Justice* is late': letter 164, FCC to HJA (18.5.1916).

p 178 'It was a square handsome house': WM *In the First Watch* (London: Faber, 1947) p302.

p 179 'Besides the factory operatives': Karl Marx *Capital*, above.
'They were sharp jolly Fleet Street men': WM *In the First Watch,* above.

p 181 'Jack, Jack' and all quotes: HJA *Driven from Home* (Butterfly 1909-1911).

p 186 'Florence Bartle': quoted in Anna Davin, *Growing Up Poor: Home, School and Street in London 1870-1914* (London: Rivers Oram Press, 1996) p77.

Chapter Fourteen

p 189 'Take a tram': Maud Pember Reeves, *Round About a Pound a Week* (London: Bell & Sons, 1913).

p 191 'Our policy was to rain': Lord Northcliffe (30.11.1919).

p 192 'The newspaper was their Sunday': Pember Reeves, above.
'It is sad to see': Lady Bell, *At The Works* (London: Nelson, 1911).

p 193 'As might be expected': Bell, above.
'The reading that comes under the hand of the workman': Bell, above.

p 195 'It seems undeniable': Bell, p241.
'Where almost everything else': Hoggart, p34.

p 196 'We forget how terribly near': Bell, p81.
'The poor live constantly': CG 20.5.1909.
Christopher Booker, *The Seven Basic Plots* (London: Continuum, 2004).

p 197 'Every reaction has its fixed counter': Hoggart, p129.

p 198 Marina Warner, *From the Beast to the Blonde: on Fairy Tales and their Tellers* (London: Vintage, 1995).

p 199 'A surprise every tenth page': MA draft preface to *The Mysterious Mr Campion.*

p 201 '"First Rate," replied Tom Tiffin': HJA *The Girl Outcast* (*Favorite Comic* 1.4.1911).

Chapter Fifteen

p 202 'Do not imagine': *Butterfly* 22.11.1913.

p 203 'In reading a letter I often try': NLJ 3.11.1906.
'I have pictured him' NLJ 27.10.1906.

p 204 'I have found that': letter 161 17.2.1911.

p 205 'I could not pay': letter 162 20.2.1911.

p 206 'The bulk of boys selected': Arnold Freeman, *Boy Life and Labour: the Manufacture of Inefficiency* (London: King & Son, 1914) p7.

p 207 'The senses of the adolescent' and subsequent quotes: Freeman, p144ff. (The *Mail* refers to the *Birmingham Mail*).

p 208 'The book whose name': Bell, p235.

p 209 'The home of HH': Freeman, p39.

p 210 'This boy was at': Freeman, p57.

p 211 'Concerning CW's jobs': Freeman, p62.

p 212 'This boy said': Freeman, p158.

p 213 'Working boys are not greatly interested': Freeman ,p63.

p 215 'These boys are mostly': Freeman, p159.

Chapter Sixteen

The *Centenary Chronicles*, a particularly good series of local history papers is available at www.bretonheath.me.uk/history

p 216 'What a beautiful land England is' and all quotes: HJA *Human Nature* (*Butterfly* 26.9.14).

p 219 'What gave rise to it I cannot remember': *OH* p183.

p 221 'I had a sudden recollection': *OH* p20.

p 223 'A time when war was life': *OH* p20.
'Five or six submarines observed': Dr JH Salter, *Diary and Reminisences* edited JO Thompson (London: John Lane The Bodley Head, 1933).

p 224 'Like a bright star to the SW': Salter, above.

p 225 'an ugly chapter': Van Emden & Humphries, *All Quiet on the Home Front* (London: Headline, 2003) p54.

p 227 'one in four of the men': Richard Holmes, *Tommy: the British Soldier on the Western Front 1914-1918* (London: Harper Collins, 2004).
JM Winter, *The Great War and the British People* (Cambridge, Massachusetts: Harvard UP, 1986).
'the lost generation': Juliet Gardiner, *The Thirties* (London: HarperCollins, 2010) p13.

p 228 'Bald figures on casualties': Van Emden & Humphries, above, p309.
'Their poor physical state': Winter, above, p49.

p 229 'The sale of our periodicals': Lord Northcliffe 4.8.1916, ADD MS62185.
'who, when their hour came': ES Turner, *Dear Old Blighty* (London: Michael Joseph, 1980) p201.

p 230 'canaries chirping in an earthquake': Frank Richards, p174.
'somewhat disorganised': letter 307, above.

p 231 'Business at the AP': Sir George Sutton, 9.8.1917, ADD MS62184A. Gross receipts rose from £1,223,400 in 1914 to £1,296,000 in 1917, ADD MS 62185.

Chapter Seventeen

p 233 'In these times it is not good': *Happy Home* 8.1.1916.

p 235 'It was in 1916': *The Record,* Fleetway House Magazine 1961.

p 236 'Before the end came': Dilnot, above.

p 237 MA 'Darings of the Red Rose' (first published *Weekly Welcome* 1930; new edition 1995).

p 239 'She must make it clear to herself': *Woman's Weekly* 18.1.1919.
'more than usually beastly': letter Philip Allingham to MA, ASL.
'Their little noses': Emmie Allingham, *None Other Gods* ,CG 1915.

p 241 'Polly Parsons is a very delightful girl': *Woman's Weekly* 8.4.1916.
'A poor girl': *Woman's Weekly* 6.5.1916.

p 243 'Aunt M was a power': MA *The Relay.*
'The enemy's fleet were out': Salter, above.

p 244 'The Old Doctor': *OH* p182.

Chapter Eighteen

Richard Van Emden's and Steve Humphries' wonderful book *All Quiet on the Home Front* led me to visit Dennis Gilfeather on 22 June 2004. Mr Gilfeather had aged and was not able to add a great deal to his previous testimony but his daughter Irene's memory of her grandmother reading her weekly serial in the *People's Journal* was invaluable.

p 246 'a happy, prosperous and *non*-military': WM to HJA 1.1.1917.

p 248 'Within the past few weeks': *People's Journal* 4.9.1915.
'The kid was in the high chair': Van Emden & Humphries, above.

p 250 'Raid came during the big fight': HJA diary 1918.

p 251 'Long after the last war': *OH* p154.

p 252 'After Dad was killed': Van Emden & Humphries, above, p277.

p 254 'A good holding story': letter 175, WH to HJA (28.5.1918).
'There's a lot of money to be made': letter 176 (30.5.1918).
'He is going to discuss': HJA diary 1918.

p 255 'Probably greatest in Scotland': Van Emden & Humphries, above, p277.
'Dear Mr Allingham': letter 177, WH to HJA (31.5.1918).

p 257 'Little trace remained': HJA *For Love of Her Bairns* (*People's Journal,* 1918).

p 258 'Your mother's in bed': Van Emden & Humphries, above, 277.
'During these last few weeks': HJA *For Love of Her Bairns*, above.
p 259 'I was just a wee boy': Van Emden & Humphries, above, p277-278
p 262 'As you know': letter 191, WH to HJA (21.12.1918).

Chapter Nineteen

p 263 'First and foremost': *Merry & Bright* 10.5.1919.
Violet Hopson, born Elma Kate Karkeek, was a major star of the silent film era and was additionally renowned for her business sense.
p 265 'Read the story with great interest': *Picture Show* 6.12.1919.
p 267 'Hollywood was Everywhere': *A History of the Cinema from its Origins to 1970* (Harmondsworth: Allen Lane, 1976) p73.
p 268 'Devised on ingenious lines': Dilnot, p47.
p 269 'Looking pleased': Bell, above.
'It seems to me unquestionable': Freeman, p133.
p 271 'An absolutely new': *Cheerio!* 17.1.1920.
p 272 'Like most big men': *Kinema Comic* 28.8.1920.
p 273 'Now he has made a start': Kinema Comic 24.7.1920.
p 274 'In England a tuppenny weekly': Harold Kellock, *Houdini, His Life Story: from the Recollections and Documents of Beatrice Houdini* (New York: Harcourt, Brace & Co. 1928) p275.
p 275 'My price too high': HJA diary

Chapter Twenty

Margery Allingham's archive at Essex University includesthe notes of the Mersea Island seances and Herbert Allingham's account of these events.

p 276 'Errands. Practised elo': MA diary 1921
p 278 'Came to London to learn to write': MA, 'I seem to have won a medal', *Homes and Gardens* 1963.
'one of those born editors': AMA p105.
'An intellectual, interested mainly in his plots': AMA p52.
p 279 'Silverdale': Mab's Gossip, *London Journal* 18.12 1896.
p 280 'I had always assumed': AMA p126.
'Right-hand writing': see MA preface to *Mysterious Mr Campion*, above.
p 281 'The glass began' and all quotes: HJA account of seances, ASL.
p 283 'You cannot call yourself an author': conversation with Joyce Allingham.
'primarily an intuitive': AMA pxviii.
p 284 'My poor father': AMA p109.

p 285 'To working class people': Hoggart, above, p138.

p 286 'I wondering': MA diary 30.12.1921.

p 287 'A curious air of unreality': editor *Red* magazine, ASL.
'things not joyous': MA diary 1924.

Chapter Twenty-One

p 290 'Work, read and potter': HJA diary 1927.
'Fire smoking, dinner poor': HJA diary 1927.

p 291 'Sutton going to the *Mail*': HJA diary 28.3.1927.

p 292 'Films in *Film Fun*': HJA diary 28.3.1928.

p 293 'serial in the *Daily Express*': *The White Cottage Mystery.*

p 294 'Draughty attic': PYC *All I Did Was This* (above).

p 296 'structure of feeling': Raymond Williams, *Marxism and Literature* (Oxford: OUP 1977) p131-132.

p 297 'He doesn't write': HJA *Tempted by Love* (typescript).

p 298 'When anyone in the Lane': Gwendoline Freeman, *The Houses Behind* (London: Allen and Unwin, 1947) p86.

p 299 'We would have': Gwendoline Freeman, p88.
'The cult of the movie star': Walter Benjamin, 'The Work of Art in an Age of Mechanical Reproduction' from *Illuminations* (London: Cape, 1970) p233.
'A commodity': Marx, above.

p 300 'A typical and extreme case': Bell, above.
'Your resilience': WM letter to HJA.

Chapter Twenty-Two

p 302 'Get as much as you can': letter 231, HJA to C&C (22.12.1932).

p 305 'I thought the instalment': letter 241, AC to HJA (8.9.1932).
'I love all the characters': letter 292, AC to HJA (8.5.1034).

p 306 'You can't gather figs': *Home Companion* 18.2.1897.

p 307 'A united': *Family Journal* issue 1, 1909.

p 308 'I am exceedingly sorry': letter 264, AC to HJA (15.6.1933).

p 310 'Watershed': Noreen Branson & Margot Heinemann, *Britain in the Nineteen Thirties* (London: Weidenfeld & Nicolson, 1971).
'There are few indeed': *Family Journal* 24.10.31.

p 311 'Heroic optimism': Warner, *above,* p xvi
'All fiction from the mushroom libraries': Orwell p531.

p 312 'I know your desire': letter 191 21.12.1918.

p 313 'Little thought was given to Milly' and all quotes: HJA *The Child She Dared Not Claim* (aka *Her Hidden Past, Family Journal* 1931*)*.
This may be a private joke. HJA lived in Ealing when first married. Tudor Street was the first office of the Harmsworth Brothers in 1888.

Chapter Twenty-Three

p 317 'The entries and detail': editor's note, Salter, above.
p 318 'Poor Emmie came home upset': letter Emily Jane Hughes to Maud Hughes, ASL.
p 319 'Turnbull came': HJA letter, ASL.
'For nearly five months': HJA *The Child She Dared Not Claim* (aka *Her Hidden Past, Family Journal* 1931).
p 323 'I can quite understand': letter 243, FA Wickhart to HJA (26.9.1932).
'I want to tell': letter 242, AC to HJA (22.9.1932).
p 324 'Mrs Cooper asks me': letter 251, Phyllis Morgan to HJA (23.12.1932).

Chapter Twenty Four

p 326 'This is not a big point': letter 223, AC to HJA (11.5.1931).
p 327 'I like your third instalment': letter 280, AC to HJA (11.1.1934).
'I can't have you as my sweetheart' and all quotes: HJA *Wife of a Wanted Man* (*Family Journal* 1934).
p 330 'You appear to have transformed': letter 281, WH to HJA (18.1.1934).
'I will of course': letter 282, HJA to WH.
p 332 'Davidson was in London': letter 304, C&C to HJA (9.11.1934).
p 333 'To help my married daughter': letter 301, HJA to AC (25.10 1934).
'One Scottish B-d': undated scrap in HJA handwriting.
p 334 'I would not bother you': letter 306, HJA to WH (n.d.).
p 335 'Surprsingly good and unlike anything else': HJA diary 1934.

Chapter Twenty Five

p 338 'Oppressed by the thought': HJA diary 18.10.1934.
'The marvel is': doctors letter to HJA, ASL.
p 339 'Mrs Martin, Jane's landlady' and all quotes: HJA *The Silence of Jane Carter* (*Family Journal* 1934).
p 342 'And Phil's shrill laugh': HJA diary 1886.
p 343 'The senior school girl': AJ Jenkinson, *What Do Boys and Girls Read?* (London: Methuen, 1940) p219.
'Full of really grand stories': *Miracle* 9.2.1935.
p 345 'Can't write, can't think': HJA diary 1935.

p 348 'Since the old man died, Marge': WM letter to MA, ASL.
'Radiant and very important': MA diary 1936.

p 349 'Master of men': Em Allingham, unpublished manuscript, ASL.

p 350 'Those who remember': *Family Journal* 1932.

p 353 'The story of Harriet Yorke': *My Weekly* 16.2.1929.
'One of the last': PYC, *All I Did Was This*, above.

p 354 'The sociological theory': Theodor Adorno & Max Horkheimer, *The Culture Industry: Enlightenment as Mass Deception* (Harmondsworth: Allen Lane, 1975).
'Every day of happiness': 'Frank Richards Replies' in Orwell, *Collected Essays*, above, p537.

p 355 'I dwelt with rapture': Ada Chesterton *In Darkest London* (London: Stanley Paul, 1926) p186.

. . . Mary picked up the telephone and spoke hurriedly. If only she could get her message through.

List of Illustrations

with original title and reprint number where necessary

East End children watching the 'moving pictures'.
Photograph from the Christian Globe 1909

FRONT COVER adapted from *She Loved a Rogue*, front cover of the *Family Journal* 1932.

BACK COVER *The Redemption of Richard Deane*, the *Christian Globe* 1895.

HALF TITLE PAGE *The Girl Who Stood by Him*, *Oracle* 1931 (6th *Justice*).

DEDICATION PAGE Herbert and Margery Allingham c.1923 (© Margery Allingham Society).

TITLE PAGE 'This is who I am,' she said slowly. 'Not a lady with servants to wait upon her, but a work-girl with only her own hands to keep her from starvation.' Illustration by Charles Horrell. *Her Own Game, Woman's Weekly* 1916 (2nd *Her Luck in London*).

FOREWORD 'She flung out her arms and pointed to the stage box.' *His Luck in London, Kinema Comic* 1927.
'She danced around the room in sheer delight.' *His Luck in London, Kinema Comic* 1927.

p XII *The Dead Secret, Merry & Bright* 1922.

INTRODUCTION '"Who are you?" she demanded.' *Driven from Home, Butterfly* 1909.

p 11 'As soon as I tried to turn I saw the packing case above my head tremble.' *The Amazing Exploits of Houdini, Kinema Comic* 1922.

p 12 *London! Favorite Comic* 1916.
p 19 '"Can you scrub floors?" she asked eagerly.' *Pluck Will Tell, Kinema Comic* 1931 (4th *Plucky Polly Perkins*).
p 20 *The Face Behind the Veil, Merry & Bright* 1922 (2nd *Lights of Home*).
p 31 'Lucy found herself suddenly released and Sal's arms around her.' *The Face Behind the Veil, Merry & Bright* 1922 (2nd *Lights of Home*).
p 32 The *Christian Glowworm* 1874.
p 45 *The Adventurers* (Margery and Phil Allingham), *Christian Globe* 1912.
p 46 Fennings advertisement, *Christian Glowworm* 1874.
p 57 CICFA advertisement, *Christian Globe* 1912.
p 58 *Billy on his Own, Merry & Bright* 1923 (2nd *Lights of London*).
p 68 *Amateur Scraps.*
p 69 The *Boy's World* 1879.
p 82 'He hung in this position.' Illustration by Robert Prowse, *Barrington's Fag, New Boys' Paper* 1886.
p 83 The *London Journal.* Illustration by Sir John Gilbert 1889.
p 95 'Merlin did not hesitate.' 'The Duffer, Detective', *True Blue* 1905.
p 96 *The Woman Who Dared, Bullseye* 1933 (8th *A Devil of a Woman*).
p 110 'I won't let my children starve.' *The Strange Disappearance of Lorna Meede, Oracle* 1933 (3rd *A Mother at Bay*).
p 111 *Pots of Money, Butterfly* and *Firefly* 1925 (2nd *Peg of the Pictures*).
p 127 'And I must ask you, Sir William Joyce, to mind your own business.' *Ruby Wray, Jester* 1910.
p 128 *True Blue* 1904
p 143 'Agile as a cat Max dashed forwards.' *Max the Magnificent, Dreadnought* 1913 (3rd *Max*).
p 144 *Ruby Wray in London. Jester* 1910.
p 155 'A yell, long and sustained, broke from the onlookers.' *The Captain's Fag, True Blue* 1905 (2nd *Barrington's Fag*).
p 156 *Sport Monkimore, Jester* 1908.

p 170 'Polly made many conquests.' *Plucky Polly Perkins*, *Butterfly* 1908.

p 171 *Driven from Home*, *Butterfly* 1909.

p 187 '"Sargeant Sims, I think you will find your man behind that screen," said the baronet smoothly.' *The Shadow of a Crime*, *Film Fun* 1923 (5th *London*).

p 188 *Romney Hall*, *Butterfly* 1912.

p 201 '"My child," said Madame Clare, "to the young all things are possible. Yes, I can make you beautiful again – if I choose."' *The Girl Outcast*, *Favorite Comic* 1911.

p 202 *Mother Love, Fun & Fiction* 1912.

p 215 'When at last Tom tore himself away.' *The Way of the World*, *Butterfly* 1916.

p 216 *Human Nature*, *Butterfly* 1914.

p 231 'Although Baron Stolly was a famous person in his own country, here he was shut up in a coal cupboard by a little London street-arab.' *Human Nature*, *Butterfly* 1915.

p 232 *Don't Leave Us Mummy! Happy Home* 1914.

p 245 'You will order Kingsley, at the point of a revolver, to descend in the German lines.' *Human Nature*, *Butterfly* 1915.

p 246 "The wounded soldier entered the shop, and he walked very slowly, leaning heavily upon a stick.' *The Way of the World*, *Butterfly* 1917.

p 262 'Nan Seymour, out of work and starving – easy prey for an unscrupulous man' *The Girl who was Somebody Else*, *Poppy's Paper* 1933 (3rd *Her Luck in London*).

p 263 'I have quite made up my mind. You will write my next play!' *His Luck in London*, *Kinema Comic* 1927.

p 275 'You won't tell anyone you saw me here?' *Pots of Money*, *Butterfly* and *Firefly* 1925 (2nd Peg of the Pictures).

p 276 *Miss Maggie MacFee*, *Puck* 1909.

p 287 '"I am Miss Sunny Ray of the firm of Michael Power," said Sunny boldly.' *The Girl Who Made Good*, *Kinema Comic* 1926 (2nd *Miss Maggie MacFee*).

p 288 *He Thought She Was His Wife*, *Mascot* 1925.

p 301 "Harvey Price stood motionless as Marion lifted the poisoned peach to her lips.' *The Woman He Feared*, *Red Star Weekly*, 1929 (2nd *Silent Lady of Deadman's Lane*).

p 302 'Only in one way could Mary escape this House of Silence and the Nurse Who Never Answered.' *Mary Marlow – the Woman Who Paid*, *Family Journal* 1933 (2nd *A Woman Cast Out*).

p 315 *Robbed of Her Child! Home Companion* 1931 (2nd *Her Stolen Bairn*).

p 316 *The Woman Cast Out*, *My Weekly* 1932.

p 324 'Mary pressed on desperately.' *Mary Marlow – the Woman Who Paid*, *Family Journal* 1933 (2nd *A Woman Cast Out*).

p 325 *The Wife of a Wanted Man*, *Family Journal* 1934 (5th *The Woman Pays*).

p 337 'Her father was the last person she wished to see.' *The Hate of a Woman*, *My Weekly*, 1934.

p 338 *The Silence of Jane Carter*, *Family Journal* 1934.

p 358 'Lucy finds a paper in her father's handwriting.' *Justice*, *Favorite Comic* 1915.

p 359 *Your Editor's Chat*, *New Boys' Paper* 1907.

p 373 'Mary picked up the phone and spoke hurriedly. If only she can get her message through.' *The Woman Cast Out* (*My Weekly* 1932)

p 381 'My darling little Madge', *The Girl who Loved Him Best* *Family Journal* 1932 (5th *Justice*).

p 386 'Oh, you silly boy!' *Plucky Polly Perkins* (*Butterfly* 1909).

p 387 '"Are you mad?" he gasped. "You will be killed!"' *The Face Behind the Veil*, *Merry & Bright*, 1922 (2nd *Lights of Home*).

p 388 *The Girl Who Loved Him Best*, *Family Journal* 1932 (5th *Justice*)

INDEX

of people, places, periodicals and stories mentioned in the text
for more extensive information about Allingham's fiction (eg alternative titles for his serials) visit www.fiftyyearsinthefictionfactory.com

'Achievements of Michael Power, The': 117-123, 132
Adorno, Theodore (and Horkheimer, Max): 352, 357
Aldine Press: 80, 82-83, 138-149, 142, 148, 175, 270
Allan-Wood, Tess (pseud HJA & EJA, various spellings): 1, 266
Allingham, Albert (HJA brother): 69, 339
Allingham, Arthur (HJA brother): 49, 65, 69, 74-75, 81, 221, 236, 339
Allingham, Claude (HJA brother): 49, 69, 236, 277, 289, 339, 347
Allingham, Elizabeth Jane (Jinny) (HJA grandmother): 14, 22-23
Allingham, Emily Jane (Hughes, Emily Jane aka Granny)(HJA aunt and mother-in-law): 22, 39, 43, 130-131, 135, 289
Allingham Emily Jane (Em', 'Emmie' HJA wife), see Hughes, Emily Jane
Allingham, Ernest ('Tod'): 69, 70, 81, 175, 179, 236, 289, 294, 339, 347
Allingham, Florence (HJA sister): 46, 49
Allingham, Florence (HJA sister-in-law): 144, 339
Allingham, Grace (HJA cousin): 182, 236, 289, 319, 322, 333, 338, 348, 349
Allingham, Haidée (HJA aunt): 22, 65
Allingham, Herbert (HJA):
appearance and personality: 1, 7, 9, 58, 76, 78, 132, 148, 175 (as 'Jeffrey' 58, 91, 130, 131)180, 251, 278-279, 289-290, 321, 340
as editor: 53, 85-86, 90-92, 98-101, 103-108, 116, 123-124, 132, 137, 146, 147-149, 175
childhood: 14, 23-25, 32, 54, 69, 70, 81, 128
education and reading: 58-64, 68, 74-75, 81, 85, 91, 116, 227, 251
fiction (themes and characters): 3-4, 7-10, 26, 28, 54, 63, 65, 76, 82-83, 85, 87, 93, 97-98, 100, 113-114, 117-123, 124, 136-138, 140-142, 145-148, 153-154, 156-158, 161-163, 168, 171, 173, 180-186, 195-201, 214, 217-220, 226, 223-235, 240, 246-247, 252, 257-261, 264-266, 284-285, 296-298, 311-316, 323-324, 328-333, 340-342
friendships; 51, 63-66, 92, 97, 133-135, 146, 159, 161, 175, 179-180, 303
life and times (general): 3-4, 6-7, 10, 16, 18-19, 37, 71, 79, 145-146, 151, 161, 166, 180, 188, 216, 220-223, 236, 244, 247, 249-253, 266, 277, 288, 296, 300-301, 309-310,

312, 323, 327, 345, 348-349, 354, 358-359
literary criticism: 64, 67, 74-75, 79, 93, 150, 279
writing style (including advertisments): 5, 31, 57, 108, 141-142, 153, 158-160, 168, 176, 183-184, 197-201, 217, 240, 256-258
pseudonyms:
Arbuckle, 'Fatty' (pseud HJA):1, 272
St Clair, Herbert (pseud HJA):1, 80, 112
Pitt, David (pseud HJA): 1, 140-141
Allan-Wood, Tess (pseud HJA & EJA, various spellings): 1, 265
Houdini, Harry (pseud HJA): 1, 271, 274
Talmadge, Norma (pseud HJA): 2, 271
Hayakawa, Sessue (pseud HJA): 2, 20, 271
Semon, Larry, (pseud HJA): 2
Strong, Victoria (pseud HJA): 2, 324
politics: 5, 44, 55, 166, 168, 182
professional life (career and relationships with editors)1-2, 4, 8-10, 12-13, 45, 80, 97, 100, 107, 113, 118, 122-123, 124, 136-139, 142, 144-145, 148, 149-151, 153-164, 169-170, 172-174, 176-178, 184, 202-205, 225-226, 230, 232-233, 237, 246-247, 253-257, 262, 263-265, 270-273, 275, 280, 288-292, 297, 300-301, 302-305, 308-310, 312, 324-325, 326-336, 343-345, 349, 351-354
relationship to children: 21, 103, 135-136, 141-142, 147, 176, 208, 266-267, 276-279, 282-287, 293-295, 321-322, 336-338, 345-348, 351
family relationships: 12, 14, 20, 72, 74, 79, 91, 103, 128, 130, 139, 175-176, 182, 236, 249, 281, 289-290, 319, 333, 338, 339-340, 343
relationship to readers: 3, 9, 26, 37, 102, 106, 109, 133, 162, 169, 174, 185-187, 202-203, 207-208, 214, 219, 229, 246, 257, 273-274, 353, 356-357
relationship to wife: 130, 132-135, 144, 147, 176, 178, 240, 295, 317-321, 350
Allingham, James (also 'William Galantry') (HJA father): 14-16, 23-26, 32-41, 43-44, 46-47, 50, 52-53, 55-57, 69-70, 72-73, 75, 79, 89-90, 111, 116, 128, 130-131, 145, 175, 289, 306
Allingham, John (a.k.a. Ralph Rollington) (HJA uncle): 12, 69, 71-73, 76-77, 79, 89, 91, 130, 138-139, 148, 151, 175, 236, 289, 303, 333
Allingham, Joyce (HJA daughter): 6, 8, 10, 15, 21, 55, 69-70, 73, 80. 90, 130-131, 133, 216, 219, 222, 239, 250, 252, 266, 283-284, 294-295, 337, 340, 343, 345, 347-348, 350-351
Allingham, Julia (Nowell, Julia) (HJA aunt): 22, 38, 75, 130
Allingham, Louisa (HJA mother): 14-15, 23-26, 32, 47, 49, 69-70, 90, 131, 289
Allingham, Margery (HJA daughter): 2-8, 10, 14-15, 20-22, 38-39, 43, 45, 58, 69-70, 73, 92-93, 98, 103-104, 130-135, 141-142, 147, 175, 177-178, 199, 208, 216, 219-223,

225, 237, 239, 243-244, 251-252, 266-267, 276-287, 289, 293-295, 303-304, 317, 319-322, 334-337, 340, 343, 346-347, 349-351
Allingham, Philip (old Phil) (HJA brother): 56, 69, 81, 175-176, 179, 233, 253, 289, 293, 339-340, 342-343
Allingham, Philip (young Phil) (HJA son): 21, 45, 130, 134, 216, 239, 252, 266, 281-282, 286, 294, 304, 317, 321, 333, 336-338, 342-343, 345-347
Allingham, Walter (HJA brother): 69, 81, 339
Allingham, William (Will) (HJA brother):49, 58, 70, 78, 289, 339
Allingham, William (also 'James Galantry') (HJA grandfather): 14, 20-23, 25, 32, 36, 42, 72, 130
Amalgamated Press, the (also the AP, also the Harmsworth papers, also Fleetway): 3-4, 93, 116-117, 136-138, 149-155, 160, 169-170, 173, 179, 203, 225, 229-231, 235, 238, 239, 242-243, 253, 264-265, 268-269, 273, 280, 287-292, 301-303, 309, 312, 343-345, 349
Amateur Scraps: 66-68, 293
Amos, Sir Maurice: 61
Anderson, William: 97, 335
Answers to Correspondents: 3, 4, 91, 93, 116-117, 123, 194, 229, 231, 235-236, 303
Arbuckle, 'Fatty' (pseud HJA):1, 272-273
Arbuckle, 'Fatty' (fictional character): 273
Arbuckle, 'Fatty' (r.n.): 272
Ardingly College: 58, 81
Arnold, Matthew: 115-116
Ashamed of His Mother: 208, 212, 263, 272
Aspasia (graphologist): 107
Aspden, Hartley: 40, 306
Atkins, Frank: 151
Baby Jess: 246, 247
Barrington's Fag (also *The Captain's Fag*): 12, 77, 79-83, 87, 91, 140-141, 151, 184, 351
Bartle, Florence: 186
Bayswater: 245, 251, 266, 276
Bell, Lady Florence: 192-197, 208, 269, 286, 300, 357
Benjamin, Walter: 299
Bennett, Arnold: 10, 37-39, 41
Birmingham: 205-206, 208, 210, 215, 228, 269, 298-300
Blackerchief Dick: 284, 286, 317
Blogg, EJ: 89, 147-148
'Bobs': 133, 218-219
Booker, Christopher (*Seven Basic Plots*): 196-197
Booth, Charles: 15, 193,
Boy Who Won Out, The: 150, 154
Boys' Cinema: 268
Boys' Friend, The: 117, 290, 292
Boys of England: 72
Boy's Own Magazine, The: 71
Boy's Own Paper, The: 55 74-75
Boys' World, The: 73-74, 77, 89
Bradley, AC and CW (printers): 56-57, 77, 89, 91-92, 96, 107, 175, 324
Brett, Edwin: 72
Brown, Charles Perry: 80, 139, 148
Burrage, AS: 139
Burrage, EH: 11, 139
Butterfly, The 1, 8, 156, 161-163, 166,

168-173, 187, 191, 202, 207-208, 210-213, 216, 219, 226, 228-235, 247, 263-264, 267, 270-272, 280, 288, 292, 303
Cambridge (city and university): 58, 61-64, 66, 74, 81, 83, 85, 91, 95, 278, 294
Camrose, Lord (also William Berry): 167, 291
Cantle, GH: 153, 157
Carter, Lilian (see Robinson, Lilian)
Carter, Pip Youngman: 4, 7, 65, 293, 294, 303, 319, 321-322, 334, 336, 338, 340, 343, 347-348, 354
Cassell's (publishers): 87-88, 162
Casuals of the Sea: 51, 92, 102, 145-147, 178, 188
Cheapjack: 336-337, 343
Cheerio! See *Kinema Comic*
Chesterton, Ada: 357
Chesterton, GK: 5
Child She Dared Not Claim, The (aka *Robbed of her Child, Her Hidden Past, Milly*): 309, 311, 313, 320, 327, 340, 351
Chips (*Illustrated Chips*): 116, 153, 161, 173, 194, 207, 208, 270, 292
Chiswick: 26, 56, 58
Christian Globe, The: 32-34, 36-38, 40-45, 50, 52-57, 73, 79-80, 89, 91-94, 103, 112, 116, 124, 128, 130-131, 145, 168, 175-176, 189, 194, 196, 206, 229-230, 232-234, 236, 239-240, 246, 268, 306
Christian Glowworm, The: 32-33, 35-36, 38, 40, 46-47
Christian World, The: 33, 50, 52
Clarke, James: 50
Clarke, TEB (Tibby): 3-4, 304

Comic Cuts 2, 4, 116, 153, 161, 173, 194, 229, 235-237
Comrades True: 152-153, 157, 160
Convict Bride, The: 173, 174, 188, 212, 226, 241, 280
'convict stories': 9, 345
Cooper, Anne St John (McGlachan): 289, 302, 304-6, 308-309, 323-328, 351, 352
Cooper, Gladys: 240-241, 265
Cooper, Henry St John: 150, 302, 303, 304, 307
Cooper, Robert St John: 303
Cordwell, Fred: 153, 168-169, 172-173, 191, 207, 225, 230, 238, 263-265, 269-275
Cotterill & Cromb (agents): 253-254, 288, 292, 293, 333, 352
Daily Express: 117, 120, 123, 293
Daily Mail: 4, 116-117, 120, 123, 136, 148, 166, 173, 225, 235
Daily Sketch: 236, 237
Dance of the Years: 20, 22-23, 38, 43, 58, 73, 91, 130-132

Das Kapital: 18, 179, 267
Davidson (Dundee editor): 333, 335, 346
Death of a Ghost: 7, 277, 335, 344
Deserted (*The Silence of Jane Carter*): 339, 340-343
Devil of a Woman: 93-100, 118, 198, 212, 218, 248, 280
Dickens, Charles: 65, 87, 199, 203, 240
Don't Leave Us, Mummy!: 233-243, 271
Dreadnought: 173, 174, 207, 212
Driven From Home (1909): 1, 171-175, 178, 180, 182, 183, 186-188, 196, 214, 244, 252, 263, 272, 280, 309
Driven From Home (1932) (*The Woman Cast Out*): 317, 321
'Duffer, The': 8, 83-85, 95, 140-142, 150-151, 154, 212, 270-271
Dundee: 16, 98, 233, 247, 249, 252-254, 292, 301, 332-335, 346, 357
Ealing: 135, 176, 240, 313
East Lynne: 208, 234, 254, 258
Edwards, Hamilton: 150-154, 156, 158, 174, 303
Egan, Pierce II: 86-88, 98
Egan, Pierce II: 76-77, 87-89
Evening Telegraph: 97, 253
Fabians: 5, 55, 132, 169, 189-192, 273
Family Journal, The: 302, 304-310, 324, 327-328, 341, 344, 345, 349, 351
Favorite Comic, The: 12, 173, 198, 200, 212, 226, 230, 247
Fellow Who Loved Violet Hopson, The (see also Hopson, Violet): 265-266, 270
Film Fun 2, 271, 291-292
Firefly, The – see Fun & Fiction
Fleet Street: 32-33, 52, 56, 73, 92, 94, 116, 120, 132, 145, 179, 253, 303, 336
Fleetway Publications – see Amalgamated Press
Flower, W Newman: 162
Forget-me-Not: 4, 117, 235-236
Fox, Charles: 73, 151
Francis, James Caradoc (see also JC Francis Agency): 56
Freeman, Arnold: 205-215, 269
Freeman, Gwendoline: 298-300, 358
Fun & Fiction (also The *Firefly*): 172-174, 202, 207, 212, 230, 269, 373
'Garden of Glory, The': 111, 124-129, 132, 159
Garrish, HJ: 152-155, 156-163, 167-169, 172-175, 184, 188, 207, 238, 253, 280, 290, 292-293
'Gaston Gaters': 8, 156-157
Gem: 152-153, 167-170, 177, 207, 213, 230, 292
Gilfeather Family: 248-249, 252, 254, 258-261, 299, 357
Girl of My Heart: 160-161, 176, 178
Girl Outcast, The (aka *Clara Brent* etc): 173, 174, 188, 196, 198, 200, 212, 280, 352
Girl Who Married a Scoundrel, The: 210, 212, 263, 271
Girl Who Trusted Him, The: 214
Girl Without a Home, The: 173, 184, 188, 196, 210, 212, 263
Girlman, Frank: 136
Girls' Cinema: 268, 283
Gissing, George: 10, 25-26, 106, 174
Green Corn: 279, 284, 287
Greenwood, James: 53
Griffth, Percy: 151-153, 158, 207
Guardian, The: 51-52
the Harmsworth papers – see the AP:

Hamilton, Charles (aka Richards, Frank and Clifford, Martin): 4, 150-155, 159, 168-169, 178, 231, 356
Hammersmith: 25-26, 56, 66, 92, 128
Happy Home, The (formerly *Sunday Hours*, then The *Mascot*): 232-235, 246-247, 252-253, 271, 288, 289, 295, 296
Harmsworth: for Alfred Harmsworth see Lord Northcliffe, for Harold Harmsworth see Lord Rothermere and for the Harmsworth papers see the Amalgamated Press.
Harvey, William: 253-257, 261, 262, 279, 297, 312, 323, 326-328, 331-333, 335-336, 352
Havant, H: 153
Hayakawa, Sessue (pseud HJA): 2, 20, 271
Hayakawa, Sessue (r.n.): 272
Hearn, George: 175, 179, 281-283, 347, 349
Her Own Game (aka *Her Luck in London*): 237, 241
Herbert, AP: 327
Hinton, Herbert: 153
Hoggart, Richard: 37, 182, 195, 197, 202, 287
Home Companion: 304, 306, 308-309, 324, 344
Home Mirror: 304
Hopson, Violet: 265-266
Horrell, Charles: 242
Houdini, Harry (pseud HJA): 1, 271, 274
Houdini, Harry (fictional character): 11, 270, 274-275
Houdini, Harry (r.n.): 2710, 274
Hughes, Emily Jane ('Granny') (HJA mother-in-law) – see Allingham, Emily Jane
Hughes, Emily Jane (also Allingham Emily Jane, 'Em', 'Emmie') (HJA wife): 82, 130-135, 144-147, 162, 175-176, 221-222, 233, 236-237, 239-240, 250, 251, 253, 265, 276, 278, 284, 287, 289-290, 293, 294-295, 317-324, 337, 339, 343, 346, 347-350
Hughes, Maud (HJA sister-in-law): 131, 161, 236, 238, 241-243, 265, 268, 270, 283, 285, 287, 293, 298, 300, 304
Hughes, Molly: 87, 115, 268
Hughes, Walter (HJA brother-in-law): 131, 139, 221, 250
Hughes, William Walter (HJA father-in-law):22, 130-131
Human Nature: 133, 178, 202, 216-219, 225-226, 231, 234, 247
Humphries, Steve (and Richard Van Emden): 228, 255
Illustrated Police News, The: 16, 208, 213
Jay, Frank: 89, 91, 93
Jester, The: 127, 144, 153, 156-157, 159, 161-162, 173-174, 194, 204
Johnson, WS: 88-89
Johnson, Winifred ('Biddy'): 235-238, 242
Joy: 268
Justice: 12, 177, 226, 321-322, 359
JC Francis Advertising Agency: 57, 89, 92, 94, 108, 135, 232
Keary, Peter: 149
Kennington: 14, 23, 25, 32, 46, 58, 69, 130, 163, 189, 192, 195-196, 340
Kinema Comic (includes *Cheerio!*): 169,

263-267, 271-275, 292
Kirkpatrick, Robert: 72
Lambeth: 25-26, 28, 69, 128, 189-190
Larter, Henry: 24
Leng, John: 16, 97, 229, 233-4, 241, 253-254, 280, 288, 290, 295, 298, 333, 352
Lights of Home, The (also *The Face Behind the Veil*): 20, 26-31, 133, 182, 188, 196, 204-205
Lights of London Town: 58, 162-162, 170
London: 14, 15, 16, 24, 25, 48, 52, 54, 67, 113, 131, 168, 184, 198, 200, 212, 223-224, 225, 250, 252, 266, 273, 289-290, 333, 343 (see individual entries for Bayswater, Chiswick, Ealing, Fleet Street, Hammersmith, Kennington, Lambeth, Walworth)
London: 226, 247, 253
London Journal, The (includes The *New London Journal*): 16, 53, 77, 83, 85-94, 97-99, 101-105, 107, 109-110, 123, 132, 135-136, 139, 145, 147, 162, 175, 194, 202, 238, 246, 279-280
Lloyd, Harold ('Winkle'): 272
Lloyds Weekly: 16
Lowe, Robert: 13
Luard Family: 222, 244, 347
'Mab': 97-104, 106-107, 109, 111, 123, 136, 147, 279
Magnet, The: 152-3, 167-169, 177, 207, 229-230, 292
Married to a Monster (*The Hate of a Woman*): 326, 331
Marx, Karl: 18-19, 179, 235, 299
Max the Magnificent: 81, 143, 148, 150-151, 154, 168, 174, 212, 272
McFee, William: 5, 51, 92, 102, 122, 133-135, 145-147, 168, 176, 178-179, 188, 227, 246, 257, 277, 280, 283, 286, 290, 300, 349
Merry & Bright: 58, 82, 172-174, 184, 207, 210, 212, 226, 228, 230-231, 263-264, 267, 269-271, 288, 292
Mersea Island: 224, 249-250, 252, 281-282, 284
Middlesbrough: 192-193, 196, 208, 269, 299, 306, 345, 357
Miracle: 304, 343-345
Miss Maggie Macfee: 122, 168, 176
Moody, Dwight Lynam: 40, 268
Mother Love (aka Spare My Children, The Wicked Guardian etc):188, 202, 207-208, 212, 214, 232, 234, 280, 354
'mother love' stories: 9, 222, 252, 271, 304
Murray, AC and CH: 81, 140-142
My Weekly: 10, 234-235, 240-242, 253, 297, 321, 331, 333 353, 356 358
New Boys' Paper, The: 69, 79-80, 82, 94, 138, 148, 162, 168, 272
Newnes, George: 88, 91-93, 113, 115, 117, 123
Nietzsche, Friedrich: 5, 227
Nineteenth Century, The (magazine): 115
None Other Gods: 239-240
Northcliffe, Lord (also Harmsworth, Alfred): 3, 4, 16, 18, 91, 92, 116, 120, 138, 149, 153, 155,169-170, 178, 191, 219, 225, 228-229, 235, 238, 281, 306, 355
Nowell Julia (see Allingham, Julia)

Oaken Heart, The: 6, 20, 22, 221
Oracle: 304, 324, 343
Orwell, George: 4, 166-169 312, 355
'Our Madge': 113-117
Pearson, Arthur: 16, 18, 91-92, 117, 140, 149, 169
Pearson's Weekly: 91, 118, 123, 137
Peg of the Pictures (also *Pots of Money*): 111, 271, 275
People's Friend, The: 10, 16, 253, 358
People's Journal, The: 16, 98, 229, 247-250, 254-256, 260-261, 297, 299, 326, 352
Pictorial Magazine (*Penny Pictorial*): 136-137
Picture Show, The: 265-266, 268, 271, 284, 290, 298, 305
Pitt, David (pseud HJA): 1, 140-141
Plucky Polly Perkins: 8, 19, 163-164, 166, 169-170, 172, 188, 204, 280, 303
Poppy's Paper: 304, 324
Pots of Money, see *Peg of the Pictures*
Presumptuous Polly: 240-241, 265
Priestley, JB: 323
Prowse, Robert: 77, 82, 139
Puck: 82, 97, 149, 151, 153, 158, 160-162, 168, 173-174, 194, 204, 212
Our Boys' Paper: 89
Red Star Weekly: 344
'Redemption of Richard Deane, The': 113
Reed, Talbot Baines: 75, 80
Reeves, Maud Pember: 189, 192, 195, 358
Regent Street Polytechnic: 266, 284
Religious Tract Society: 55, 74, 80
Reynolds GWM: 87
Reynolds Weekly; 16
Richards, Frank – see Hamilton, Charles
Robinson, Lilian (Carter, Lilian): 63-66, 293-294, 344
Robinson, Nellie: 63-66, 68
Rod of the Oppressor (aka *The Fateful Hour*): 188, 293, 352
Rollington, Ralph – see Allingham, John
Rothermere, Lord (also Harmsworth, Harold): 4, 16, 18, 91, 92, 117, 138, 169, 172, 178, 191, 306, 354
Royal Surrey Gardens: 25, 39-40, 69
Ruby Wray: 127, 144
Salter, Dr JH: 222-224, 243-245, 250, 290, 295, 317-319, 323, 334, 343, 347, 350
Sankey, Ira: 40, 268
Sell, Henry: 52
Shaw, GB: 5
She Sinned for her Children (*For Love of her Bairns*): 257, 262, 297
Shelley (Dairy House): 319, 321, 322, 323
Shurey's Illustrated: 97, 145
Sible Hedingham: 289
Sisley, Charles: 136
Smith, JF: 86-90, 102, 147
Society of Authors: 143
Spare Moments: 92-93, 96, 103, 107, 175, 324
Sport Monkimore: 156-157, 161, 292
Spurgeon, CH: 39-40, 41, 266, 268
St Clair, Herbert (pseud HJA):1, 80, 112
Starr, Richard (friend of HJA): 214, 289
Starr Richard (Starr-Bowkett Building Society): 38
Stead, WT: 90
Stead, WT Jnr: 56
Stiff, George: 85-88, 104

Strand Magazine: 117, 123
Strong, Victoria (pseud HJA): 2, 324
Sunday Companion: 117, 306
Sutton, Sir George: 191, 228, 230, 238, 264, 291
Talmadge, Norma (pseud HJA): 2, 271
Talmadge, Norma (r.n.): 272
Talmadge, Rev T de Witt: 40-41, 266
Thomson, DC: 16, 97, 234, 241, 253-254, 290, 292-293, 295, 324, 344-345
Thorpe Bay: 323-324, 336, 346, 349
Thyrza: 25-26, 106, 174
Tiger in the Smoke: 7
Times, The: 4, 18, 22, 169
Tit-Bits: 88, 91, 113 194
Tolleshunt D'Arcy: 223-225, 295, 317-319, 343
Tracy, Louis: 123
True Blue: 81-84, 96, 128, 139-143, 149-151, 270, 271
Turner, ES: 52, 229
Tyrer, Walter: 344

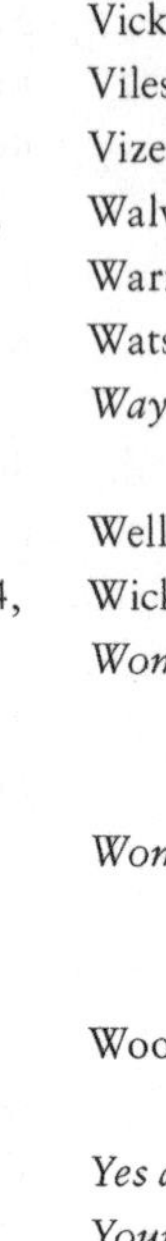

Vickers, George: 85
Viles, Arthur: 148
Vizetelly, Henry: 86, 93
Walworth: 14, 22-25, 28, 37, 190, 298
Warner, Marina:198-201
Watson, Albert: 273-274
Way of the World, The: 170, 178, 215, 226, 230, 246
Wells, HG: 5, 10, 51
Wickhart, FA: 96, 145, 324, 359
Woman Pays, The (also *Wife of a Wanted Man*, *Wife of a Hunted Man*): 262, 326, 328
Woman's Weekly: 10, 232, 235-240, 242-244, 246, 247, 252, 265, 266, 268, 358
Wood, Edward (Teddy): 238, 251, 289, 298, 304, 333
Yes and No: 145
Young Folks Paper: 66, 76, 78